Psychoanalysis
at the
Political Border

Rafael Moses, M.D.

Psychoanalysis at the Political Border

Essays in Honor of Rafael Moses

Edited by

Leo Rangell
and
Rena Moses-Hrushovski

International Universities Press, Inc.
Madison Connecticut

Library of Congress Cataloging-in-Publication Data

Psychoanalysis at the political border : essays in honor of Rafael
Moses / edited by Leo Rangell and Rena Moses-Hrushovski.
p. cm.
Includes bibliographical references and index.
ISBN 0-8236-5110-X
1. Social sciences and psychoanalysis. 2. Political psychology.
3. Moses, Rafael, 1924- . I. Moses, Rafael, 1924-
II. Rangell, Leo. III. Moses-Hrushovski, Rena.
BF175.S65P78 1996
150.19′5—dc20 95-47649
CIP

Manufactured in the United States of America

At the time this book went to press, the leaders of two nations, representing human divisions at spiritual war with each other for millenia, shook hands in an unprecedented symbol of a genuine intention for peaceful resolution. The world was relieved and in anxious expectancy.

Before this book was published, one of these men of vision and moral courage lay dead at the hand of an assassin's bullet. The civilized world, although not unfamiliar with such acts, was stunned and mourned.

This book is dedicated to that segment of humanity which cherishes the steps taken in the cause so abruptly set back. Since its spiritual center, not only in the name of its honoree but in the hearts of its contributors, is in the Middle East, the book is directed to the living concept that while affects and ideas are to be helped toward their optimum expression, the approaches to action need to be guarded by the rational ego.

—Leo Rangell, M.D.

We psychoanalysts know more about aggression, wars, abuse, conflicts, and emotional obtuseness than about how to develop love, care, respect, openness to complex needs and the capacity to compromise, reconcile or bring about social change.

I dedicate this book to my mother who continues to be involved, interested, and caring for the present without forgetting the past; who bravely overcomes wars and losses and succeeds in creating a life of quality and dignity while growing old.

At the same time I dedicate this book to Yitschak Rabin whom we all mourn. His openness to perceive changing circumstances and his courage to bring about revolutionary change accordingly; his determination and his deep commitment to strive for peace, all these planted in us the hope for a better world which he began to bring closer.

It is from individuals like my mother on a personal level and Yitschak Rabin on a national and international level that we can learn more about the psychoanalytic aspects of the ability to change, about resilience and the peaceful resolution of conflict in individuals, groups, and nations.

—Rena Moses-Hrushovski, Ph.D.

TABLE OF CONTENTS

Contributors ix

Part I Rafael Moses: The Man and the Psychoanalyst

1. Rafael Moses, Psychoanalyst of the Middle East
   Leo Rangell 3
2. A Personal Note
   Rena Moses-Hrushovski 17

Part II Within the Individual

3. Psychoanalytic Footnotes on Love
   Joseph Sandler and Anne-Marie Sandler 23
4. The Secret Seed of Hatred in a Delinquent Adolescent
   Harold P. Blum 35
5. Fear of Love
   Yecheskel Cohen 49
6. Freud's Theory of Motivation and Others
   Arnold D. Richards 69
7. The Interminable Uncanniness
   Yolanda Gampel 85
8. The Nonverbal Communication of the Analyst to the Patient
   Harold Stewart 99
9. Endings
   Nina E. C. Coltart 117

Part III Toward the Group

10. Ambivalent Sibling Rivalry: Latent Concerns in Anna Freud's Candidacy Paper
    Rivka R. Eifermann 133
11. Ideology and Psychoanalysis
    Charles M. T. Hanly 147
12. Remaining in the Bunker Long After the War Is Over: Deployment in the Individual, the Group, and the Nation
    Rena Moses-Hrushovski 165

13. Can You Not, Father, See the Erlking? Psychoanalytic Observations on Goethe's Ballad, "The Erlking"
Hermann Beland 189

Part IV At the Psychopolitical Border

14. Moral Conflicts, Public Opinion, and the Political Process
Leo Rangell 213

15. The Leader and the Led—Their Mutual Needs
Ronnie Solan 237

16. Intergenerational Transmission and "Chosen" Traumas: A Link Between the Psychology of the Individual and That of the Ethnic Group
Vamik D. Volkan 257

17. The Working Through of the Nazi Experience in the German Psychoanalytic Community
Martin Wangh 283

The Writings of Rafael Moses 303

Name Index 313

Subject Index 319

CONTRIBUTORS

HERMANN BELAND, M.A.
Training and Supervising Analyst, German Psychoanalytic Association, Berlin Psychoanalytic Institute; Former President, German Psychoanalytic Association.

HAROLD P. BLUM, M.D.
Clinical Professor of Psychiatry and Training Analyst, New York University College of Medicine; Executive Director, Sigmund Freud Archives; past Editor-in-Chief, *Journal of the American Psychoanalytic Association.*

YECHESKEL COHEN, Ph.D.
Training Analyst, the Israel Psychoanalytic Institute; Past President, the Israel Psychoanalytic Society; Executive and Clinical Director, the B'nai B'rith Women Residential Treatment Center.

NINA E. C. COLTART, M.A., M.B., B.S.
Member and Training Analyst, British Psychoanalytic Society; Past Director, London Clinic of Psychoanalysis; Past Vice-President, The British Psychoanalytical Society.

RIVKA R. EIFERMANN, Ph.D.
Supervising and Training Analyst, Israel Psychoanalytic Society and Institute; Past President, the Israel Psychoanalytic Society; Associate Professor of Psychology, The Hebrew University of Jerusalem.

YOLANDA GAMPEL, Ph.D.
Senior Lecturer, Department of Psychology, School of Psychotherapy, Tel-Aviv University; Training Analyst, Israel Psychoanalytic Association; Past President, Israel Psychoanalytic Association; Co-Director, Jerome International Study of Organized Persecution of Children, Sands Point, New York.

CHARLES M. T. HANLY, Ph.D.
Training and Supervising Analyst, Canadian Psychoanalytic Society, Toronto Psychoanalytic Institute; Emeritus Professor of Philosophy, University of Toronto.

RENA MOSES-HRUSHOVSKI, Ph.D.
Training and Supervising Analyst, Israel Psychoanalytic Society.

LEO RANGELL, M.D.
Past President (twice), American Psychoanalytic Association; Past President (twice), International Psychoanalytical Association; Clinical Professor of Psychiatry at University of California, Los Angeles; and Clinical Professor of Psychiatry (Psychoanalysis) at University of California, San Francisco.

ARNOLD D. RICHARDS, M.D.
Training and Supervising Analyst, New York Psychoanalytic Institute; Editor, *Journal of the American Psychoanalytic Association.*

ANNE-MARIE SANDLER, Lic. es Scs.
Training and Supervising Analyst, British Psycho-Analytical Society; President, British Psycho-Analytical Society; former President, European Psycho-Analytical Federation; European Editor, *International Journal of Psycho-Analysis* and *International Review of Psycho-Analysis.*

JOSEPH SANDLER, Ph.D., M.D., D.Sc., Hon. LL.D.
Training and Supervising Analyst, British Psycho-Analytical Society; Freud Memorial Professor of Psychoanalysis, University of London; President, International Psychoanalytical Association; former President, European Psycho-Analytical Federation; former Editor, *International Journal of Psycho-Analysis* and *International Review of Psycho-Analysis.*

RONNIE SOLAN, Ph.D.
Training Analyst, Former Chairperson, Israel Psychoanalytic Society; Supervisor and Lecturer, the Israel Psychoanalytic Institute; Lecturer, Postgraduate Psychotherapy Section, Faculty of Continuing Medical Education, Sackler School of Medicine, Tel-Aviv University.

HAROLD STEWART, M.B.B.S., M.R.C.S., L.R.cP., F.R.C.Psych.
Training and Supervising Psychoanalyst, British Psycho-Analytical Society; Consultant Psychotherapist (retired) in the Adult Department, Tavistock Clinic, London.

VAMIK D. VOLKAN, M.D.
Medical Director, Blue Ridge Hospital, Professor of Psychiatry, Director of the Center for the Study of Mind and Human Interaction, University of Virginia School of Medicine; Training and Supervising Analyst, Washington Psychoanalytic Institute; Chairperson, Committee on International Relations of the Group for the Advancement of Psychiatry; Actively involved in numerous conflict resolution programs in the Mid East, Hungary, the Baltic countries, and other regions.

MARTIN WANGH, M.D.
Supervising and Training Analyst, New York Psychoanalytic Institute (on leave of absence); Supervising and Training Analyst, Israel Psychoanalytic Institute; Scholar, Sigmund Freud Center, Hebrew University, Jerusalem; Emeritus, Clinical Professor of Psychiatry, Albert Einstein College of Medicine, Bronx, New York.

Part I

Rafael Moses: The Man and the Psychoanalyst

1.

RAFAEL MOSES, PSYCHOANALYST OF THE MIDDLE EAST

Leo Rangell, M.D.

The two participants in the analytic dyad, who are focused on the analysis of the patient's intrapsychic processes, are surrounded by their common cultural ambience in the broad sense of the term. In the usual flow of the analysis, this environmental influence operates silently, and comes under analytic scrutiny only as it infiltrates into the patient's associations, and thus enters the field of clinical observation.

Psychoanalytic understanding, however, has a long reach, and can, under circumstances other than in the clinical psychoanalysis of patients, be utilized directly for the wide-ranging insights it is capable of bringing to social and group phenomena. Psychoanalytic thinking, from Freud onwards, has been used with varying degrees of satisfaction for the understanding of psychobiography, psychohistorical events, war, cultural and social oscillations and mores. Its use has been less in evidence until recent years for the observation and attempted explanation of political crises and more ordinary, ongoing psychopolitical phenomena.

The wide political or sociocultural world becomes a subject of the analysis either when it impinges on the individual analysis or when it is sufficiently pathological to attract analytic thinking on its own account. A psychoanalyst working in Germany during the period of its malignant history would have had to direct his instrument of observation outward to encompass and account for the pathology at work. The same goes for an analyst in Prague during the communist regime, or a would-be analyst in the former

Soviet Union. Waelder has pointed out that conditions in such political systems are in fact incompatible with the conduct of individual analyses (1960). Psychoanalysts in the United States, however, and to a great extent in Britain, have been faced with quite other problems, and opportunities, in which the political atmosphere is not as directly involved.

The Middle East is in the unusual position of being an area of intense conflicts, while at the same time it has contained and nurtured an active psychoanalytic atmosphere and community. Regarded as the flash point of international tension and danger during the entire memory of the current generation of psychoanalysts, it is also the site of the Sigmund Freud Professorship of Psychoanalysis at Hebrew University in Israel. The area's role as a source of international conflicts has been continuous and ubiquitous. The civilized world, suffering chronic trauma, and numb from recurrent wars and human atrocities over the lifetime of the present population, has been apprehensively focused on this small region, where three continents converge, as having the potential to explode into further hostilities and human slaughter. Only in the last few years has a distinct document promising peace been signed by opposing sides, and can the hope for a new beginning be reasonably entertained. At the time of writing, the astonishing exchange between King Hussein of Jordan and Itzak Rabin, Prime Minister of Israel, before the Congress of the United States in 1994 brings a new atmosphere of promise which was previously close to impossible.

It is in this milieu that the analyst whose life and work is celebrated in this book has spent his analytic life. Rafael Moses is the quintessential psychoanalyst of the Middle East. I do not mean a psychoanalyst who lives in the Middle East, but who in his central interests and analytic image epitomizes the application of the psychoanalytic view to the understanding of the Middle East and its indigenous conflicts.

Born in Berlin in 1924, Rafael Moses emigrated with his family to Palestine in 1937 as a boy of 13. For two years before that, he had been sent, for safety, along with an older brother, first to a Jewish boarding school in Italy for half a year, after which he moved with his family to London for eighteen months. During this time, his father, a distinguished lawyer, who was President of the

Zionist Organization of Jews in Germany, commuted between London and Berlin, initiating a new profession, that of Public Auditor, helping emigrating Jews transfer their funds from Germany to Palestine. He later became the first State Comptroller in the new State of Israel, with cabinet rank, overseeing proper accounting and ethical conduct in government offices.

This early composite exposure of Rafael's, from Germany to schools in Italy and England, along with his later training in the United States and subsequent frequent visits there, has imparted to him a distinctly international voice, language, and tone. It is a unique combination and presentation, and merges with his character and interpersonal stance. Rafael's mien, demeanor, and behavior is cross-cultural, international, open on all sides.

Living his adolescence in that tense, turbulent, uncertain geographic region, Rafael began premedical courses at Hebrew University, which he left to serve in the British Army for four years during World War II. From 1942 until 1946, when he was between 18 and 22, he was in the Palestine Infantry, Jewish Brigade. A citizen of Israel when the new State of Israel was born, he remained in the Israel Defense Army Reserves for the next thirty-five years.

Rafael had wanted to be a doctor since he was a young boy. At the age of 15, influenced by a close uncle who was a Jungian analyst, he decided to be a psychoanalyst. In 1946, the path to these goals took him to Switzerland, first to the University of Fribourg, then to Zurich. He secured his M.D. from the University of Zurich in 1951. After internship and a first psychiatric residency back in Israel, in 1953 he came to the United States to continue his psychiatric training. He served two more residencies, one year at the Brooklyn State Hospital, and two years at Yale University, as well as one as Instructor and Chief Resident. During these years, Rafael established roots in America which were to become a source of a sturdy second identity. He was spurred on in these early years by such figures as Drs. Mo Kaufman of New York's Mount Sinai Hospital, Milton Rosenbaum, Theodore Lidz, Jules Coleman, and Frieda Fromm-Reichmann, all of whom helped and encouraged him along his course. Never relinquishing his primary roots in the history and fate of Israel, Rafael was to become a frequent visitor and familiar figure in the United States, particularly in later years when a strong affective bond was fortified by his and Rena's children also training and living for periods in this country.

In 1957, at 33, Dr. Moses returned to Israel to Hebrew University, where he taught psychiatry. Rafael trained in psychoanalysis in the late fifties and early sixties at the Israel Psychoanalytic Institute, graduated in 1964, and went on to leadership in the Israel Psychoanalytic Society. Before that, between 1961 and 1964, he was Secretary of the Israel Neuropsychiatric Society.

Then in 1964, he returned to the United States on a sabbatical for two years, one year at Albert Einstein Medical College, in New York, and one as a Visiting Scientist at the National Institute of Mental Health in Washington, focusing on family research and therapy. He also worked in mental health for the underprivileged community.

He returned to Israel in 1966, where he has since served in a settled and committed way, living and becoming a psychiatric and psychoanalytic fulcrum for the mental sciences there. In the Israel Psychoanalytic Society and Institute, he went on to leadership positions, becoming Scientific Secretary, twice President, a member of the faculty, Training and Supervising Analyst, and Chairman of the Education Committee. He continued his applications to broader social issues, serving as a consultant to the Adoption Service of the Ministry of Welfare, and to the Rehabilitation Office of the Ministry of Defense.

From then on, Rafael's travels, which are steady and generally brief, have been as a visiting psychoanalyst. From 1988 to 1989, he served for a year as the Erik Erikson Resident Scholar at the Austen Riggs Foundation in Stockbridge, Massachusetts. In Israel, before and after that assignment, Rafael taught at Hebrew University-Hadassah Medical School, in the Department of Psychiatry and the Social Mental Health Unit and at the School of Social Work; at Ben Gurion University of the Negev, where he chaired and was visiting professor at the new Division of Psychiatry and Human Development; at the Jerusalem Mental Health Center; and as Medical Director of the Summit Institute. Before his year at Austen Riggs, Dr. Moses served as the Sigmund Freud Professor of Psychoanalysis at Hebrew University. He had previously been a founding initiator and supporter during the years of the setting up of that historic chair. He was the first Israeli appointed to that position, which he built up in a creative and productive scientific way.

His scientific pursuits and leadership led Rafael to take part in international scientific conferences, on "Why War," on "Leadership and Authority," at the Tavistock Institute of Social Relations, on "Insight in Psychoanalytic Treatment," at the European Federation of Psychoanalysis. He served on numerous editorial boards, including *The Israel Annals, Samiksa, The International Journal of Psycho-Analysis,* and was Associate Secretary of the International Psycho-Analytic Association from 1977 to 1981. He was a broad educator; besides teaching candidates in psychoanalysis, he taught in many departments in related fields—medical students, residents, social workers, psychologists, political scientists, at the graduate and undergraduate levels.

Above all, Rafael Moses stands out as a psychoanalyst with a special orientation toward the most sensitive group issues and problems at international, interpolitical, intersocial, and interethnic levels. His eye is particularly attuned to the vicissitudes of the Arab–Israeli conflict, which happens to make the Middle East the world's most sensitive, enduring, and potentially explosive trouble spot. The entire civilized world of nations has been concerned about this region for many decades and has held its collective breath for the lifetime of all who live in the modern age. Rafael Moses represents understanding of and reflection about these complex issues. There might be many solutions, but there must be rationality and insight. This, to my way of thinking, is not unlike Fenichel's (1945) statement regarding psychoanalytic therapy, that there can be many treatments, but only one understanding. Moses has always stood for understanding, reflection, reason, and actions based on these. I hesitate to include moderation, because there are times when moderation is not the best course, and can even result in untoward suffering; for example, hesitation and moderation toward the Holocaust. There are instances in individual lives as well, and in small and larger group interactions, where the same principles and orientation might apply, where moderation leading to passivity produces harm rather than good.

A relevant comment, which may raise eyebrows as much as induce reflection, appears in a letter from Ernest Jones to Freud during their long-standing, voluminous correspondence. In a letter in 1914, as the First World War is about to divide and separate the small groups of early analysts on both sides of the combat, Jones writes to Freud:

> [T]he capacity of human prediction as to human affairs has at present very definite limitations. It is a consolation, however, to think that in time our work must reduce these limitations, perhaps very greatly. If there is ever to be any salvation of the world from these nightmares, it will surely be psychoanalysis that will point the way. That is why I feel that if the future of psychoanalysis had to be weighed with the future of my own country, I should side with the former [Paskauskas, 1993, p. 308].

Moses' scientific contributions began early during his training days at Yale, continued with regularity throughout his cumulative experiences, and covered a wide array of situations as his interests expanded and widened. The subjects ranged from observations on individual mechanisms and psychopathology, to group issues, to the widest psychopolitical processes, and combinations of all of these. To some extent this book will follow this sequence and organization of subjects and interests.

Dr. Moses has written on such subjects as suicide, psychological aspects of lactation, psychosomatic gastrointestinal disorders, delinquency, homosexuality, sensory deprivation, levels of awareness in cancer patients, combat reactions in the Yom Kippur War, and bereaved war widows. Early there were papers on group processes, on reactions in a Kibbutz, problems of immigrants, parental education, crime in developing countries, bureaucracy, mental health, and cultural values. Later there were papers on theoretical or technical issues, an ego view of form and content, structural elements of the organizing processes of the ego, psychological aspects of aggression, and adult psychic trauma. From the eighties on, Moses' writings took on a wider, global character, in which the essence of psychoanalytic thinking was applied to the most pressing problems of the psychopolitical world. In other hands, these could well have been regarded as bordering on the grandiose, but his contributions were received as modest, sincere, believable, and usable. Some of these publications dealt with such subjects as obstacles to the peace process in the Middle East, with particular reference to narcissism, ideological polarization in Israel, the group self and identity in Arab–Israeli relations, guilt in the political process, a fifty-year look at Israeli–German relations, empathy and disempathy in the political process, the leader and the led, dehumanization in victim and aggressor, psychological problems in forced evacuation of a small town at the tip of the Sinai, the perpetuation of victimization, denial in the political process, mutual perceptions of Arabs and Israelis, psychological dimensions of the negotiating process, psychotherapy and world peace. A staggering brew.

Rafael Moses welcomed the first International Psychoanalytic Congress held in Jerusalem in 1977, and in Hamburg in 1985 addressed the first International Psychoanalytic Congress to return to Germany after the War. A unique group of contributions, which can be recognized as Rafael's by their titles and subjects, open vistas of thought and understanding from individual to the largest group pathological reactions. Of special significance is the book he edited consisting of papers that originated at an unusual conference held under his sponsorship during his tenure as Sigmund Freud Professor on "Persistent Shadows of the Holocaust: The Meaning to Those not Directly Affected." The thoughtfulness and diversity of this courageous interchange has been widely appreciated.

Of special note are a series of recent contributions on subjects which serve as a theoretical and clinical bridge between the intrapsychic and the interpersonal. These deal with his ideas and those of Rena on entitlement, acknowledgment, deployment, and shame. All of these phenomena and conditions point to a population under chronic stress and danger living under the conditions in which the Moseses live and which they face routinely. The very titles point to the Moseses' writings, just as envy and (my paraphrase, lack of) gratitude bring Melanie Klein automatically to mind. These are traits deeply rooted in the individual, which reach out for fulfillment to the person's relationship with the group and sociability, and which tend to characterize a person's styles of relatedness. The Moseses' explanation for all of them stem from a combination of psychoanalytic thinking and sociologic, including moral, orientations.

Each of these psychological traits and problems begins in childhood and operates in groups. All of them carry us in our thinking from the individual to the psychology of people in groups. From how these operate developmentally in the child, to how they become prevalent and unadaptive, even dangerous within pathological groups, how they apply and produce resultant effects from the individual to a nation, all have theoretical and clinical implications and lessons. To feel entitled, a subject which is to be theoretically understood, to acknowledge, "the balm of narcissistic injuries," an action which has reparative and therapeutic consequences, can all well be added to the analyst's cognitive and clinical armamentarium. The Moses' relate this spectrum of states and subjects to shame, humiliation, and threats to self-esteem more than to anxiety. Deployment, so thoroughly covered in Rena Moses' contribution to the present volume, centered in psychic energies, is obviously related to defenses, a global defense probably a composite of multiple more discreet and specific defense mechanisms. A further task will be, in my opinion, to relate these new, interpersonally operative insights, to the inner, intrapsychic drive-anxiety-defense sequence more conventionally utilized.

Rafael can be influenced by others as much as he influences and leads others. He reverberated strongly to my descriptions (1976, 1980) of the Watergate complex as residing in the people, not in one President who forged the syndrome. The "syndrome of the compromise of integrity," I have written a number of times since 1974, "is as ubiquitous as neuroses in human affairs." Rafael picked this up and carried it along. He equally led the way to an active application of psychoanalytic theory for understanding international tensions and conflicts, the use of defense mechanisms, acting out, and symptoms by nations as by individuals. A virtual industry grew around these insights and attitudes, in the United States as also in and around the Middle East, among diplomats, social and political scientists, even if less so among the participating policy makers and responsible government officials themselves. A prominent such group or nucleus is, of all places, at the University of Virginia, and its Blue Ridge Hospital, in Charlottesville, Virginia, under the spirited leadership of Vamik Volkan and his interdisciplinary group of colleagues.

I remember my own experience when, in 1962 and 1963, I was spending a year as a Fellow at the Center for Advanced Study in the Behavioral Sciences at Stanford, California. I was working, among other subjects, on intrapsychic conflict, its internal structure, and its resolution. A special and serendipitous occasion during that year occurred when I presented my thoughts and material to the Political Science Department at Stanford University, aiming to integrate the principles involved in understanding individual intrapsychic conflict and its resolution with large-group political conflict between nations. My enjoyment and satisfaction at the stimulating interaction which ensued was matched in retrospect by my regrets that there was no follow-up or continuity by either side.

But I did find my own way deeper into the psychoanalytic psychopolitical interface. This presented itself in a peak way ten to fifteen years later, during the unfolding of the moral crisis of Watergate in the early seventies, that involved the presidential office at the very apex of our national government. What I became mainly interested in was the relations and continuity between the actors at the top and the public at the base of the population pyramid. The interaction between the levels was the subject of my study, not the psychology of one man. My description of "The Mind of Watergate" was not a psychobiography of Richard Nixon. I have objections to the methodology which makes claim to such biographic studies from afar. It was rather a study of mass psychological reactions from data in the public domain. The Watergate complex, the choice of expediency over principle when the ego stakes are high enough, was postulated as ubiquitous and timeless in human affairs. A decade later, Rafael Moses continued about the Watergate as a universal phenomenon, writing of further social aspects of the bribing of the superego and the subverting of the ego ideal. We had formed a common bond at the psychopolitical border with the understanding to be made by the psychoanalytic view of human life.

Following this introductory chapter is an appreciation of Rafael Moses by his wife, Rena Moses-Hrushovski.

The papers to follow in this volume, directly and indirectly, relate to the work and interests of Rafael Moses in applying psychoanalytic thinking and the objective and uniquely fair stance and orientation of the analytic attitude, from conflicts within the individual to the most sensitive areas of human conflict on a world scale. The chapters are grouped in accordance with this organization, and carry out the sequence from individual dynamics to issues related to group interactions, moving from small group processes in everyday life, to problems and pathology in large group behavior. These reach up to the tensions, conflicts and warring between nations, and attempts to approach the understanding of these on the basis of psychoanalytic understanding.

The contents of Part II are centered on intrapsychic psychology and psychopathology within the individual, pointing and leading to relationships to others. In the first paper, Joseph and Anne-Marie Sandler present a number of important observations and reflections on love, extending Freud's statements on the subject, and provide interesting insights into the ties that bind love objects together. These can serve as a fertile motivational base for amplification into the bonds of group formations. As a contrast, Harold Blum explores the seeds of hatred in intrapsychic life, in a patient who displays its social derivatives of delinquency and criminal tendencies. On the same subject of instincts and intimacy, Yecheskel Cohen studies the fear of love and the preference to deal with problems of aggression, in life, in patients, in transference and countertransference reactions, and in the arts.

Arnold Richards writes on motivation in psychoanalytic theory, traces its comparative explanations in classical and alternative theoretical systems, and concludes, as I do, that a total integrative theory can best lead out of the dilemmas posed by conflicting theories. Yolanda Gampel expands the meaning of "the uncanny" beyond primary repressed infantile traumata to the dread and horror of social violence transmitted between generations. Harold Stewart describes the effects of nonverbal communication from analyst to patient, and its influence on the course of the analytic process. Derivatively, these can similarly exert an affective irradiating effect in any interpersonal exchange. In a final paper of Part II, Nina Coltart writes philosophically and psychoanalytically on endings, in a spectrum from separating to mourning, to terminating analysis, to death.

Part III consists of a group of papers centering on intrapsychic conflicts but which come closer to object relations and issues of the individual within the group. Rivka Eifermann writes of the dialogue between the author of a paper and the audience to whom it is directed (written or spoken). Her subject comes from the very history of psychoanalysis, concerning Anna Freud's paper on "Beating Fantasies and Daydreams," which she presented to the Vienna Society at her inauguration as a psychoanalyst. What was taking place subliminally was a latent dialogue between Anna Freud, her sibling analysts and her analyst father, with an intertwining of theoretical issues and sibling relations. In the next paper, Charles Hanly writes of the power of ideologies and idealized transferences to cause conflicts in the life of groups in general and specifically in the psychoanalytic world. In many if not all Institutes, such mechanisms subvert the goal of data collection and objectivity, thwarting the advance and theoretical progress of psychoanalysis.

Rena Moses-Hrushovski introduces the use of deployment as a global defense, extrapolating from a large group of narcissistic patients (Moses-Hrushovski, 1994) to explain rampant pathological behavior in both large and small groups. This mechanism is a system of self-programming of attitude and roles designed to protect against previously experienced and now expected humiliation and loss of dignity and control. It has the widest applicability in the lives of groups and nations. Herman Beland next contributes an analysis of Goethe's ballad "The Erlking," demonstrating a creative work predating Freud by over a century, which contains in its substructure the predecessors of the Oedipus complex. The myth of Laius, and his homosexual love for Chrysippus, whom he drove to suicide, the subsequent Oedipus tragedy, and Freud's description of the prehistoric trauma of man in the ice age are all presaged and condensed in this epic poem, which in its own way demonstrates the inability of individuals and groups to live by cognition and reality.

Part IV is at the psychopolitical border, and beyond, dealing more squarely with group psychopathology as derived from intrapsychic conflicts of individuals in the aggregate. The first of these is my paper on the political and group process, and the psychology of public opinion, as affected by moral as well as instinctual conflicts coalesced on a mass scale. The subject matter studied involves a successive series of public events occurring in the United States in the last decades which in each case galvanized a huge national audience and elicited various forms of psychopathological reactions. These included the McCarthy years, the Watergate burglary, the Hill-Thomas hearings, two rape cases by celebrity defendants, the Rodney King trial and its violent aftermath, between them all, the psychology of the electorate in selecting their national leaders, and finally a notorious ongoing murder case, with a national, almost a world audience. Ronnie Solan, exploring psychological issues between leaders and led, studies their mutual intrapsychic needs, and highlights the fates of self and object representations in the participants on each side. As the previous chapter, this paper casts particular light on the roles of the followers and their inner motivations in choice of leader, as well as how this process progresses developmentally, from narcissistic to mature object-choice.

Vamik Volkan follows with a plea for more active participation by psychiatrists and psychoanalysts in sociopolitical affairs and ethnic conflicts behind the chronic state of recurrent wars in certain of the world's most incendiary regions. Citing the work of Rafael and Rena Moses and himself in these areas, he describes a mode of intergenerational transmission of self and object representations affectively connected to ethnic conflicts, in which, for example, the father deposits these "psychological genes" into the son for safekeeping and for the resolution of future conflicts. The final paper, by Martin Wangh, addresses the timeless and bottomless task of trying to work through the Nazi experience both by the victims and the perpetrators of the most evil period in the history of man. Against the background of the Mitscherlichs' "The Inability to Mourn," Wangh recounts the history of the psychoanalytic movement in Germany during and after the War, and the problems and progress in the return of German psychoanalysis into the international psychoanalytic community. He makes recommendations for enhancing mutual trust between the present generations, some of which have begun to be fulfilled.

I am happy to be introducing and presenting this volume by his friends and admirers to Dr. Rafael Moses in the year of his 70th birthday.

REFERENCES

Fenichel, O. (1945), *The Psychoanalytic Theory of Neurosis.* New York: W. W. Norton.

Moses-Hrushovski, R. (1994), *Deployment: Hiding Behind Power Struggles as a Character Defense.* Northvale, NJ: Jason Aronson.

Paskauskas, R. A., Ed. (1993), *The Complete Correspondence of Sigmund Freud and Ernest Jones, 1908–1939.* Cambridge, MA: Harvard University Press.

Rangell, L. (1974), A psychoanalytic perspective leading currently to the syndrome of the compromise of integrity. *Internat. J. Psycho-Anal.,* 55:3–12.

——— (1976), Lessons from Watergate. A derivative for psychoanalysis. *Psychoanal. Quart.,* 45:37–61.

——— (1980), *The Mind of Watergate. An Exploration of the Compromise of Integrity.* New York: W. W. Norton.

Waelder, R. (1960), *Basic Theory of Neurosis.* New York: International Universities Press.

2.

A PERSONAL NOTE

RENA MOSES-HRUSHOVSKI, Ph.D.

Two terrorists bombs killed 19 people on Sunday, January 21st, in Israel, throwing Israel's beleaguered government "into a crisis it looked uncertain to survive" (*International Herald Tribune*, January 23rd, 1995). This has been the spirit for a long time: from the joy of hope that something moved at last, that peace agreements are signed—to the despair when terror strikes; from crisis to crisis. Yehuda Amichai, a modern Hebrew poet, said: "In Jerusalem people lived 'inside prophecies' that have come true as inside a thick cloud after an explosion" (Elon, 1991, p. 12).

In such an atmosphere it is not easy to persistently pursue psychoanalytic studies that aim at shedding light on the psychological conditions and obstacles to peace as Rafael does. Special qualities and attitudes seem to be needed. As we become more aware of the importance of our attitudes and personal qualities in our psychoanalytic work in general, I think that they are particularly crucial in the area of psychopolitics. I see these attitudes as a kind of professional self-ideal that can be developed and worked through when its relevance is recognized.

Barron (1950) notes some of the attributes that scholars share with creative social entities: freedom of expression and movement, a lack of fear of dissent and contradiction, a willingness to break with custom, a spirit of play as well as of dedication to work and purpose on a grand scale (p. 288). I think that Rafael, who is deeply involved in working, thinking and writing about intrapsychic, interpersonal and psychopolitical processes has succeeded in acquiring such attributes. Their contribution to his work is considerable.

MacKinnon (1962) in his study of American architects writes that what is most characteristic of the creative architect is a high level of effective intelligence, openness to experience, freedom from petty restraints and impoverishing inhibitions, an aesthetic sensitivity, a high level of energy and an unceasing striving for creative solutions to the ever more difficult architectural problems which he constantly sets for himself (p. 310). I am not neutral or objective. But I hope that it is not only idealization when I think that such attributes characterize him well, when he functions like the architect of the mind and soul. I think that such attitudes and attributes enable him to invest and maintain infinite patience, persistence and trust—in spite of all resistances—that individuals, groups and societies will open up eventually.

Dalia Rabicovitch (1976), a well-known Israeli poet, wrote a poem she called "Pride":

Even rocks crack, I tell you, and not because of age.
For years they lie on their backs, in the heat and the cold,
So many years
It almost seems peaceful.
They don't move, so the cracks stay hidden.
A kind of pride.
Years pass over them, waiting
Whoever is going to shatter them hasn't come yet
And so the moss flourishes
The sea weed swirls,
The sea pushes through and rolls back
And it seems they are motionless.
Till a little seal comes
To rub against the rocks
Comes and goes away
And suddenly the stone is split.
I told you, when rocks crack, it happens by surprise.
And people too.

One of the messages I perceive in this poem is similar to our credo: that as heavily deployed as individuals, groups and societies may be—often to counteract humiliation and shame—there is always the hope that an opening will be made.

My participation in the Festschrift for Rafael is a good opportunity for me to thank him for the fulfilling experience which I sense in me and between us. It is like a river that keeps flowing; it affects our being and working together. One of the directions of our endeavor is to study more systematically attributes and attitudes of the analyst and how his mind works.

REFERENCES

Barron, F. (1950), The disposition towards originality. In: *Creativity*, ed. P. E. Vernon. London: Peguin Education, 1970, pp. 273–289.

Elon, A. (1991), Jerusalem—*City of Mirrors*. London: Fontana.

MacKinnon, D. W. (1962), The personality correlates of creativity: A study of American architects. In: *Creativity*, ed. P. E.Vernon. London: Peguin Education, 1970, pp. 289–312.

Rabicovitch, D. (1976), Pride. In: *The Outer Voice*, ed. J. Bankier et al. New York: W. W. Norton.

Part II

Within the Individual

3.

PSYCHOANALYTIC FOOTNOTES ON LOVE

JOSEPH SANDLER AND ANNE-MARIE SANDLER

Freud could be eloquent on the subject of love, and one has only to read his letters to his fiancée, Martha Bernays, to be convinced of this. On the other hand, his theoretical, so-called metapsychological, formulations on the subject were, in essence, extremely simple; but from the point of view of what we know today, simplistic. Love for another person, the love object, was conceived of as the investment (cathexis) of the object with libido. This investment with sexual energy was referred to as genital love, but the sexual libido could undergo a change, and become, as Freud put it, aim inhibited or desexualized. Thus he says, in "Civilization and Its Discontents" (1930):

> People give the name "love" to the relation between a man and a woman whose genital needs have led them to found a family; they also give the name "love" to the positive feelings between parents and children, and between the brothers and sisters of a family, although *we* are obliged to describe this as "aim-inhibited love" or "affection." Love with an inhibited aim was in fact originally fully sensual love, and it is so still in man's unconscious [pp. 102–103].

In 1920, Freud, in "Beyond the Pleasure Principle," modified his view of libido and referred to *Eros* as a life force, a binding energy, as opposed to *Thanatos,* the death drive. But his theory of love continued to be formulated in terms of sexual as well as aim-inhibited libido. This theory, of love as the investment of another person with psychic energy, whether sexualized or desexualized, has by now outlived its usefulness, and psychoanalysts have had to seek other theoretical formulations. This brings us to our first footnote.

A major turning point in psychoanalytic thinking occurred shortly after World War II, with the differentiation, by the psychoanalysts Heinz Hartmann and Edith Jacobson, of the idea of the mental representation of the self from that of the ego. Previously, "ego" had referred to a psychic agency, to the organizing, controlling part of the mind, an agency in touch with and affected equally by the instinctual drives, the superego, and the external world; but it had also referred to the person's own self as an object, one that could be invested with libido. From the time when the differentiation between the two meanings of ego was made, the term *ego* could be restricted, in the Anglo-Saxon literature at least, to its reference to a mental agency, to a part of the mental apparatus. However, the term *self representation* (often reduced to the shorter form of *self*), the mental representation of the self, could be contrasted with the idea of the mental representation of the object, of the "other person." Love for the *self* (narcissism) can then be seen more clearly to parallel love for the *object*. When Narcissus fell in love with his own reflection, what he fell in love with was *the representation of his own self* as experienced first in the sphere of perception. Similarly, when one loves the object one loves the mental representation of the object, a representation that can exist in perception, fantasy, or memory, and which can be conscious or unconscious. Equally, of course, when one hates an object, what one hates is the mental representation of the object.

In this context we need not speak of investment of libidinal energy in a self or object representation, but it is more profitable theoretically to think in terms of an affective investment, a feeling investment (an *affective cathexis,* if one wants to use the term), a cathexis of value attached to the self or object representation. In talking of affective cathexis we are talking of the attachment of love values or value signs to a conscious or unconscious mental representation, affective value signs which provide us with a whole range of possibilities that constitute a scale of emotional values that can be attached to self or object representations, or to attributes or possessions of the self or object. Such values include those intimately connected with attachment behavior. They also include such affective investments as those of safety or security, and we must add, of course, that negative affects, such as those of distaste, pain, and hate, should also be included. It would perhaps be worth while contemplating, on another occasion, the task of relating attachment values to love. In this connection we should not forget the role of the values attached to those activities we call sublimations, because they are not simply the products of inspiration, but involve, in a sense, an object relationship to the activity, a relationship which is not so different from that of love. By love in this context we do not mean infatuation or the temporary or socially acceptable delusional psychosis of "falling in love."

Love, or the emotional values which constitute love, are not only attached to one's self or to external objects. The concept of "internal objects" is one that has proved extremely valuable to psychoanalysts, and we can love those unconscious internal objects as much as we do objects in the external world. Of course, just as we can attach affective hate values to the representations of external objects, so can we hate our internal objects or simultaneously love and hate them. It is important to note that the concept of ambivalence applies equally to external and internal objects. It is worth adding that these internal objects, the descendants of the important objects of our childhood, may be loved (or hated) with greater intensity than objects outside ourselves. Very often they are externalized onto others, who become the unconscious representatives of internal love objects. Such externalization of internal object relationships is the basis for the phenomenon of transference, and the relationship between transference love and love in general has been a subject of great interest to psychoanalysts; but a word of qualification is necessary at this point. The loved internal object may in certain circumstances not be externalized in any way that resembles the unconscious fantasy object, but rather as its opposite. We think of a patient, reared in the deep South of the United States, who continually chose as love objects fair-haired, blue-eyed, and light-skinned women. During the course of his analysis it was discovered that he had loved and internalized a love relationship with a black woman who had worked in his parents' household, and who had in fact substituted for an uncaring alcoholic mother. But as an adult the conscious acceptance of a black woman as a love object was quite unacceptable to him, and so he had constructed a fantasy love object that was exactly the opposite. It is not surprising to learn that in fact all these object choices turned out to be unsatisfactory, because, of course, they were too close to the real mother. After some years of analysis he found a satisfactory compromise in the form of a brown-eyed brunette of impeccable European origins.

Let me now turn to our second footnote, which has to do with some special forms of love. We all know narcissism as love for the self, but there is a form of what can be called narcissistic object love which is in essence a pseudolove. This is a love attached to an object which is purely a narcissistic extension of the self. The men who choose beautiful women, or the women who select handsome, rich, or powerful men may do so because the object represents a narcissistic extension of the self. Admiration by others of the object becomes admiration for oneself. One could say that there is narcissistic gratification obtained through the feeling that if one possesses such an admirable object, one must be admirable oneself. If the object's prized attributes fade, and there is nothing to compensate for them, the love is lost, because it was never really there in the first place. We hasten to add that not every man who loves a beautiful woman, nor every woman who chooses a rich, handsome, or powerful husband has made a narcissistic object choice. Our lives would be at risk if we made such an assertion. But life is full of contradictions, and, in a rather different sense, it could be said that *all* love is narcissistic; but we shall postpone discussion of this aspect until a little later.

Our third footnote has to do with the issue of the idealization of the love object, and one cannot help but be reminded of Freud's remarks on this question in "Group Psychology" (1921) in connection with what he calls the overevaluation of the object. He says:

> [T]he love object enjoys a certain amount of freedom from criticism, and . . . all its characteristics are valued more highly than those of people who are not loved, or that its own were at a time when it itself was not loved. . . . The tendency which falsifies judgement in this respect is that of *idealisation*. . . . We see that the object is being treated in the same way as our own ego [self], so that when we are in love a considerable amount of narcissistic libido overflows on to the object. It is even obvious, in many forms of love-choice, that the

> object serves as a substitute for an unattained ego ideal [we would now say ideal self] of our own. We love it [the object] on account of the perfections we have striven to reach for our own ego, and which we would now like to procure in this roundabout way as a mean of satisfying our narcissism [pp. 112–113].

It is necessary to point out, of course, that the ideal that is externalized onto the object in the process of idealization may be the ideal self as represented in the person's fantasy, but it may equally be an ideal object, perhaps an ideal mother that had been fantasied in childhood. Probably in normal love the idealization of the love object is predominantly the outcome of externalization of some form of an idealized parental representation.

Parenthetically, it should be said that idealization of the object has at times the function of being a defense against hostility toward the object. It is always worth asking whether an abundance of idealization of an admired object conceals a substantial degree of hate which, if it gained access to consciousness, would cause intolerable conflict. The idealization serves to reinforce the suppression of the unconscious hostility.

The externalization of an ideal is not only seen in heterosexual love, but in homosexual love as well. One might speculate whether in male homosexuality it is predominantly an aspect of the ideal self which is externalized onto the love object, while in lesbian love it might be predominantly an unconscious maternal ideal; certainly this area deserves further exploration.

We want to comment in our next footnote on the role of the interaction between self and object. If the love object is not one with which the subject interacts—if it is a pop star or film idol, for example—then we can speak of love for an internal fantasy figure which has been externalized onto the image of the loved one. It would be difficult to characterize this as "true love" in any sense of the word, although the person in such a state of love would vigorously dispute this last statement. It is certainly a reflection of either a form of self-love or love for an internal object, love for an ideal self or an ideal object, which has been projected outside oneself. The choice of the object must, of course, fit with the unconscious internal fantasy figure for, as we know, it does not simply occur at random.

If we consider the question of object choice a little further, taking interaction between self and object into account, then we come across an interesting phenomenon. We know that not all unconscious wishes are instinctual, that is, they are not all reducible or sexual or aggressive drive impulses. What characterizes unconscious wishes above all is that they involve a fantasied *interaction* between self and object. There is a role for the self as well as a role for the object in the wishful fantasy. Here we are able to learn something of importance from the analytic experience of the patient's transference and the analyst's countertransference. Some years ago, in a book published with two coauthors (Sandler, Dare, and Holder, 1973), a comment was made in this connection. It was said then:

> [T]ransference need not be restricted to the illusory apperception of another person. . . , but can be taken to include the unconscious (and often subtle) attempts to manipulate or to provoke situations with others which are a concealed repetition of earlier experiences and relationships . . . when such transference manipulations or provocations occur in ordinary life, the person towards whom they are directed may either show that he does not accept the role, or may, if he is unconsciously disposed in that direction, in fact accept it, and act accordingly. It is likely that such acceptance or rejection of a transference role is not based on a conscious awareness of what is happening, but rather on unconscious cues. Transference elements enter to a varying degree into all relationships, and these (e.g. choice of spouse or employer) are often determined by some characteristic of the other person who (consciously or unconsciously) represents some attribute of an important figure of the past [p. 48].

In a later work on "Countertransference and Role-Responsiveness" (Sandler, 1976), it was suggested that the patient's attempts to manipulate or to provoke situations with the analyst were "an important part of object relationships in general, and . . . enter in 'trial' form into the 'scanning' of objects in the process of object choice. In the transference, in many subtle ways, the patient attempts to prod the analyst into behaving in a particular way and unconsciously scans and adapts to his perception of the analyst's reaction" (p. 44). We went on to say that "The analyst may be able to 'hold' his response to this 'prodding' in his consciousness as a reaction *of his own* which he perceives, and we would make the link between certain countertransference responses and transference via the behavioural (verbal and non-verbal) *interaction* between the patient and the analyst." But, of course, in ordinary life the person who is unconsciously prompted to assume a role toward the subject does not normally behave like an analyst who has to deal with the transference and who has to check and examine his or her countertransference.

In the choice of an object who might be a candidate for love the individual will normally scan the objects with whom he or she comes into contact for unconscious complementary responses and, as we have suggested, this is an important aspect of so-called object choice. What determines the later course of events is, of course, another question. In interactions of this sort we see what can be referred to as the attempt by each member of the couple to impose an intrapsychic role relationship on the other. There is a role in which each casts himself or herself, and a complementary role in which the other is cast at that particular time. Then there is an attempt to impose an interaction, an interrelationship, and we can say that in a sense each party attempts to *actualize* the fantasied relationship in a disguised way, within the framework and limitations of what is socially appropriate and acceptable.

The attempt to actualize a role relationship may lead to acceptance of the role, but it may equally lead to a rejection of that role—and all of this goes on, for the most part, quite unconsciously. We want to emphasize that we are speaking here of a normal process leading to a choice of an object, a process which can be a bridge to the development of a wholly satisfactory love relationship.

It can be said that, in the course of a developing love relationship, we see the formation in each party of what can be called an object-complementary aspect of the self, and by this we mean that aspect of the self representation that "fits" the representation of the object. It is this aspect of the self that enters into the love attachment to the other, and in the unfortunate circumstance of one of the two parties being lost through death or for some other reason, what the individual loses, in addition to the object, is an aspect of his or her own self; that is, it is the object-complementary aspect of the self that is lost when the object disappears. In the normal and appropriate mourning for the lost object, there is also a process of mourning for the object-complementary aspect of the self. So, however strong the love one has for another, such love always has a narcissistic root—indeed, some would say that fundamentally all object love is narcissistic. This is also a point worthy of discussion.

Our final footnote relates to the question of the mutual identification between the two partners in love. We have seen how projection and externalization enter into the love relationship, and how idealization of the partner can play a significant role in the love relationship, representing, in one way or another, a fulfillment of a certain wished-for ideal for oneself. In connection with this the Kleinian concept of projective identification can be extremely useful, if the concept is used in a relatively specific way, not as a general and vague notion of "putting something into another person"—a usage which is, unfortunately, very common (Sandler, 1987).

We normally understand identification (we refer here to so-called introjective identification) as the modification of the self representation on the basis of the representation of an object—real or fantasied. Some aspect of the object is copied into the real representation, and becomes part of oneself. The opposite process, that of projective identification, can be seen as a modification of the object representation by making the other person identify with an aspect of oneself. It can be, and often is considered, as a mechanism of defense, as a way of getting rid of some unwanted aspect of oneself by, so to say, "forcing" it into the other person, which means projecting it into the other person or rather into the representation of the other, and then manipulating the other person so that he or she in fact does come to function in a way which represents an unwanted characteristic of one's own. One can then attack that characteristic as if it belongs to the other person instead of attacking it in oneself. However, we have to consider projective identification also as being a very *normal* process which is an integral part of *all* emotional relationships, and a vital part of love relationships in particular. We see it in the way a parent can live through the lives of his or her children—something which, if too marked, can have unfortunate consequences. We see a similar phenomenon when a partner in a love relationship lives to too great a degree through the other, again something which can lead to frustration and disappointment if the other party does not conform to the allotted role. But in spite of the fact that projective identification is largely used as a defense, idealized aspects of the self can also be externalized through the use of this mechanism, and we may ask ourselves what benefits the processes involved in projective identification bring to the individual, processes which, we should like to stress, are, within limits, entirely normal.

We want to take the opportunity to attempt to provide a possible answer to this question. In order to do this we need to say something first about the notion of primary identification, or primary confusion, between self and object. This was described by one of us (J. Sandler, 1987) in the following way:

> In representational terms [primary identification or primary confusion] could be said to relate to the state which exists before a firm boundary between self and object (or self and object representations) has been established. It has also been described . . . as a state in which the infant cannot differentiate the representational aspects of his own self from those of the object. In relation to pathology, the state of primary identification has been described as a regressive one in which a "de-differentiation" of self and object occurs and so-called "ego boundaries" ("self boundaries") have been lost or put out of action. This is most commonly seen in severe psychotic states (Jacobson, 1964). However, [and this is what concerns us now] a "fleeting primary identification" or "fleeting confusion" between self and object has been described as a ubiquitous normal phenomenon (Sandler, 1959; Sandler and Joffe, 1967). This phenomenon relates to what Weiss has called "resonance identification" (Weiss, 1960), which can be regarded as a basis of empathy [pp. 9–10].

We see this state of confusion between self and object when, for example, we see someone slip in the street, and immediately right ourselves, or when we watch ice-skating or show-jumping on television, or cowboy films at the movies, when we find ourselves moving in identification with the movements we perceive on the screen. This is an absolutely normal phenomenon, which can occur extremely rapidly, or endure for a longer period of time when we are not paying attention or are relaxed or fatigued. What is relevant to our present discussion is the fact that very fleeting states of primary identification or primary confusion, in which the boundary between self and object is lost, occur whenever we relate to another person, and this is, in our view, the essential basis of the process of projective identification.

What follows from this is that we have to account for the fact that when projective identification is used, we need to be aware that what we have projected is a quality or characteristic of our own in order to feel that it is not our own. If, for example, we could get rid of an unwanted quality by simply locating it in another person, then turning our backs on that person, life would be very much simpler. Unfortunately things do not work out that way. We need to establish an ongoing relationship with the person in whom we have located this unwanted quality, and we have to keep on disidentifying ourselves from what we have projected into the other. Similarly, if we project a so to speak "good" part of ourselves, an idealized quality of our own, we also need unconsciously to own it as our own, to recognize that it is in some way our own in order to enjoy it in the other person. Our suggestion in regard to this apparent paradox of simultaneous identification and projection is that the fleeting primary identification, the fleeting confusion between self and other, allows for an extremely rapid and continual to-and-fro: an unconscious alternation between the momentary state of "oneness," of primary identification or primary confusion on the one hand, and a process of boundary-setting, of sorting out differences between self and object, on the other. What was one's own a short moment before is now located in the object. What is projected is fleetingly "mine," but then, a microsecond later, reassuringly "not mine."

The more we are in a reciprocal love relationship with a partner, the more important these processes become, and we can see the way in which confusion between self and other occurs in its most extreme form at the height of the sexual act, at the point of orgasm, when for a short moment it becomes impossible to say which partner one is. Projective identification, of the sort we have described, is a significant basis for empathy, and the development of the capacity for such empathic identification is an important ingredient in the state of reciprocated love.

REFERENCES

Freud, S. (1920), Beyond the pleasure principle. *Standard Edition*, 18:3–64. London: Hogarth Press, 1955.

——— (1921), Group psychology and the analysis of the ego. *Standard Edition*, 18:67–143. London: Hogarth Press, 1955.

——— (1930), Civilization and Its Discontents. *Standard Edition*, 21:59–145. London: Hogarth Press, 1961.

Jacobson, E. (1964), *The Self and the Object World*. New York: International Universities Press.

Sandler, J. (1959), Identification in children, parents and doctors. In: *Psychosomatic Aspects of Paediatrics*, ed. R. MacKeith & J. Sandler. London: Pergamon Press, 1961, pp. 16–26.

——— (1976), Dreams, unconscious phantasies and "identity of perception." *Internat. Rev. Psycho-Anal.*, 3:33–42.

——— Ed. (1987), *Projection, Identification, Projective Identification*. New York: International Universities Press.

——— Dare, C., & Holder, A. (1973), *The Patient and the Analyst*. New York: International Universities Press.

——— Joffe, W. G. (1967), The tendency to persistence in psychological function and development. In: *From Safety to Superego: Selected Papers of Joseph Sandler*, ed. J. Sandler. New York: Guilford Press, pp. 208–220.

Weiss, E. (1960), *The Structure and Dynamics of the Human Mind*. New York: Grune & Stratton.

4.

THE SECRET SEED OF HATRED IN A DELINQUENT ADOLESCENT

HAROLD P. BLUM, M.D.

The roots of delinquency and criminal tendencies, first sought entirely in constitutional factors, are now known to be largely found in psychological and social determinants. Delinquency is associated with acting out, especially the acting out of narcissistic fantasies which simultaneously express hate, poorly controlled aggression, and infantile demands for love and nurturance. Omnipotence coexists and alternates with feelings of inferiority and humiliation. There may be disturbance at all levels of development, though early childhood disorder and early traumatization predispose toward aggressive and violent tendencies. The child and adolescent may also act out the unconscious delinquent fantasy of the parents and the parents' wish to punish or be punished.

Hatred, too, an affective form of aggressive dislike, tends to be closely linked to disturbances in psychic structure when it is intense, unmodified, unremitting, and a powerful motive force. Freud (1915) postulated that hatred was an ego response and stated, "The ego hates, abhors, and pursues with intent to destroy all objects which are a source of unpleasurable feeling for it" (p. 138). Hatred is thus not specifically tied to fear or frustration, but to all unpleasant affect and experience. It requires sufficient ego development for persistent affective states associated with differentiation of self and object representations. The enactment of self or object directed hatred in the form of violent destructive aggression is a particularly malignant phenomenon.

Hate is the negative pole of ambivalence which cannot be resolved when hate is preponderant over love. Object constancy requires the modulation and integration of infantile love and hate, associated with stable, cohesive self and object representations. Love may moderate and defend against hate, and hate may defend against love. In the delinquent, ambivalence is usually extreme with violent swings of mood and behavior. Hate and aggressive loss of control may be augmented through learning and identification. Underlying rage and hate may be readily mobilized and expressed because of constitutional factors and developmental disorder with deficient ego and superego regulation. It may be noted here that individual and group delinquency and violence are favored by regression, by group condonement and incitement. The state, the leader, the peer group may readily corrupt the corruptible and foster delinquent tendencies and externalized hostility (Rangell, 1980).

Psychoanalysis takes into account unconscious intrapsychic conflict and trauma in particular, but also considerations of psychic structure and its deformations or deficits, and biological, psychological, and social forces which influence psychic structure and development. Traumatic overstimulation and deprivation may predispose to later violent behavior. Illness, injury, object loss, and probably all forms of noxious, developmental experience may contribute to traumatic repetitions. Identification with the aggressor and his aggression with hatred and hating objects, foster tendencies toward destructive behavior. It is of interest that studies of terrorists have shown a frequent history of severe childhood illness characterized by protracted pain, immobilization, and isolation. Reversing the childhood situation, they subject their helpless victims to their enduring rage and hostility. Abused children, if they do not succeed in mastering severe early trauma, all too often become abusive parents and prone to other forms of aggressive assaults and self-injury.

Individuals with central nervous system disorders and brain damage may be particularly prone to violence. The violence is often both the cause and the consequence of head injury and brain damage. Milder forms of cognitive, linguistic, and affective defects may also predispose to hate and aggressive behavior. Substance abuse may adversely influence superego regulation, ego integration, and judgment, and may seriously interfere with underlying brain function. Those who are prone to aggressive behavior for psychological reasons are often particularly susceptible to the detrimental effects of alcohol and other pharmacological agents. Although violence may occur as part of an organic brain syndrome, what I am emphasizing here is the role of the underlying personality disorder which leads to or is aggravated by substance abuse. So much of today's individual and urban violence is rooted in the lack of self-control, compounded by the lack of external control (e.g., the lack of gun control). Many impulse-ridden character disorders and withdrawn, hostile individuals lacking in the capacity for sustained, affectionate relationship and lacking self-esteem and empathy for others have an increased potential for violent behavior. In many of the so-called borderline personalities with severe structural and developmental disorders with impaired ego functioning and object relations, aggression is untamed and poorly modulated. A childhood history is often replete with traumatic deprivation and overstimulation. If the child has not been directly subjected to abuse and violent punishment, he has often witnessed sexual and aggressive attacks on other persons, pets, or property. Lack of control in the form of enuresis, fire setting, and disruptive behavior at school or in play may augur later aggressive behavior.

There are also far more subtle forms of disturbances which predispose to hate, poorly controlled aggression, and later violence. Aggression is normal and necessary for psychic function and survival, and in many instances, the reasons for an aggressive personality disturbance are not comprehensible on the surface. These are not the children of violent or addicted parents or children who have been abused, abandoned, or neglected. The individual's disorder personality and violent tendencies may appear to be inexplicable until there is an opportunity for analytic exploration. Parents, friends, and relatives may be utterly bewildered, and there is often a shared overlay of denial, distortion, and rationalization.

Such was the case of M, a 15-year-old delinquent male who had become estranged from his parents. His parents reciprocally regarded him with shame, fear, and contempt—their problem child whom they no longer knew and who was a "stranger." He was the "black sheep of the family." These white, middle-class parents and their teen son were confused, and there was a long history of confusion, misunderstanding, and denial of the serious implications of M's personality disturbance. M presented a syndrome of truancy, lying, drug use with reported marijuana and probable use of amphetamines and barbituates, theft of money from his mother's purse and his father's wallet, and burglary. He was, on rare occasions, given to outbursts of temper and had tried to choke his sister.

Arrest for his repeated burglaries evoked denial and rationalization that it was just an adolescent problem which he would outgrow. From the outset, the treatment was complicated by the fact that the patient had an arrest record, and on probation, and could face more serious consequences, including possible prison and expulsion from school. He had been a school problem for many years, an underachiever but of superior intelligence who was always trying to outwit the authorities, whether parents, teachers, or later the police. Psychological tests when he was a preteen revealed a combination of narcissistic issues, a sense of inferiority combined with a sense of grandiosity, narcissistic entitlement, and predelinquent signs of rebellious identification with delinquents and criminals. He was attracted to antisocial gangs, to peer groups which disparaged education and social conformity and which were part of a drug and theft subculture. M did not reveal his involvement in an ongoing series of delinquent acts which ultimately led to his apprehension by the police.

He had had brief therapy once a week some two years before my meeting him, but had broken off the treatment without revealing his incipient involvement in delinquency. His conduct and school performance had temporarily improved, and he and his parents, ever ready to assume that improvement would be sustained, readily terminated the treatment.

At the time of my initial contact, M was a medium-built youth, superficially affable, well-dressed and groomed, guarded, and carefully responsive. He gave a history of being aloof, frequently withdrawn, sullen, and suspicious. He avoided communication with his family and was preoccupied with a delinquent peer group whom his family feared and despised. In school he was unmotivated, underachieving, and frequently truant with disruptive behavior in class. The schoolmates he chose had similar problems.

His group consisted of angry, alienated "coconspirators" who rationalized a defiant hostility and their attraction to drugs and delinquency. While claiming he wanted treatment because of his problems at school and with his parents at home, he really felt coerced into treatment as an unofficial condition of probation. Behind his pseudocooperation and courtesy, there was a barrier of negativism and distrust. He could be pseudocompliant, but no real therapeutic alliance was obtained. He briefly revealed a sadomasochistic fantasy system of play with swords and knives as a swashbuckling hero and a daring desperado. He wanted to impress girls; he thought of them in terms of narcissistic exhibitionistic conquest, but was tight-lipped about his other inner fantasies, feelings, and attitudes.

An attempt to engage M in twice-a-week psychotherapy proved to be frustrating, disappointing, and ultimately futile. His severe narcissistic entitlement, his extreme sensitivity to the shame and humiliation associated with his police record and the ashamed, shaming, and outraged reactions of his family all contributed to a barrier of aloof antagonism. What he really wanted was for his parent and the authorities to be "off his back." He adopted pseudocompliance and pseudocooperation in order to be removed from the supervision of parents and probation officer. He had a capacity to be disarmingly charming and to convey the impression that he was a changed person on his way to achieving constructive goals. Underneath this facade he was devious and manipulative and derisive toward authorities who could be easily hoodwinked. His frequent contrived smiling concealed his underlying motives and attitudes. Omnipotent and at the same time so narcissistically vulnerable, he maintained a readiness to react to any injury with demands for compensation and reparation and with hateful vindictiveness. He was able to use his large vocabulary and linguistic gifts, his ample resources of information, and a deft awareness of the needs and frailties of others in the service of persuasion and manipulation. The treatment effort rapidly foundered, although M probably would have continued treatment if he considered it socially or legally advantageous.

A year after the superficial improvement engendered by his flight into healthy conformity and perhaps with some contributions from the benevolent therapeutic contact, M's school difficulties and antisocial tendencies reemerged. He rejoined, and probably had never really left, a drug-taking peer group. This time his mother again consulted me in a state of depression and near panic. She was sure that her own problems had somehow impacted upon her son; the problem within the entire family had contributed to her son's serious disorder. She kept hoping he was going to improve, but part of her felt that he was on his way to catastrophe. She was desperate even if her husband had given up on the child and was passively dissociated. M seemed nonchalant and unconcerned, bristling with anger at any parental supervision, and his mother felt he was totally outside of parental control. In any case, M's mother needed help because she was on the verge of a "nervous breakdown." In addition to being at "the end of her rope," she felt a very deep anguish for herself and her son. She wanted intensive help and did not want to be referred to another analyst. She was struggling with feelings of shame, guilt, and disgrace. She felt that I knew M and some of the problems she faced, and felt that this knowledge would enhance rather than diminish her own treatment.

The further data to be presented were obtained in the course of analytic work with M's mother. I shall not focus on M's mother's treatment and transference, per se, but rather on the data that clarified and illuminated, to some degree, the enigma of her son's delinquency.

M's mother, Mrs. N, could hardly wait to tell her story. There was so much she needed to "get off her chest," so much that she had held back that she should have talked about long before with a therapist. Her associations and account of her life began with a "bombshell." M was not the child of her husband but had been conceived through artificial insemination with donor sperm. After approximately a decade of marriage, she and her husband had given up on the hope of having their own child, especially since his sperm count was very low and had never been restored in years of medical investigation and treatment. They embarked on artificial insemination, with great reluctance, and with the greatest secrecy; only they and their doctor knew. So far as family and friends were concerned, she had been impregnated by her husband, and he was, without question, the father of M. Her public pregnancy facilitated a level of secrecy that may not be obtainable with adoption.

Actually, she had asked for a donor who was a member of her own Christian religion and from similar genetic stock so that the child would resemble herself and her husband. She was sure that M came from different stock, that he didn't resemble their family, physically or psychologically, even though M's physical appearance did not set him apart from their families. He came from the sperm of a stranger, and he had become a stranger. Fantasies of the "bad seed" were on the surface, and she preferred to believe that M harbored a genetic tendency toward criminality, while, at the same time, denying that criminals are born rather than made. There was internal split in the representations of the child and of the parent into "good and bad."

In retrospect, she deeply regretted having participated in this "misconception." She had always felt somehow that it was illicit and illegitimate, an act of adultery which doubtless injured and angered her husband. She had fantasies of an affair with a fertile father figure, connected with unconscious prostitution fantasies and primal scenes. Her husband had been, from the outset, ambivalent, and she wondered if he had acquiesced in order to maintain the marriage. She suspected that on the one side he was pleased to have had M and the opportunity for a family, but that on the other hand he harbored a grudge against her and M. Had she harbored a grudge against her husband because of his infertility? Did she not resent his putting her in the untenable position of either not becoming a mother or accepting donor sperm? Her own needs for biological motherhood were so great that she had refused to contemplate adoption. They were actually both opposed to adoption since her husband wanted her to be publicly pregnant bearing his child. She thought her husband had rationalized that at least one of them would be a biological parent but that he had repressed his injury and his anger. In the cross-currents of injury, anger, and hostility, she slowly became aware of evidence, not only of her own ambivalence, but of her husband's unacknowledged hatred for their son. Remarkably, and in keeping with their secret solution to the problem of her husband's infertility, she went on to repeated artificial insemination and had more children. However, there was a major difference. They had decided and insisted upon repeated trials with her husband's semen, so that M's siblings were the presumed biological offspring of both parents.

These siblings were treated quite differently from M by both parents, but especially the father. The next sibling to be born, two-and-one-half years after the patient, was clearly the father's favorite child. The father was a workaholic, and although he paid insufficient attention to the family, he was always more readily attuned and available for his daughter rather than his son, especially this daughter. In fact, the mother gradually came to understand the prejudiced familial relationships. Her son was unconsciously aware of and sensitive to the prejudice and favoritism. The father made half-hearted efforts to respond to his son, but quickly withdrew and for the most part evaded emotional interaction and limited physical contact. This father was estranged from his son and a stranger to him. In her treatment, M's mother struggled with her need to deny her husband's alienated and antagonistic attitudes toward the boy. This later grew into a mutual antagonism between father and son. Underneath social amenities and ritualistic father–son exchanges, it was quite probable that the two had a deep-seated hatred for each other. This had been complicated and aggravated by Mrs. N's need to protect her son from his father's coldness and distance and to compensate for the lack of effective, unambivalent maternal protection. In turn, the boy became very possessive of his mother and quite resentful of her involvement with her husband or the other children. She had, in her way, doted on him while sorry for herself and for him, and felt very guilty about having brought him into the world. Her special attention to her son further antagonized her husband.

The seeds of prejudice, hatred, and violence were already present when M was in utero. I refer to his mother's ambivalence, her fantasy of bad girl impregnated by bad seed, and to his father's negative attitude and feelings toward his son whom he at least, in part, did not accept as a son. His son's rivalry, grievances, and hatred of his father were rooted in response to his father's hidden rejection, as well as oedipal rivalry. Moreover, it was especially difficult for the mother to acknowledge her ambivalence toward this child and for the child to deal with this hostility toward his mother on whom he was so dependent for affection and emotional support.

It further developed that tendencies for violence and excited interest in harsh punishment were to be found in the mother herself. She was very guilty over the death of a close relative. This unmarried female became pregnant, and Mrs. N advised her to have an abortion rather than to marry. Her relative died as a result of the abortion, and Mrs. N never forgave herself, only to identify with this woman in her own illicit impregnation. She was now being punished through her child, and she was also unconsciously stimulating the child to enact delinquent behavior and to provoke punishment for her guilt. He was now the delinquent—not her or her relative. This was an unconscious "illicit" excitement and punishment they shared together. Both were also temperamental, and mother could respond to M's own tantrums with screaming, shouting threats, and hitting the child. Later when the child would attack his siblings, his mother would lash out at him verbally and physically. By the time M was a teenager, she had threatened to "throw him out of the house" because of violent assaults on his sisters and hitting his mother when she had struck him in exasperation.

His mother had both overprotected M and overstimulated him with an excessive closeness, and she had been inconsistent in setting limits and maintaining discipline. She felt she had also capitulated to his possessiveness. M was also overstimulated in the early years by being allowed to observe sisters in the nude in bedroom and bathroom with "relaxed" rules and regulations concerning brother and sister dress and play. It is quite likely that his anger at his sisters arose from his feelings of rivalry, replacement, and his father's prejudice in their favor. However, his "manhandling" of them, and his violent temper in which he threw their possessions about, may also have been related to unconscious, incestuous sexual temptations and frustrations. His stealing from his sisters, his not feeling guilty for often being mean and malicious toward them, and fights with his mother in which he had to have the last word, were among the childhood signs of delinquent trends. These delinquent trends were manifest at school in lying, truancy, petty larceny, and disruptive behavior, always well rationalized with self-exoneration and blame of teachers and other children. He treated and mistreated his classmates as he had his sisters. The pattern was probably continuous between home and school.

His mother's recognition of his delinquency, his narcissistic entitlement, and his destructive and self-destructive attitudes was quite discontinuous and limited. Mrs. N initially avoided conscious shame and guilt and any conscious awareness of her responsibility in parental contributions to the child's increasingly severe personality disorder. The convergence of the father's enmity, the mother's guilt, ambivalence, and seductive overprotection, and the intensification of sibling rivalry, all point to a crucial period between 2 and 3 years of age when his first sibling was born, and possibly earlier. There was probably a disturbance in the primary object relationship and in affect regulation and communication. The series of disturbances, infantile traumas, and narcissistic injuries, his father's rejection, his mother's attempts to mediate between pleasing her husband and placating her son, all contributed to the foundation of M's later narcissistic and delinquent disorder. M's superego was prone to regression, disharmony, and excesses of permission and punishment. He was unable to anticipate the impact of his aggression and appeared to lack empathic concern.

The network of communication and shared fantasy in every family setting was particularly intense here where it tended to be so exclusive and extended. This mother and son had probably never fully separated, further impeding M's individuation and his personal and sexual identity (Mahler, Pine, and Bergman, 1975). He identified with his mother as unconsciously delinquent and deserving of punishment. He remained alert and suspicious about the feelings and intentions of others, beginning with his parents. He was extraordinarily sensitive to the slightest form of insult or rejection. The core of omnipotent infantile rage was probably associated with intense aggression, with anal phase threats of object loss, and impaired separation-individuation at the time his sibling was born. Narcissistic demands, oedipal rivalry, transgression, and guilt were reactivated and intensified in adolescence. His chosen peer group represented a type of pseudomasculinity in which bravado and defiance were idealized and compassion, concern, or remorse were denigrated and associated with weakness and femininity. He was led toward them and also by them. His tendencies toward delinquent, violent behavior stem from a variety of sources including the repetition of infantile traumas, rejection and rage, and unconscious parental incitement to act out, all with condoning acting out when it occurred. His acting out encompassed the unconscious delinquent fantasies of his parents (Johnson, 1952).

A still deeper and more refined understanding of the familial contribution and the specifically maternal influence in M's psychopathology might have emerged with further treatment. Regrettably, Mrs. N's analysis itself was aborted as she began at a deep level to uncover her own role in her son's disorder. She also began to understand the complexities in the father–son relationship and the buried tensions in the marriage. Her husband was now tremendously aggravated by his son's recidivism and his slide back into antisocial behavior. He was ready to emotionally disown the boy as an ingrate who was unable to benefit from or utilize any and all that they had given to him. In parallel, M's father was increasingly threatened by his wife's changing views and the altered emotional climate in the marriage. Afraid of change, he *insisted* upon change, but a geographic change. He had worked too hard to sacrifice everything to save his son, and now he thought his son could only be saved by removing him from his antisocial delinquent and drug-taking peer group. Mrs. N resisted the effort to sabotage her treatment and the simplistic notion of removing the youth from the noxious environment as a solution to his problem or to their marital problems.

However, the difficulties were brought to a head by a new arrest as a repeat offender. M was now older, and it was a serious threat that M's wish for punishment through the judicial system could be gratified. Fearful of their son's criminal record, fearful for his future, and wanting to avoid further shame and humiliation and to protect their daughters' constructive development, Mrs. N finally capitulated. The family opted to leave the area. They decided to move to another rural part of the country where the father would semiretire and where M would, it was hoped, be away from antisocial group activity and substance abuse. With this decision, calm was temporarily restored, and M went through a period of rapid, outward improvement. Mrs. N recognized that the adolescent threat of independence and separation contributed to M's regressive decompensation. She was ready to find a new environmental structure and new treatment opportunities. This move presumed that M would live at home in the new community. The threat of adolescent separation was diminished for mother and son. For M, the "solution" may have temporarily helped to restore a narcissistic equilibrium and maintain parental controls. Other adolescent conflicts were either unchanged or perhaps intensified.

The family secrecy surrounding M's delinquency and reasons for flight was unconsciously linked to the secrecy of his paternal origins. Secrecy and evasion interfere with spontaneous parental empathy, and, in this case, the absence of the paternal "blood bond" was a serious, continuing narcissistic injury. Hidden feelings of shame and stigma, shared by both parents, were unconsciously transmitted to their son. His mother's unconscious guilt and her compensatory overprotection and seduction further corrupted M's superego, while he was punished for her fantasies of prostitution and sibling murder. The secrecy contributed to M's bewilderment and parental confusion about genealogy and progeny (Blum, 1983). The ambivalent attitudes of each parent contributed to and represented the internal split of good and bad, victim and aggressor in mother and son.

What is not verbalized and not integrated within the adult personality tends to be unconsciously communicated within the family and communicated as well as defended through enactment. Family secrets resonate with and often represent core conflicts (Jacobs, 1991), in this case, the conflicts surrounding infertility and donor insemination. The delinquency of this adolescent reflected the parental sense of transgression, "borrowed guilt," and the need for punishment and violent inner rage associated with concealed maternal seduction and paternal rejection. That this child was raised with deception about his origins is likely to have been a continuous, silent influence in his dishonesty and delinquency.

This case illuminates intrapsychic and intrafamilial factors contributing to delinquency. Parallel to the study of delinquency, the case also demonstrates the complexities associated with artificial insemination with donor sperm. It does not lead to generalizations concerning artificial donor insemination and does not imply that this choice by an infertile couple will necessarily have a pathological outcome. The controversial issue of genetic versus environmental etiology of delinquency and crime was not resolved. This case clearly indicates the importance of childhood experience, but allows for constitutional factors. A differently endowed child might well have chosen different defenses and modes of reaction. Unconscious rage, traumatization, and inappropriate, inconsistent limits might, in another child, have resulted in severe inhibition or masochistic character. The innate and experiential, nature and nurture, interweave and interact throughout development. Psychobiological disposition may favor tolerance of anxiety or frustration, but excessive exposure to unpleasure, and to object related hatred or violence will favor hostile and violent tendencies.

Finally, the question may be asked whether M did not have some dim awareness or unconscious knowledge of his secret paternity. Did he not overhear, register some hint of "vibrations," some unconscious communication of the secret and its reverberations? This could not be demonstrated or ruled out. His need to expose his parents in his delinquency does not presuppose that he knew what they had concealed on any conscious level, though he may have known it in his "heart." Had he been analyzable it would have been fascinating to ponder the question of the reconstruction of his secret seed of hatred. In this connection, Marise Choisy's (1963) report of her three consultations with Freud is pertinent. After pondering an obscure dream and associations, Freud told her that she was an illegitimate child. The patient thought this was impossible and rushed back to Paris. There her aunt confirmed Freud's dream interpretation (that she was an illegitimate child). She was frightened of Freud and his seeming magic power and did not return to him. Instead, she later converted to Catholicism, and after her own training analysis, attempted to develop a church-approved brand of psychoanalysis. The revelation of the family secret was followed by panic and a compromise between being an illegitimate offspring of psychoanalysis and having the legitimized acceptance of the church. It is similarly intriguing to conjecture what the effects upon her adolescent son would have been if Mrs. N had revealed "the truth" to M about his origins.

REFERENCES

Blum, H. (1983), The psychoanalytic process and analytic inference: A clinical study of a lie and loss. *Internat. J. Psycho-Analysis*, 64:17–33.

——— (1989), Punitive parenthood and childhood training. In: *The Psychoanalytic Core: Essays in Honor of Leo Rangell*. Madison, CT: International Universities Press, pp. 167–185.

Choisy, M. (1963), *Sigmund Freud: A New Appraisal*. London: Peter Owen.

Freud, S. (1915), Instincts and their vicissitudes. *Standard Edition*, 14:111–140. London: Hogarth Press, 1957.

——— (1921), Group psychology and the analysis of the ego. *Standard Edition,* 18:67–143. London: Hogarth Press, 1955.

Jacobs, T. (1991), *The Use of the Self.* Madison, CT: International Universities Press.

Johnson, A. (1952), The genesis of antisocial acting-out in children and adults. *Psychoanal. Quart.,* 21:332–344.

Mahler, M., Pine, F., and Bergman, A. (1975), *The Psychological Birth of the Human Infant.* New York: Basic Books.

Rangell, L. (1980), *The Mind of Watergate: An Exploration of the Compromise of Integrity.* New York: W. W. Norton.

5.

FEAR OF LOVE

YECHESKEL COHEN, Ph.D.

As a concept and a phenomenon, love is the subject of endless debate. Everyone talks about love; it is an integral part of our daily lives, the subject of works of art and literature, and philosophical treatises. Yet despite all this, it seems to be very difficult to understand. Moreover, the willingness to experience love seems to pose a problem, particularly when the concept of love is translated into the actual experience of living and being with another person. These difficulties have long been of concern to me because of the manifold problems of patients who complain of difficulty in forming personal connections and in functioning in the social realm. It was an excerpt from the book *Forces of Destiny* by Bollas (1989), that prompted me to write this paper. Bollas asserts that psychoanalysts tend to deal with the patient's feelings of aggression and hatred toward the therapist while relating only secondarily to the positive transference and the love felt toward that same figure.

Bollas posits that the reluctance of therapists to relate to the patient's positive feelings toward them stems from a fear that this might be interpreted as offering gratification to the patient. In contrast to his colleagues, however, Bollas enjoins the therapist to

---

The German version of this chapter was presented in November 1993 at the seventh Sigmund Freud annual lecture of the Sigmund Freud Stiftung, Frankfurt-am-Main and the Sigmund Freud Institut at the Johann Wolfgang Goethe University, Frankfurt.

Acknowledgments. The author wishes to express his gratitude to Sibylle Drews (Frankfurt) and Dr. Rivka Eifermann (Jerusalem) for their significant help in bringing this paper to its final version.

Thanks are also due to the following colleagues for their substantial suggestions: Raanan Kulka, Sarah Moses, and Mati Ben-Zur.

draw the patient's attention to his positive feelings toward the treatment and the therapist, a sort of affirmation of how enjoyable it is to be together and to do something jointly out of pleasure. Thus, he says to one of his patients: "We're not a bad team, are we?" (p. 90). It appears that therapists take great pains to avoid expressions that might hint at ties or connections that overstep the commonly accepted bounds of the patient–therapist relationship. Therefore, according to Bollas, the therapist feels safer when dealing with the patient's manifestations of aggression, even if such a focus means that only part of the patient's total personality is being addressed.

Although Bollas' very definite assertion ostensibly relates to the unique situation of psychotherapy, his words prompted me to wonder if perhaps this is not the exclusive problem of therapists, if perhaps it is not only they who feel that they are treading on safer ground when dealing with hatred and aggression. Is it possible, despite the paradox inherent in this view, that people as a rule feel more protected when confronted with occurrences of hatred and rejection than with love? The more one ponders this question, the more associations arise with regard to the level of attention paid to aggression and to the scope of aggression, hatred, and destruction in interpersonal relations and in relations among groups, societies, and peoples.

Freud tried to find parallels between his innovative discoveries in the psychic realm and the scientific realms of physics and biology. Thus he used terms such as *energy, drives,* and the like in order to explain psychic phenomena. But he also kept a central place for mental issues and terms in which "love" has a unique role. It was his followers who increasingly shied-off from dealing with love with all its complexities. This refrain is clearly exemplified in the psychoanalytic lexicon of Laplanche and Pontalis (1973) where there is, amazingly, no separate definition for "love"; instead, it lies buried in other definitions such as "libido," "life instincts," and "eros." It is only since the late 1970s that psychoanalysts have begun again to refer to "love" as a psychic phenomenon that deserves and needs clarification and investigation.

Freud (1912) postulated that the survival instinct dictates the primary attachment and is responsible for the formation of bonds of love between people, ties that are based on this primary attachment, the same erotic and sexual bond that people search for throughout their lives. Freud saw, therefore, in love relationships a manifestation of life impulses, and argued that each "finding" of a love object is nothing more than a "re-finding," since man continually seeks out his primary love figures. But the subject is a great deal more complex than this. Even Freud in other works is of the opinion that love is not such a primary and formative element as one is given to understand from the above hypotheses taken from his writings. In his work on narcissism (1914), he states that love is the apex of development, while in 1915, he asserts that love is a type of defense mechanism: "It might be said that we owe the fairest flowering of our love to the reaction against the hostile impulse which we sense within us" (p. 301).

Bak (1973) argues that the ability to love depends upon the separation of the self from the dual union of mother and child. In other words, love develops out of a need to rectify what the individual, the infant, feels as a result of the experience of separation. Love is actually intended to turn the clock backward and to enable a return to this state of union. A similar view was expressed by Zuckerberg (1988): "An ongoing wish then in human adulthood is to be reunited in symbiotic harmony with the mother, perhaps the foundation of love" (p. 149).

Melanie Klein (1937) views love as a kind of counterreaction, a mechanism aimed at safeguarding all of the "good" in the face of the "bad" and the destructive. Thus, we see that Klein does not treat love as a primary element, and that she places it in opposition to hatred. This was also expressed in a paper by Person (1992) in which the author claims that love restores narcissistic injuries. She even states that love emerges and develops the more society stresses the uniqueness, the separateness of the individual. Thus, she says, that in Japan, where the group element of life is stressed, the experience of love is not widespread.

Bergmann's (1987) view is quite similar to that of Bak. He notes that love is "The yearning to be forever united with another person" (p. 259). Bergmann (1987) summarizes the psychoanalytic approaches to love by claiming that there are three theories. First, there is a refinding of some hitherto repressed aspect of the parent.

Second, there is the recalling, however dim, of the very early symbiotic phase. Third, there is the inclusion of the other within the boundaries of the expanding self, thereby undoing some degree of separateness.

Despite those who have tried to view love as an outgrowth of development, everyone finds a connection between love and primary experiences of attachment, union, and merger, on the one hand, and separation, detachment, and withdrawal, on the other. In this way Gediman (1981) explains the sadomasochistic element present in all love relationships. The course of love consists, inter alia, of obstacles and difficulties that form an integral part of the ongoing drama characteristic of loving attachments, the tension between approach and withdrawal. Some commentators have tried to attribute the obstacles of a sadomasochistic nature within love relationships to oedipal fears, and have presented these obstacles as symbolic of the obstructions barring access to the forbidden maternal object. Gediman tends to view the erection of obstacles (as in the story of Tristan and Isolde) as a manifestation of the preoedipal struggle, the struggle of rapprochement, the struggle between the desire for attachment and merger and the desire for separateness and individuation.

I believe that love is characterized by four structural elements: (1) Love is an erotic–emotional and affective experience that is comprised also of physiological and cognitive factors. The main aim of this experience is to be together with the love object, be it a human being, nature, an inanimate substance, or an aesthetic experience. (2) The features of this experience will change during the developmental process. This developmental principle has been elaborated by Stern (1993) who claims as follows: "My reading of infants is that they do fall in love and do so several times over as development progressively gives them a new set of capacities with which to fall in love all over again or 'deeper.' The form is largely established. New contents will be poured into it" (p. 178). (3) This experience is based on continuing conflict between safeguarding self-boundaries and merging with the object of love. (4) The experience of love encompasses an inherent struggle between the wish to enrich, expand, and broaden the self-perception on the one hand, and the wish to preserve self-definition and self-identity in its limited status quo.

In what follows I will confine myself to the last two points, namely the conflict between protecting self-boundaries and merger with the love object on the one hand, and the conflict between self-definition and total identification with the love object, on the other hand.

THE CONFLICT BETWEEN SEPARATION AND MERGER

Within the experience of love lies buried the primary desire to return to the fetal state, to reexperience the state of warmth and coziness that began inside the mother's womb, a state which we continue to seek all our lives, a state that Balint (1968) defines as "harmonious mix-up." Fulfillment of the desire for union with the love object carries various risks; for example, it can lead to infantilization, to a type of debasement and depletion, since the individual who loves feels that he or she is no longer a complete entity.

Since love is such a complex and all-embracing phenomenon, it encompasses numerous psychic powers and motivating forces: libidinal and aggressive drives, the power of the superego, and various defense mechanisms. Disruptions in the functioning of these factors are liable to disturb the necessary balance and to skew the struggle in a particular direction. Thus the experience may lead to an exaggerated sense of union, a kind of merger, and to what Kernberg (1977) calls a "oneness," in which there is a risk of blurring of boundaries and loss of individuality. The experience of love in conjunction with such an imbalance may arouse in the individual an exaggerated need to preserve his boundaries, a need that can ultimately limit all attachments, and lead to an excessive turning inward and to withdrawal. In extreme cases, reciprocity between the individual and the love object ceases.

In this framework of separation versus merger it seems to me pertinent to mention Blass and Blatt (1992) who differentiate between two kinds of what they call "union"—that of "merger" and that of "fusion." The former indicates a mutual connection of some kind, such as the healthy bonding between mother and infant, in which, despite its being based upon union and nonindividuation, the mother recognizes the fact that the infant is also a separate entity (what Balint calls "primary harmonious mix-up"). In the second state, that of fusion, however, there is a perception that the other is an integral part of the self; in other words, proper development demands of the mother a way of relating to the baby that is based from the outset on merger rather than fusion—harmonious mix-up in other words.

Case Example

Roni, a 10-year-old, is the second of three children, all boys, born to illiterate parents. The father is a municipal worker and an alcoholic. He has outbursts of rage during which he beats his wife and his son, Roni.

The mother is a cousin of the father. She married him due to family pressure and against her will. She is a gentle and passive woman who has worked in the past as a cleaning-woman and studied hairdressing, but is not currently working. Roni was born prematurely when the first-born was a year old. Two years after Roni's birth, the youngest son was born. At birth he was found to suffer from a heart defect that necessitated emergency treatments including three angiograms. The parents were preoccupied primarily with this child. Behavioral problems emerged with Roni at age 3 and intensified when he entered school. As these increased, so did the beatings which he received, mainly from his father, along with harsh punishments such as locking him into a bomb shelter and other forms of isolation. The beatings he suffered were severe enough to require hospitalization. At the age of 7, he began to demonstrate self-destructive behaviors, such as suddenly darting out into a busy street or loitering in dangerous areas. At times, he would leave the house and wander about in the very early morning, taking his little brother with him. After studying for approximately one year at a special education facility, at 7, he was referred for residential treatment. Both parents expressed great relief at this and exhibited no anxiety or ambivalence whatsoever. In contrast, they engaged in a detailed description of the medical treatments necessary for the third child, although these descriptions as well were not accompanied by any expressions of emotion. While the father has avoided regular, ongoing contact with Roni since his placement in the residence, the mother visits him more regularly. Her attitude toward the boy, however, also exhibits extreme swings: at times she forgets to call or visit Roni when scheduled to do so. Both parents expressed strong opposition to the residence's insistence that they visit Roni weekly. Even after one year, the father still objects strenuously to regular visits, and argues that the boy is a lost case in any case.

Upon entering the residence, Roni was labeled by his counselors as a wild child who expressed even positive emotions through aggressive behavior. Thus, for example, he snuck up behind his counselor and kicked her while jumping on her and wrapping his arms around her. Expressions of any sort—a request, joy, anger—were made in an aggressive and violent fashion. For one-and-a-half years, Roni exhibited behavioral characteristics and emotional expressions that fit the definition of "fear of love." He frequently responded violently to any frustration or rejection but also behaved similarly when approached on a personal and individual level. He avoided all physical contact, fought hard with the other children, provoked them, and brought out a great deal of aggression in them. Roni caused adults as well to avoid "dealing with" him, since the dominant feeling was that whatever one did with him would provoke opposition, withdrawal, and verbal and physical aggression. His personal counselor stated, after working with him for half a year, that Roni managed to arouse in him feelings of anger and fury that could not be compared with his usual feelings of anger. In numerous discussions with staff members, it became clear that from an objective point of view Roni's actions were not of a different nature from those of the other children; despite this, the angry feelings that he evoked were infinitely stronger than those aroused by the actions and responses of the other children. It gradually emerged that Roni's responses arouse in his teachers and caregivers the desire to totally reject him. It is as if he were constantly yelling: "Do not dare to come too close to me."

In this entire relational system it is apparent that Roni identifies intimacy with aggression and destruction; the latter provide the avenue of expression for his desire for union and intimacy without his being able to distinguish between intimacy and destruction, violence and rejection. It seems that the more Roni feared the crisis that he was unable to integrate into his personality, the more he avoided any true intimacy founded upon love relationships.

The following is taken from a treatment session conducted about a year after Roni began psychotherapy. The therapist came to pick him up from his classroom as had been the practice from the beginning. Roni hid behind the door and when the therapist found him he said to him: "Do you know where I was? . . . I hid myself from you." On the way to the treatment room, Roni asked the therapist to pick him up and carry him. When he did so, Roni pulled on the therapist's arm, at the same time pretending to fall, and expecting the therapist to pick him up. Roni asked for the keyring to unlock the door to the clinic where his treatment room was located. Meanwhile another psychologist arrived and asked to enter the clinic, but Roni stalled her by making her look for the right key. After they entered the clinic, Roni went outside and tried to lock the door so that the therapist would stay locked inside. This game is reminiscent of the period when Roni would be locked in his house, except that this time there was a role reversal. After this game, they both entered the treatment room. Roni immediately suggested role-playing, with the therapist taking the role of Roni's brother and Roni shooting at him. Right after the shooting, the "brother" (the therapist) was brought to a doctor where he received good treatment. But later on, the medical treatment became unbearable and extremely painful although eventually he was cured. Then came the process of payment, with each party paying: the "brother," for the treatment, and Roni, for the pleasure that he derived out of causing the patient pain. Next, Roni told the therapist to go visit his "girl friend" (Roni) and to lie down "next to her" while "she" embraces him after hearing everything that has happened to him. Suddenly the "girl friend" turned into a magician who took away the therapist's wound (which had been caused by the gunshot) and transferred it onto the ceiling. Then the magician-girl friend changed into various animals including a snake that wrapped himself around the therapist leaving him unable to react. Following this incident, Roni changed into a small monkey that the therapist found lying in the road with a gunshot wound. The therapist healed the little monkey (the infant), and the monkey enjoyed his treatment. At the end, the mother chimpanzee came and heard the whole story. She handed over the little monkey to the therapist and Roni said: "Then she leaves the monkey with you, and you're happy."

It would seem that this treatment session contained many echoes of the rapid transitions from activity to passivity, from child to adult, from the battered, wounded child to the cared-for child, and so on. But out of all this, it is apparent that there is an ongoing struggle between approach and withdrawal, between realization of the desire to be cuddled and to be "with," and the fear that this cuddling will cause a disaster of aggression and destruction to befall him.

THE CONFLICT BETWEEN THE WISH TO EXPAND THE SELF VERSUS PRESERVING SELF-IDENTITY

The more complex form of love encompasses mutuality, inasmuch as it relates to, and is directed toward, human objects; this is romantic love, which can include genital sexuality but can also be based on nonsexual eroticism. It can be directed toward an individual object—not necessarily exclusively—just as it can be directed toward a collection of human objects (as in love for a group, community, or people). This serves as a means of expressing the desire for a broadening experience that lies embedded within the love relationship, in other words, the wish to create unions that are more and more wide ranging and complex. The desire for a broadening experience also finds expression in the thirst for aesthetic experiences or the wish to experience a certain landscape. These are all activities and experiences which, if they are undertaken out of a feeling of love, are also capable of expanding a person to the point of encompassing the beloved object within his self identity, within his self entity.

Davis (1988) claims that "A loving relationship is one in which the self of each partner, while connected in a shared identity, also flourishes and is enhanced individually" (p. 162). But this wish for self expansion and enrichment can be fulfilled as long as love is not fixated, or as Setzman (1988) says: "love that is freed from primitive needs and phantasies can give birth to tremendous feelings of creativity, productivity, and mature dependence and mutuality" (p. 132).[1]

[1]This principle is well exemplified by the comparison between Berlioz's "phantastic symphony" and the ninth symphony by Beethoven. In both we have a repetition of themes. But Berlioz's leitmotif repeats itself without any elaboration, the motif is somehow fixated,

In a constant thrust for self-expansion lies a risk of loss of individuality and self-identity. Thus, there is also an opposing force operating within the individual, the force that strives to preserve the status quo and not to expand, and, above all else, to ensure that the self-identity remains intact and well defined. But it sometimes happens that this ongoing, eternal struggle between the two opposing forces can lead to situations of loss—temporary or even extended—of the individual identity.

On the personal level, this condition can lead to schizoid phenomena, with fears and anxieties surrounding any interpersonal contact whatsoever. A schizoid personality disorder is liable to develop, during which we see the emergence of various idiosyncratic characteristics intended, so to speak, to preserve the person's individuality. These pathological phenomena may be accompanied by acts of aggression whose purpose is not only to safeguard individuality from within, but also to protect it by eliminating anything that is different and therefore perceived as a threat to individuality from without. Racist movements of various types belong, of course, to this category.

This exaggerated self-definition is one pathological outcome of the fear of love in this conflict, so we may also face the other extreme, that of overidentification with the love object, through which the individual relinquishes his own self-identity. This is sometimes encountered in cases of suicide motivated by the desire to rejoin significant objects that have been lost (Volkan, 1981). Also included here are personality disorders of the "as if" type, or disorders that stem from taking roles that are expected of one (referred to by Sandler as "role responsiveness"). To this category belong, of course, several kinds of addictions. On the societal level, this framework of loss of self-identity encompasses certain group religious conversions and group or mass participation in various messianic movements. But we can also include on this level phenomena of total and indiscriminate identification with sports teams or singing groups which to a certain extreme in pathological cases, lead to acts of violence, assorted addictions, and even suicide.

---

which leads the lover finally to hell. The motifs in the ninth symphony by Beethoven appear repeatedly in the last movement but in an elaborated and more complex way which finds fruition in the final song of joy and unity.

Case Example

Dror, 39 years old, came in for treatment complaining that he was unable to form a connection with a mate. Dror had had relationships with many women during his life, but these were always broken off after a short time, in most cases at his instigation. Very soon he would feel that the girl didn't interest him anymore, and then he would cut back on the frequency of their dates until they stopped altogether. Even when he met a new woman, he would not see her often, and when the woman expressed a desire to date more intensely, he would avoid doing so. In his sexual relationships with women, he felt no problem whatsoever but he found sleeping together with a partner difficult. Here he related various manifestations of that difficulty: fear that he would wake her up with his movements, that she would fall asleep with her head on his arm, or that she would leave behind things in his apartment. These indicate the separation that he makes between sexual relations and loving attachments. When he was involved in loving relationships, he was reluctant to express attachment, physical or spiritual; when he saw signs of this developing he experienced a feeling of "real strangulation."

Most of his complaints were directed toward his parents who never expressed an interest in his actions, his interests, his friends, or his girl friends. His mother's guiding principle to this day is noninterference in the lives of others, including her children. Even when he has made an effort, and tried to tell his mother about a new woman he had met, she did not ask him even one question, despite her worry at his being unmarried. His mother exhibits extreme obsessive behavior which, he believes, safeguards her principle of noninvolvement, a principle that is perceived by Dror as inattentiveness to him and alienation. As he continued to dwell on this issue, his sorrow around the lack of physical contact comes up more and more often. He never witnessed any physical contact between his parents, nor did he enjoy a pat or a hug from either of them. A singular memory surfaced around this issue: when he was a little boy, the family traveled abroad where he saw his aunt for the first time. She hugged and tickled him, a unique experience that he never forgot.

Various memories relate to receiving things from his parents; these were generally given to him only after he burst into tears.

When he got them, he would quickly abandon them as objects in which he had no interest. At work here, apparently, was the principle that something that is not given out of a loving attachment cannot serve as a transitional object. This is also the way he behaved toward women: after forming a connection with them, he would lose interest in them quite rapidly. Frequently he attempted to form ties with women who, it emerged after the initial meeting, were involved with another man. This pattern repeated itself many times until it became clear that in some way he knew from the onset that these girls were engaged in a relationship with someone else, and perhaps the other man served as his "safety valve" against overattachment. True, there is some replay of the oedipal state in the above, but it seems to me that the problem is different, for here there is a repetition of the "I have no mother" trauma; in other words, he feared that any attachment would ultimately bring with it the experience of the alienating mother.

His entire appearance indicates great control and restraint, all in the guise of good manners. For example, when I called his attention to the fact that he had not responded at all to the increase in the treatment fee, he said: "So what can I do? At most, I could leave treatment." In other words, any expression of opposition, of rebellion, is immediately perceived as total destruction, as if there exist only two alternatives: complete surrender or complete destruction. This total self-restraint has led him into difficult situations which have caused him to remain outside of the performance track or the circle of more important people at his workplace, due to some hidden message that he gives off that he is uninterested in all sorts of assignments, contacts, or positions. On the one hand, he has a strong desire for attachment, appreciation, and union, but, on the other, what predominates is his fear of the danger that these relationships could arouse resistance in him that could only end in destruction and annihilation. He adds: "I have a tendency to run people over." In other words, there is a risk that he will annihilate the object and end up alone; thus it is better, so to speak, to stay away from forming an attachment to the object. And indeed, after two years of treatment, when he allowed himself to feel love toward a woman, he wondered if rather than loving her he was actually clinging to her, meaning, he drew a parallel here between love and the primary bond of attachment.

It is apparent that in his case, two feelings are part and parcel of any relationship that involves attachment: either that attachment involves a risk of engulfment, meaning annihilation, or, alternatively, it is liable to arouse destructive traits in him. So, for example, when he was invited to stay at his current girl friend's home, he claimed that he didn't feel comfortable "since this wasn't my territory," but when he invited her to his home he was unsure about whether to make room for her in his closet—a sort of feeling that she was about to become a part of him. Directly after this, he told of his aggressive outbursts directed toward people at work, who appeared truly frightened by him. In his behavior, we see an unmistakable manifestation of the ongoing struggle between the desire for union and the desire for separateness, where there is actually no interim space, no potential space, in his feelings. He still lives with the feeling that there exists only the possibility of engulfment or that of being engulfed, without there being a simultaneous coexistence of union and separateness.

This state of affairs was demonstrated through the following vignettes. The first was a dream that he recalled after telling me about his sexual inhibitions toward his girl friend. In the dream, as a soldier, he flees with two comrades from the enemy's territory. They then go toward a very narrow canyon in which they were sure that they would meet the rest of their unit. To their surprise they encounter enemy soldiers who capture them.

The second vignette concerns the trip he and his girl friend took abroad to visit her parents and entire family. He tells how wonderful the visit was, though he was quite often embarrassed as everybody was asking about their future. Then he told about her moving finally into his apartment and about a long conversation they had in the evening. They were sitting on the balcony and surprisingly he initiated the topic of their possible joint future. His girl friend raised her hesitations yet she also talked about her wish not to postpone too much as she is over 30 and still wants children of her own. He too shared with her his uncertainties. He is not sure whether he loves her and if he is capable of handling the responsibilities that are part of marriage. Finally he said that he was also apprehensive about the ceremonial aspects of getting married. This conversation lasted for a long time and he reported it in quite a gloomy mood. I told him that it struck me how easily he could pronounce the word *marriage,* which he had refrained from doing previously. Whereupon his expression suddenly changed and amused he said that when they were getting up the other morning his girl friend had asked him in a funny and quite cynical way: "So, Dror, are we getting married?" Upon which I could show him how easily, openly, and happily he could relate to this question of hers just because it was somehow not serious, and in this sense not real, which meant not frightening.

ETIOLOGY

In his work entitled *Fear of Breakdown* (1974), Winnicott asserts that the origins of the fear of breakdown lie in the initial stage of life when traumatic events took place; but because of the earliness of their occurrence and the initial development of the self, they were not perceived by the infant as part of his own being. The person who fears breakdown is unaware, so to speak, that the traumatic incident that he fears has already taken place. Until he integrates this into his personality, he will continue to fear that this breakdown indeed awaits him. Only when he acknowledges that it has already happened at some point in his past, and he is able to "include" the event or experience in his personality, can he relinquish the fear and the defense mechanisms that he has activated against this fear. In reality, what we have here is a state of lack of control, wherein the individual is terrified of a loss of control when this traumatic event that he is so afraid of comes to pass. Consequently, he employs massive defense mechanisms whose purpose it is to protect the self from the breakdown that awaits him if indeed this trauma occurs. The assumption is that the unconscious actually recognizes the traumatic phenomenon since it already took place in the distant past, but that the event, as stated above, was not integrated into the framework of the person's self and his control, thus rendering him incapable of seeing it as a part of the fabric of his self.

I would like to argue here that the fear of love also serves as a defense mechanism against the repetition of a traumatic event that took place in the distant past but was not perceived by the individual as an experience of the self, under the control of the self, and one that he himself underwent. I believe that the drives to form a primary attachment, *archaic love,* evoke traumatic experiences such as potential annihilation stemming from extreme rejection or, alternatively, extreme incorporation, while preventing the development of a separate and individual self. The fear of either of these two possibilities can lead to a total defense system that blocks the development of real love relationships.

Winnicott asserts in this work that agonies from the early childhood period are related to anxieties surrounding an endless fall, death, or a return to an unintegrated state. It is interesting to note that various languages commonly connect love with these concepts of agony, as in the case of the English expression "falling in love," the Hebrew slang "I'm nuts about him" which translates literally as "I'm dying" over him, the slang expression, "I could eat him up," and others, so that it can be assumed that love also arouses numerous forms of anxiety.

The nonintegration of the trauma into the self is a result of overly abrupt transitions from a state of nondifferentiation to that of differentiation. This transition is actually accomplished by means of an interim space known as "potential space." This concept, which was defined by Winnicott (1971b) and developed by Ogden (1985), explains the inception of development as being based on an interim space created between the infant and his mother. The transition from an inadequately defined state wherein mother and baby live in an undifferentiated system, to a state in which the differentiation between the two is more defined, must be accomplished gradually. In the course of this gradual transition, a situation will be created in which mother and infant are simultaneously both an undifferentiated and a differentiated unit, both an imaginary and a physical state. Within this potential space the infant slowly learns that when he lies snuggled in the arms of his mother he is also separate from her, that he has a different existence from hers, and that he is also united with her. It is only within this space that the infant can safely integrate his sense of self. A rapid, abrupt transition from undifferentiated union to absolute separateness can arouse a fear of love, a fear that the renewed "coziness" within the state of love will bring him back to the state from which he was prematurely driven out. There are cases where children were unable to develop such a space between themselves and their mothers because the mother was preoccupied with herself and was unaware of the need to develop a unique language of communication between herself and the infant, or particular facial expressions or positions for holding and feeding the baby that were unique to the two of them, along with other phenomena that make up this unique space that is different for each child. It can also happen that the mother relates to the baby as an extension of herself, as a reflection of her, and does not allow the formation of any wedge between them, a wedge where the potential space might have been able to develop.

While love, as we perceive it, means a return to the state of potential space where there exists a state of union which is also separateness, and separateness which is also union, development characterized by an abrupt transition does not permit the individual to develop love relationships due to this same fear of losing boundaries and self-identity.

In conclusion I would like to illustrate the issue presented in this paper by an example from the world of music. In Mozart's opera *Don Giovanni,* we encounter the famous lover who, according to the writings of his servant Leporello, has had hundreds of lovers. Despite this, we find only one love duet in the entire opera that includes Don Giovanni. We do have, however, the Serenada, a love song that he sings beneath the window of the maidservant Donna Elvira. If we examine the libretto of the Serenada, we see that it is wholly and completely dedicated to his preoccupation with himself and the benefits to be gained from his love for this woman:

When troubled would I not call—only you
Sweeter to me than honey are your lips
Do not withhold from me your good heart,
Reveal to me your beauty,
Your voice for it is sweet—make it sound for me.

In other words, the woman has no existence of her own, apart from what she can offer to him. She becomes an integral part of Don Giovanni who does not recognize her independent existence. One form of Don Giovanni's "love" is the incorporation of the other and that person's transformation into an integral part of himself. But this, too, he can only accomplish from a distance, namely, when she is hidden in her home and he is declaring himself from the street outside. This psychic state is expressed also in the sole duet that Don Giovanni takes part in with Zerlina. Here we see a verbal and musical integration of the idea that I would like to propose. As they stand together, Don Giovanni asks her to come with him to his house and there they will be together. In other words, he does not give her the feeling that they are together here and now, but defers it until a time when they will be in his house. Moreover, from the musical point of view, both partners in the duet sing their parts separately. Instead of singing together, each one sings as if being far from and cut off from the other, despite the fact that this is supposed to be a love duet. Only at the conclusion of the duet does Mozart join the two and have them sing at the same time; however, their music is completely identical, as if they had merged. But again, this is not a union of the *merger* type (to use Blatt's term) but a union based on *fusion* (again, Blatt's usage).

In contrast, in the duet sung by Ottavio and Donna Anna, some parts are sung separately and others by both of them, but without such obvious symmetry as in the duet of Don Giovanni and Zerlina. Yet even when Ottavio and Donna Anna sing together, one can hear that the individuality of each one is preserved. This notion is also expressed in the words of Don Ottavio's aria:

Only if she is tranquil
Can I find rest.
Only if she is joyous
Does strength beat in my breast.
If she is suffering
I shall know death.
If she is sighing
My heart groans.
If she is seething
My heart is afire;
All things good in my life
Come only from her.

The words of this aria show that the lover feels himself as separate from the object of his love, just as he feels that the love object has an existence separate from his own; each of them possesses a personality, emotions, and a unique individuality. However, we also hear echoes of a union based on merger, a sort of loss of individuation. In my opinion, the words of the aria are an excellent example of the coexistence of attachment and separateness, of union and individuality, which are the true expression of a love that contains no fear. Of course, one may also ask why Don Giovanni falls in love with hundreds of women. It seems to me that these love relationships, despite their falsity, demonstrate a defense against the fear of real love. The large number of so-called loves gives the lover the feeling that no harm will come to him if he does indeed fall truly in love—a sort of counterphobic act that ultimately falls so short of solving the problem on a basic level that Don Giovanni is ready at the end to join the denizens of the underworld.

I do not know what drove Don Giovanni to respond so willingly to the summons of the stone statue of the Commendatore and thus consent to give up his life and join the legions of the dead. But Mozart may have wished to say that a man whose entire existence is based upon the semblance of a love life, while deep within himself he is afraid of love, is a man who is not alive. Thus I believe that it is wrong to say that "love is as strong as death"; rather, we should assert that "love and life are one and the same."

REFERENCES

Bak, R. (1973), Being in love and object loss. *Internat. J. Psycho-Anal.*, 54:1–8.

Balint, M. (1968), *The Basic Fault*. London: Tavistock Publications.

Bergmann, M. S. (1987), *The Anatomy of Loving*. New York: Fawcett Columbine.

Blass, R. B., & Blatt, S. J. (1992), Attachment and separateness. *The Psychoanalytic Study of the Child*, 47:189–203. New Haven, CT: Yale University Press.

Bollas, C. (1989), *Forces of Destiny*. London: Free Association Books.

Davis, H. B. (1988), The self and loving. In: *Love—Psychoanalytic Perspectives*, ed. J. F. Lasky & H. W. Silverman. New York: New York University Press, pp. 159–172.

Freud, S. (1912), On the universal tendency to debasement in the sphere of love (Contributions to the psychology of love). *Standard Edition,* 11:177–190. London: Hogarth Press, 1957.

——— (1914), On narcissism: An introduction. *Standard Edition,* 14:69–102. London: Hogarth Press, 1957.

——— (1915), Thoughts for the times on war and death. *Standard Edition,* 14:273–302. London: Hogarth Press, 1957.

Gediman, H. K. (1981), On love, dying together, and liebestod fantasies. *J. Amer. Psychoanal. Assn.,* 29:607–630.

Kernberg, O. (1977), Boundaries and structure in love relations. *J. Amer. Psychoanal. Assn.,* 25:81–114.

Klein, M. (1937), Love, guilt and reparation. In: *Love, Hate and Reparation,* ed. M. Klein & J. Riviere. London: Hogarth Press, pp. 306–343.

Laplanche, J., & Pontalis, J. B. (1973), *The Language of Psychoanalysis.* London: Hogarth Press.

Ogden, T. H. (1985), On potential space. *Internat. J. Psycho-Anal.,* 66:129–141.

Person, E. S. (1992), Romantic love: At the intersection of the psyche and the cultural unconscious. In: *Affect: Psychoanalytic Perspectives,* ed. T. Shapiro & R. Emde. Madison, CT: International Universities Press, pp. 383–412.

Setzman, E. J. (1988), Falling in love and being in love: A developmental and object-relations approach. In: *Love—Psychoanalytic Perspectives,* ed. J. F. Lasky & H. W. Silverman. New York: New York University Press.

Stern, D. N. (1993), Acting versus remembering in transference love and infantile love. In: *On Freud's "Observations on Transference-Love,"* ed. E. S. Person, A. Hagelin, & P. Fonagy. New Haven, CT: Yale University Press, pp. 172–185.

Volkan, V. D. (1981), *Linking Objects and Linking Phenomena.* New York: International Universities Press.

Winnicott, D.W. (1971a), The use of an object and relating through identifications. In: *Playing and Reality.* New York: Basic Books, pp. 101–111.

——— (1971b), The place where we live. In: *Playing and Reality.* New York: Basic Books, pp. 104–110.

——— (1974), Fear of breakdown. In: *Psychoanalytic Explorations.* Cambridge, MA: Harvard University Press, 1987, pp. 87–95.

Zuckerberg, J. O. (1988), The struggle of love: Reflections and permutations. In: *Love—Psychoanalytic Perspectives,* ed. J. F. Lasky & H. W. Silverman. New York: New York University Press, pp. 147–158.

6.

FREUD'S THEORY OF MOTIVATION AND OTHERS

ARNOLD D. RICHARDS, M.D.

While the problem of motivation must be central to any psychoanalytic theory worthy of our interest, the actual literature on motivation within the classical psychoanalytic tradition has been sparse.

Within the Freudian canon, the most comprehensive statement between Freud's death and the 1980s was David Rapaport's "On the Psychoanalytic Theory of Motivation," written in 1960 and stimulated in part by R. W. White's effort to enlarge the analytic concept of motivation by incorporating Piagetian observations on early exploration in his paper of 1959, "Motivation Reconsidered: The Concept of Competence." The most ambitious attempt to tackle the problem of motivation in the recent post-Freudian literature is that of Joseph Lichtenberg, first in *Psychoanalysis and Motivation* (1989) and now in its sequel, coauthored with Frank Lachmann and James Fosshage, *Self and Motivational Systems: Toward a Theory of Psychoanalytic Technique* (1992). Lichtenberg's work follows from his effort to integrate the findings of infancy research into a broader psychoanalytic theory and is offered as a comprehensive alternative to Freud's theory of motivation. In spite of its striking intuitive clarity, the notion of a motive becomes extremely elusive when one attempts to pin it down with rigorous definition. It may be useful, therefore, to go back to Rapaport's classical paper and use it as a touchstone for our discussion.

According to Rapaport, the concept of psychic energy is fundamental to the psychoanalytic theory of motivation. It is an entity which is scalar and directionless, analogous to physiological energy yet not correlated with it in any direct manner. This view is a departure from the traditional theory, which views psychic energy as embodying motivational aims—the qualitative, directional component of behavior. The latter position would later count George Klein (1967) and Robert Holt (1967) among its adherents.

Although Rapaport views psychic energy as directionally nonspecific, he postulates qualitative differences—libidinal, aggressive, and neutral energy—likening these to the differences in physics between heat and light. This reasoning was found faulty by both Schafer (1968) and Rosenblatt and Thickstun (1977). It might be said that Rapaport's thinking is not clearly formulated in this area. He seems to be suggesting not that psychic energy is an activator in strict parallel with physiological energy, but rather, that it acts as a trigger serving a directing and regulating function. The implied analogy is with information theory rather than with physics. Rapaport does make careful distinctions between those forces determining behavior that are motives and those which are not. He distinguishes also between types of motivational forces.

Keeping Rapaport's pioneering statement in mind, let us reconsider the problem of motivation by first considering several broad trends bearing on the theory or theories we now term *psychoanalytic.* First and foremost is the push toward a consensus that "orthodox" or "classical" Freudian theory is defunct. Stephen Mitchell (1992), in a recent issue of *Psychoanalytic Dialogues,* adopts this position in claiming that the "battle against orthodoxy has been largely won, the real vitality and creativity in the field have shifted to efforts to develop postclassical, broadly relational approaches to mind, development, and the analytic situation" (p. 443). This passing is hardly mourned, as the Freudian / drive model is deemed mechanistic and biological, and hence oblivious to humanistic issues of content and meaning. Relational models, on the other hand, are held to be nonmechanistic and psychological, and hence concerned with human values and meaningful interpersonal interactions. This dichotomous view fuels a number of current controversies, though on reflection we can see that this bifurcated approach has been played out repeatedly throughout the history of our science.

The second broad trend follows from the first. With classical theory under attack on many fronts we are witnessing a rush to theoretical pluralism. Many analysts, that is, do not merely tolerate, but endorse, the peaceful coexistence of rival theories: classical analysis, self psychology, object relations theory, intersubjectivity theory, interpersonal analysis, relational analysis, Kleinian analysis, and so forth.

The third trend follows from the second. In response to theoretical pluralism, many analysts have turned to metatheory in an effort to make sense of the diverse viewpoints that collectively constitute contemporary "psychoanalysis." Within this realm of metatheory we can identify four major positions.

1. *Clinical common ground.* The main exponent of this viewpoint is Robert Wallerstein, although others, including Joseph Sandler, are also identified with it. Wallerstein accepts theoretical pluralism as a given, but then distinguishes "clinical theory," through which all analysts accept certain fundamental postulates, such as the existence of transference and resistance, from "general theory," which for now is necessarily metaphorical. He maintains that the prevailing pluralism pertains only to the latter, the "various scientific metaphors that we have created to satisfy our variously conditioned needs for closure, coherence, and overall theoretical understanding" (1992, pp. 52–53). Our common ground is our clinical ground: we all do pretty much the same things regardless of the metaphors we espouse at the level of our general theoretical commitments. Wallerstein, be it noted, stresses that acceptance of diverse theories is a pragmatic and temporary expedient. He expresses the hope that our multiple perspectives will over time "evolve beyond the metaphoric" and therefore scientifically untestable status that characterizes them at present.

2. *Total composite theory.* This viewpoint, introduced by Leo Rangell, is embraced by many classical analysts formerly identified with American ego psychology. Rangell argues that from the very beginning, analysis has advanced by accretion, the filling in of gaps in Freud's broad theoretical system, rather than by the repetitive promulgation of what he terms "new partial theories."

Via instances of theory building by accretion—Rangell offers his own notions of "unconscious choice conflict," "unconscious ego decision making," and "unconscious ego will" as examples—psychoanalysis successfully enlarges its domain to include the selective emphases of "new partial theories." This approach is considered preferable to embracing the new theories in toto, since the latter tend to focus on one aspect of human experience at the expense of others: deficits at the expense of conflicts; preoedipal issues at the expense of oedipal issues; annihilation anxiety at the expense of castration anxiety; and so forth. As such, the emphases of new partial theories—the environmentalism of Horney, the interpersonalism of Sullivan, the object relational focus of Fairbairn—represent the fallacy of pars pro toto: these theories select one pole of what in life is a duality rather than a dichotomy.

3. *Drive/relational dichotomies*. This metatheoretical approach has been most extensively set forth by Stephen Mitchell, initially with his collaborator Jay Greenberg, and subsequently in Mitchell's *Relational Concepts in Psychoanalysis: An Integration* (1988). According to Mitchell, classical psychoanalysis, rooted in Freudian drive psychology, and contemporary relational psychoanalysis, rooted in object relational and interpersonal theory, are alternative explanatory visions that encompass development, motivation, and psychopathology. The two visions are neither complementary nor amenable to integration. Rather, they are in principle incompatible, since each is coextensive with the entire domain of human psychology. Simply put, drive and relational perspectives are incompatible because each represents an explanatory paradigm that covers the same range of phenomena.

4. *Eclecticism, or theoretical common ground*. The final metatheoretical approach, elaborated most notably by Fred Pine in *Drive, Ego, Object, Self* (1990), considers each of our competing theories to be itself inadequate, given its restricted domain and limited explanatory strategies. His approach is advanced as a pragmatic one that aims not at theoretical unification, but at the more modest goal of phenomenological synthesis. His advice, in brief, is that analysts should follow their clinical material wherever it leads, drawing selectively on the four major psychologies of drive, ego, object, and self according to the clinical exigencies of the moment. The four psychologies thus became experience-near approaches to clinical data which, in their additive totality, correspond to reality. Arnold Cooper has advocated a variant of this approach in holding that different theories "fit" different diagnostic categories: object relations theories fit borderline patients; conflict theories fit neurotic patients; self psychology fits narcissistic patients.

The problem of motivation may now be considered through a critical appreciation of the motivational assumptions, explicit and implicit, to be found in these perspectives. We may begin with Pine. His advocacy of the four psychologies approach is premised on the claim that classical psychoanalytic theory has not dealt successfully with the problem of motivation, having made successive attempts to assign motivational primacy to trauma, sexual instinct, instinct of self-preservation, aggression, and primary and secondary ego functions. But this state of affairs has been rendered more confusing still by efforts to make superordinate other kinds of motivation; attachment (Bowlby), mastery (Hendrick), and effectance pleasure (White). Pine's response is to construct a unified model that encompasses four discrete but interrelated motivational systems, each associated with one of the four psychologies. This seemingly straightforward, additive approach to motivation, however, is fraught with problems. Foremost among them is Pine's failure to achieve the neat motivational distinctions his approach seems to call for. He acknowledges, for example, that sexuality, an obvious motivator within drive psychology, is inherently problematic. Following George Klein, Pine recognizes that the search for sexual experience can have ego, object relational, and self organizational uses as well. Much the same can be said of aggression, which certainly implicates ego, self, and object relational issues. Moreover, the motivators that Pine links respectively to ego and to self psychologies—the tendency to continue to function in a familiar manner to avoid psychic pain, on the one hand and the homeostatic tendency to "maintain a comfortable subjective steady state" on the other—are themselves linked. Finally, the motivational principle assigned to the psychology of the object—the repetition compulsion, the push to repeat in current relationships object relational configurations from the past—seems to be an organismic tendency rather than an intentional dynamic force propelling people to act in certain ways.

A comparable confusion enters into recent relational contributions to the problem of motivation, whether they argue for a nondrive theory of motivation, or one with new, relationally informed "drives." Greenberg espouses the latter viewpoint in his book, *Oedipus and Beyond: A Clinical Theory* (1991). He begins by arguing that traditional Freudian psychoanalysis contains four motivational principles: (1) psychic determinism; (2) the primacy of unconscious over conscious motivation; (3) multideterminism, the centrality of conflict and compromise formation; and (4) the primacy of "biologically rooted" and "phylogenetically determined" sexual and aggressive drives. Greenberg submits that the quarrel between contemporary Freudians and relationalists revolves around the last of these. With respect to biological drives, he argues Freudian analysis is burdened with a "theory of drive without meaning," along with a failure to recognize that there is more to human motivation and to life generally than sex and aggression. Greenberg's solution is to propose a dual-drive theory that assigns motivational primacy to the drives for safety and effectance, respectively. But a close reading of his book reveals that this dualism encompasses the very same wishes, including love and hate, that contemporary Freudians speak of in modern reformulations of traditional drive theory. So it may well be that Greenberg's quarrel with them is semantic rather than substantive, and based on a misunderstanding of just what they mean by the notion of "drive."

Consider in this connection, Charles Brenner's remarks (1982) on the nature of drive in contemporary classical psychoanalysis. Questioning Freud's psychobiological notion of drive as a frontier phenomenon between mind and body, he redefines drive in purely psychological terms. The conscious and unconscious wishes of patients revealed by the psychoanalytic method of observation, he holds, are the sole "evidential basis" for drive theory. Every such observation is "personal and unique" and bears out the fact that contemporary drive theory refers always to "the wish of a particular patient for a particular kind of gratification from or at the hands of a particular person under particular circumstances. . . . It is a wish that has a uniquely personal history, a uniquely personal form, and a uniquely personal content. Nor is a wish ever just 'an aggressive wish.' It is always a wish to do something to somebody, again with a special history, a special content, and a special form" (pp. 19–22). The interrelation of drive and object is integral to this reformulation; the notion of drive is articulated in a way that is intricately tied to the relational matrix in which people live. It is difficult to apprehend what Brenner leaves out, relationally speaking, that Mitchell captures in his relational recasting of a theory of motivation:

> I regard object seeking in Fairbairn's sense or interpersonal integrating tendencies in Sullivan's sense as superordinate motivational principles that are powerfully active. I also believe that people seek pleasure, power, exercise of function, security, and all sorts of other things. I think it is more useful, however, to regard these other motives, although irreducible, as shaped and structured in the context of the relational matrix that provides a sense of self in relation to others [1988, p. 464].

Neither Mitchell nor Greenberg nor any other relational analyst, it may be argued, has to date developed a comprehensive motivational system whose explanatory breadth exceeds, or even equals, that of the Freudian system. Joseph Lichtenberg, by contrast, attempts to formulate just such a comprehensive alternative. He proposes five primary motivational systems aiming, respectively, at: (1) psychological regulation of physiological needs; (2) attachment; (3) exploration-assertion; (4) aversive reactivity; and (5) sensual enjoyment. Each of these five motivational systems is hierarchically organized, beginning with a neurobiological base central to ensuring the infant's survival. Next comes learned responses (which Lichtenberg terms "perceptual-affective-action patterns") that originate in interactions with caregivers and develop into increasingly complex programs of plans and intentions. The third stage in the motivational hierarchy accompanies the evolution of symbolic representation. This cognitive capacity follows a more flexible reorganization of experience and the development of aims and wishes in the psychoanalytic sense.

With the advent of language and the attendant capacity for greater abstraction and categorization after the first 8 months of life, interactions organized around the five basic systems become recodified into primary and secondary process modes of thought. As such, these interactions become subject to defensive permutations. However, some of the original content of these system-specific interactions are generalized and encoded in procedural memory, with the potential to emerge as reenactments. Affect is seen as an amplifier of motivational behaviors, with positive affect reinforcing certain motivational interactions, and negative affect discouraging others. Affects likewise provide the thread of coherence between presymbolic and symbolic activity. This continuity provides the rationale for making statements about the inner life of the infant. At each developmental stage, Lichtenberg holds, the needs associated with each of the five motivational systems can either be met successfully or frustrated. If the former, a selfobject experience occurs; if the latter, self-cohesion is threatened. Ongoing frustration of the requirements of specific motivational systems and ensuing fragmentation of the self—rather than intersystemic conflict—become the source of later psychopathology.

Shevrin has written critically about the central role which affect plays in Lichtenberg's system. He cites Lichtenberg's statement: "The sexual drive derives its motivational power not from any energy but from the affects it triggers" (1989, p. 224). He sees Lichtenberg's emphasis as part of a broader trend in contemporary psychoanalytic theorizing to view affect as the "cause of motives." Included in the affect-motivation group are such theoretically diverse contributors as Dahl, Emde, Kernberg, and even Brenner. He cites Schwartz, who contends that a drive is not "intrinsically dangerous and only becomes so by virtue of the affect associated with it." Shevrin then summarizes what he contends are the propositions of the affect motivational "school." Affects are "1) The primary motivators of behavior, 2) They provide motivation with its urgency and strength, 3) They define what is psychologically dangerous" (private communication).

This approach tends to downplay the biological drives by considering them as "physiological needs," and elaborate affects as the operative psychological motivators. Shevrin points out that for Kernberg (1982) affects are "dynamic entities" and the key players in selfobject mental structures. Both Kernberg and Lichtenberg give wishes and impulses short shrift, a position which is shared by relational psychoanalysts with their stress on "relational configurations" as the central motivational construct. Kernberg's construct, "object-relations" and the term *intersubjective experience* used by Lichtenberg and Stolorow have, according to Shevrin, the common emphasis on the primacy of "affective interactions with caretakers." Self psychology is rooted in a similar premise: The cohesion and stability of the self is determined by empathic (affective) experience with caretakers who are in tune with their charges. Drive manifestations are the disintegration products of the uncohesive, fragmented self.

Weinstein (1994) has identified some further problems in the underlying premises of Lichtenberg's approach. Particularly notable is the lack of any data that explain how infant–caregiver experiences are encoded in what, for the infant, constitutes procedural memory "akin to a motor program like skating." In order for interactions to be encoded, she holds, a fairly sophisticated degree of self / object differentiation is required. She goes on to critique the notion of attachment motivation. To show hierarchical continuity, attachment categories would have to demonstrate stability over time, apart from environmental circumstances, and predict later adaptive behavior as well. Such categories would have to reflect core groups of unconscious fantasies, which would then act as structures that further organize behavior as the child shifts to an organization based on symbolic processes. Yet, as Lamb and his colleagues (Lamb, Thompson, Gardner, Charnov, and Estes, 1984) have pointed out, neither aspect of hierarchical continuity has been demonstrated, in part because the attachment categories are too broad and heterogeneous. While classification of adult into attachment categories does predict adolescent adjustment and marital satisfaction, the classification of adult attachment is based on self-reported retrospective memories, often centered around the oedipal period. It is not at present known whether these memories reflect the same categories measured in infant attachment studies; the necessary longitudinal studies to make this determination are only now being conducted.

Finally, Weinstein raises questions about Lichtenberg's definition of motivation—"Anything an infant does consistently"—that are equally germane to the definitions put forward by Pine, Mitchell, and Greenberg: The definition does not distinguish between motives and externally caused behaviors; if motivation can be aroused either internally or externally, and pleasurable affect is the reinforcing agent in dyadic interactions, the model comes close to a stimulus-response paradigm. It leaves unexplained the tenacious nature of object choices and the very special type of learning that enters into these highly cathected interactions. Despite its breadth and sophistication, Lichtenberg's contribution, like that of the other post-Freudian revisionists, is predicated on the assumption that contemporary Freudian theory is experience-distant and rigidly mechanistic. Like the relationalists, Lichtenberg confuses drive as a theoretical concept with the drive derivative. As Weinstein observes:

> It is doubtful that terms like perceptual-affective-action patterns are less mechanistic or theoretical nor is the clinical use of heuristic tools such as shifting motivation sets or model scenes more personal. Is it clinically more effective to talk in terms of switches in motivation set rather than attempting to understand the dominant unconscious fantasies which structure the patient's behavior? [1994, p. 63].

Weinstein's criticism is applicable in certain respects to recent relational and self psychological theories of motivation. Freud's early notion of tension reduction as an overarching motivational principle is not consistent with mature Freudian theory, whether as developed by Freud himself or as amended and elaborated by contemporary classical analysts. Freud's case histories, whether clinical or in the realm of applied analysis, hardly rely on tension reduction as an explanatory construct. Rather, in these writings, as Mackay (1988) notes, Freud addresses motivational questions through a mixture of mechanistic, anthropomorphic, purposive, and experiential concepts. The individuals about whom he writes are motivated by wishes, desires, and a striving toward objects. To be sure, Freud thought in terms of tension reduction when he tried to develop a neurophysiological model of brain function. The abstraction, Arlow has argued, guided him to his understanding of actual neurosis, a concept important to Freud but generally discarded by later theorists, classical or not. In any case, as Mackay has noted, "a philosophy of physicalism does not eliminate a philosophy of purpose and intentionality" (p. 77). The two can exist in a dialectical tension, and it is precisely this tension that imparts explanatory richness to Freud's writings (Friedman, 1965).

In contemporary classical theory, drive psychology rests on the foundation of the dynamic unconscious; it pertains to the "drivenness" that often suffuses unconscious fantasies and wishes organized around important childhood memories and experiences. It follows that drive derivatives necessarily implicate the experiential, relational world of people who feel "driven" for different reasons and under different circumstances. Thus, when Mitchell invokes the "relational matrix" as a force shaping the form and content of human motives, he is espousing the same fundamental attitude toward human behavior as Brenner, an exemplar of contemporary classical thought. So the dichotomy between an object seeking drive and a drive toward gratification, which for Mitchell serves as the basis for a radical distinction between classical Freudian and post classical thinking, is too simplistic to be persuasive. Object seeking is obviously related to gratification and pleasure of some sort, and the search for pleasure is obviously structured by the experiential possibilities (past and present, fantasied and real) of the relational worlds in which people live.

What can be said is this: a fully adequate psychoanalytic theory of motivation must embrace the drivenness of human behavior, unconscious wishes and fantasies, and bodily experience. Contemporary classical analysis fully accommodates these factors while allowing for the shaping impact of early object relationship and resulting relational patterns. Classical analysis does not, in the manner of the interpersonal tradition, impute superordinate status to the quest (or drive) for relational intimacy, but it does not thereby devalue it. For classical analysis, the need for intimacy is simply one of the many driving forces suffused with unconscious wishes and fears; it is a need that can be satisfied only when one's sense of morality, the resources of reality, and the affects that accompany intimacy are taken into account. Can one impute the same awareness of complexity and overdetermination to the motivational framework of relational theory? There are certainly grounds here for skepticism. The notion that personality, normal or pathological, is a product of the relational matrix seems to downplay the way in which bodily experience fuels wishes and fantasies; relational theory is less than convincing about the drivenness of human behavior. Arguing, as does Mitchell, that biological and physiological factors are contained *within* relational configurations seems to make such factors epiphenomenal to the creation and maintenance of human relationships.

Now, we can all be grateful to the relational theorists for highlighting the motivational *valence* of object seeking (in the sense of Fairbairn) and of interpersonal integrating tendencies (in the sense of Sullivan). But to proclaim such motivational principles "superordinate," with "pleasure, power, exercises of function, security, all sorts of other things" derivative of the relational matrix as does

Mitchell, is to lose more than is gained. To say that contemporary classical analysis can be enriched by relational theory is not to undercut the contemporary classical theory of motivation. Classical analysis does not in principle separate drive from object, so it has no difficulty with Mitchell's apt reminder that motives "are shaped and structured in the context of the relational matrix to provide the sense of self in relation to others" (1988). We all understand that motives are structured interpersonally, with a resulting impact on a person's sense of self in relation to others. The writings of contemporary relationalists, self psychologists and social constructivists usefully underscore the range of such structuring, and especially the manifold ways in which entrenched relational patterns, at once adaptive and maladaptive, are implicated in psychopathology. But the relational theory of motivation, taken to its extreme, threatens to throw out the classical baby with the nineteenth century mechanistic bathwater. It dispenses not only with the tension-reduction drive–discharge model that is largely irrelevant to contemporary classical analysis, but with the appreciation of the dynamic unconscious, unconscious wishes and fantasies, and intrapsychic conflict that is quintessential to it. For contemporary classical analysis, these interrelated factors not only interact with, but share ontological primacy with, relational experiences. It may be noted in passing that the relative weight of endogenous factors and relational experiences is a question that divides even "postclassical" theorists. Greenberg (1991), Thomas Ogden (1992a), and Slavin, Morris, and Kriegman (1992) have all argued that some form of drive theory is essential to explaining individual development and psychopathology. This issue has kept theorists like Ogden, and Slavin, Morris, and Kriegman outside of relational theory proper and has moved Greenberg from its center to a broader, more integrated perspective that he characterizes as "representational."

The current state of theoretical pluralism represents, I believe, a great peril to psychoanalysis to the extent that it is based on dispute—divergent and conflicting theories of motivation. Psychoanalysis, if it is to remain relevant, must provide a system of explanation of human behavior, a coherent theory of motivation. Our patients consult us because they assume that we have expertise in this area and that there exists some consensus about the determinants of psychological life. How can we expect them to accept that there are multiple rules, a "drive" truth, a "relational" truth, a "self" truth, an object relations truth, etc.?

Do we tell them, "You pays your money and you takes your choice?" In my view the only way out of our dilemma is to adopt an integrative position, "total composite theory" (Rangell, 1985). Rafael Moses' distinction in regard to form and content is also helpful. Motivational forces are given form by ego processes that mediate and shape the drive, relational self, and defensive expressions.

Implicit in this recommendation is the principle of multiple function, which is both a descriptive or classificatory concept, and a supraordinate motivational concept. The idea is that we are motivated to act in such a way as to satisfy as many considerations as possible, and behavior acquires strength when it satisfies more functions—whether drive discharge, anxiety reduction, guilt relief, or adaptation. The centrality of compromise formation in Brenner's theory reflects this idea. Outside psychoanalysis proper, the psychiatric idea of a biopsychosexual model also takes off from the principle of multiple function and overdetermination.

A question to consider is why this approach is ignored by theories such as self psychology, relational psychoanalysis, and intersubjectivity. Each of these theories offers its approach as a replacement for classical psychoanalysis, which they define "reductively" as drive theory.

In closing it should be emphasized that a future adequate theory of motivation will be one that brings an integrative perspective to bear on the dialectic process that captures the complexity of the biopsychosocial determinants of human experience.

REFERENCES

Brenner, C. (1982), *The Mind in Conflict*. New York: International Universities Press.

Friedman, L. (1965), The significance of determinism and free will. *Internat. J. Psycho-Anal.*, 46:515–520.

Greenberg, J. (1991), *Oedipus and Beyond: A Clinical Theory*. Cambridge, MA: Harvard University Press.

——— Mitchell, S. (1983), *Object Relations in Psychoanalytic Theory*. Cambridge, MA: Harvard University Press.

Holt, R. (1967), Beyond vitalism and mechanism: Freud's concept of psychic energy. In: *Science and Psychoanalysis, Vol. II*, ed. J. Masserman. New York: Grune & Stratton, pp. 1–41.

Kernberg, O. (1982), Self, ego, affects and drives. *J. Amer. Psychoanal. Assn.*, 30:893–917.

Klein, G. (1967), Preemptory ideation: Structure and force in motivated ideas. In: Motives and Thought: Psychoanalytic Essays in Honor of David Rapaport, ed. R. Holt, *Psychological Issues*, Monogr. 18 / 19. New York: International Universities Press, pp. 78–128.

Lamb, M., Thompson, R., Gardner, W., Charnov, E., & Estes, D. (1984), Security of infantile attachment as assessed in the "strange situation": Its study and biological interpretation. *Behav. & Brain Sci.*, 71:127–147.

Lichtenberg, J. (1989), *Psychoanalysis and Motivation*. Hillsdale, NJ: Analytic Press.

——— Fosshage, J., & Lachmann, F. (1992), *Self and Motivational Systems: Toward a Theory of Psychoanalytic Technique*. Hillsdale, NJ: Analytic Press.

Mackay, N. (1988), Motivation and Explanation: An Essay in Freud's Philosophy of Science, *Psychological Issues*, Monogr. 56. Madison, CT: International Universities Press.

Mitchell, S. (1988), *Relational Concepts in Psychoanalysis*. Cambridge, MA: Harvard University Press.

——— (1992), Commentary on Trop and Stolorow's "Defense Analysis in Self Psychology." *Psychoanal. Dial.*, 2:443–453.

Moses, R. (1968), Form and content: An ego-psychological view. *The Psychoanalytic Study of the Child*, 23:204–223. New York: International Universities Press.

Ogden T. H. (1992), The dialectically constituted / decentered subject of psychoanalysis. I. The Freudian Subject, *Internat. J. Psycho-Anal.*, 73:517–526, II. The Contributions of Klein and Winnicott. *Internat. J. Psycho-Anal.*, 73:613–626.

Pine, F. (1990), *Drive, Ego, Object, and Self*. New York: Basic Books.

Rangell, L. (1985), On theory in psychoanalysis and its relation to psychoanalytic therapy. *J. Amer. Psychoanal. Assn.*, 33:59–92.

Rapaport, D. (1960), On the psychoanalytic theory of motivation. In: *The Collected Papers of David Rapaport*, ed. M. Gill. New York: Basic Books, pp. 853–915.

Rosenblatt, D., & Thickstun, J. T. (1977), Energy, information, and motivation: A revision theory. *J. Amer. Psychoanal. Assn.*, 25:537–558.

Schafer, R. (1968), *Aspects of Internalization.* New York: International Universities Press.

Shevrin, H. *Psychoanalysis as the Patient: High in Feeling, Low in Energy.* Unpublished manuscript.

Slavin, M. O., Morris, X., & Kriegman, D. (1992), *The Adaptive Design of the Human Psyche.* New York: Guilford Press.

Wallerstein, R. (1992), One psychoanalysis or many. In: *The Common Ground of Psychoanalysis,* ed. R. Wallerstein. Northvale, NJ: Jason Aronson.

Weinstein, L. (1994), Review of *Psychoanalysis and Motivation* by Joseph Lichtenberg. *J. Clin. Psychoanal.,* 3:55–64.

White, R. W. (1959), Motivation reconsidered: The concept of competence. *Psychoanal. Rev.,* 66:297–333.

7.

THE INTERMINABLE UNCANNINESS

YOLANDA GAMPEL, Ph.D.

Freud (1919) introduced the term *uncanny* in an attempt to conceptualize qualities of feeling which arouse dread and horror. While Freud recognized its connection to that which excites fear, he wished to distinguish within the field of what is frightening, a special core feeling of uncanniness.

The uncanny is not a symptom, behavior, or neurotic organization. It is a lived experience ("Erlebnis"), without significations, which cannot be translated into words. "Heimlich," "belonging to the house or family, intimate, friendly, comfortable," is a familiar term, but "unheimlich," to the contrary, refers to what remains hidden, "concealed, kept from sight, withheld from others." Freud added to the notion of hidden, the dangerous "eerie, weird, arousing gruesome fear" (Freud, 1919, pp. 222–224). However, as Freud gave us to understand, the uncanny represents something primary already experienced. It is as if the experience of the uncanny is a sort of dialectic between reminiscence and forgetting.

Thus, I suggest expanding upon the term *uncanny* to describe precisely those experiences which cannot be expressed in words, in particular, memories of dread and horror aroused by experiences of extreme social violence, and not just primary infant experiences that have been repressed. Further, within the social historical context, the uncanny—the dread and horror of social violence—is something primary, already experienced in the history of our century, that belongs to the familiar and is hidden and dangerous having been transmitted from generation to generation. This is inscribed in the transsubjective space.

Experience of such horror and violence can lead to the blurring or destruction of the distinction between the impossible and that which might indeed come to exist. Such an assault on the boundary between fantasy and reality becomes traumatic in itself and leads to great fear of one's thoughts and expectations.

Janine Puget (1988) understands social violence to be "the eruption of contents and meanings that cannot be approached or understood by the mind because of their traumatic character (direct attacks), and because of the paradoxical nature of their messages" (p. 100). In my search for a way to give a name to the emotions aroused by the traumatic experiences of the Shoah, I found the term *uncanny* to be helpful despite its built-in paradoxes. The experience of uncanniness, in the situation with which we are concerned, the Shoah, brings to light the unthinkable and the unrepresentable.

These formulations can be applied to a discussion of the Shoah whose uncanny experiences could not, in any way, be assimilated into the individual's range of inner representations. Individuals who experienced the Shoah as children were faced with an astounding, unbelievable, and unreal reality that was incompatible with everything they had previously known before the Shoah. As a result, they no longer fully believed their own eyes; they had difficulty distinguishing between this unreal reality and their own imagination. They lacked previous experiences which might have served as preparation for the "situation in extremity."

For Bleger (1967), the uncanny is not only something familiar and known which becomes ambiguous, but it is also the sudden appearance of the ambiguous which, undoubtedly, exists in all that is familiar. We move within a familiar environment comprised of discriminated objects, situations, and individuals. However, within this familiar and discriminated environment there always exist ambiguous aspects which must remain hidden and secret in order for events to remain familiar.

For Bleger the most regressive, ambiguous and nondiscriminated levels of the personality tend to remain fixed and unknown, hiding behind the known, or the more integrated ego. Bleger further points out that the uncanny is not a state of doubt or uncertainty but a state of disorganization or reorganization which the ego suffers. For Bleger it is a destructuralization of the integrated ego and the formation of a new ego structure of an ambiguous nature.

Applying Bleger's understanding of the uncanny to the Shoah underlines the paradox of the nondiscriminated and unknown human legacy which lives silently within us at the same time that culture and civilization build structure and discrimination. Nazism, with its brutality, social violence, and inhumanity, brings to light the split, undifferentiated, and ambiguous aspects of humanity. The individual who experienced the Shoah, suffered the attacks of the ambiguous and undiscriminated aspects of humanity, coming from the external world. While all individuals harbor within themselves this silent and hidden legacy of aggression, it is very important to underline that the individuals who went through the Shoah were forced into acquaintance with terrible aggression by a brutal, external world and not because of their own hidden aggression.

Bleger (1967) speaks of a break, a split between the "me" and the "not-me" and not just a simple return of the repressed. For Freud, the uncanny is the return of the repressed. Repression requires the intervention of the schizoid division, implying discrimination. Through Freud's description of the uncanny, we can discuss the presence of repression in "unheimlich" experiences. The presence of repression is inscribed in the structure of the word *unheimlich*. The prefix *un* points out the contrary of that which is being signified. This is to say that while *unheimlich* is the contrary of *heimlich* it is also conceived by it. Repression effaces thoughts while at the same time preserving them. It makes them known and recognizable in the return of the repressed, in fragmentary obsessional manifestations, or in incomprehensible impulsive acts which kill thoughts, leading to a feeling of uncanniness. The repressed material sometimes appears in the form of a metaphor as an attempt to recover or denounce the repressed. When the experience of the unheimlich crops up, that which was hidden becomes visible, that which was familiar becomes frightening and strange. The repressed is lifted and turns into its opposite—its content is the contrary of that which was repressed. This double movement is released by a situation, object, or special event that has some relation, by association, with the unconscious content.

THE UNCANNY AS REVIEWED IN CLINICAL PSYCHOANALYSIS

The traumatic events caused to particular children by the Shoah are not always remembered by the survivors. Repressed, these traumatic events appear as uncanny feelings, experienced as madness by the survivor. The following clinical example illustrates the experience of the uncanny aroused by traumatic events as reviewed in a psychoanalysis.

Case Example

During the first hours of work with T one of the aspects of the concept "uncanny" was raised. In her fourth session, she said she had to tell me something about which she was very embarrassed. Despite her embarrassment, she wanted to tell me since she had come to tell the "whole truth." She explained:

> When I left here last time, all of a sudden I saw my father in the car behind me. I felt what I always feel when I see them unexpectedly and out of familiar context. I did everything so that I could turn left at the first turn. Whenever I see my mother or father outside the framework in which I am prepared to meet them, I have a very uncomfortable feeling. Whenever this happens, I do everything to avoid the meeting—like some crazy person. Isn't this totally crazy? It is such a strong feeling that all my rational thinking cannot help me overcome it.

I asked her if the feeling is one of "unheimlich" (the patient knows German and the word in German expresses the point better than in Hebrew or English). "Heimlich" is related to home, and "unheimlich" is something not from home, which perhaps frightens her. She said, "Yes, perhaps that is the precise word." This experience is accompanied by an unbearable feeling of panic, horror, and desperation. "But," she says, "it is only my parents!"

We may understand this feeling by addressing T's past. She was born in 1943, in a concentration camp in Europe. It was a camp with people of "status," who thought they might save themselves by using their money and their position. However, they realized very quickly that this was not the case. T's parents had escaped and hidden in the homes of non-Jews. They were "wanted" by the Germans, and therefore it was too dangerous to continue together. When T was 2 months old, her parents left her with a childless non-Jewish couple who were delighted to receive her. T's parents hid separately.

At the end of the war, after a year and a half with this couple, T's parents came to take her. From stories T was later told, she knows that she cried terribly; her "adopted" parents had become like parents for her, and she loved them deeply. T's mother explained that despite her own desire for T to adjust to her, T did not want to look at her mother's face. The mother forced T to look at her face for hours in order to become accustomed to her.

T added that her parents had always spoiled her and had tried to prove that she was emotionally healthy and successful, despite the fact that she had not been with them during her first year. Although T had wanted to seek therapy for many years, she had not dared to do so. It would have shattered her parents' illusion that the war had not hurt her. Today, T hides the fact that she comes to therapy from her parents; with me, as with the family that hid her, she feels "at home."

We hypothesized that perhaps each time she sees her parents outside the expected framework it is as if she returns, either in thought or in language, to a situation that she has previously experienced.

T's parents were very "heimlich" and "homelike"; however, when she saw them suddenly, they quickly became something "uncanny." We related this to the strange faces that had arrived to take her when she was one year old. They had removed her from her home, and forced her to look in their eyes so that she might "adjust" to them. T would burst into tears, turn her head, and close her eyes.

As a child, she could not escape from this situation. Today, she can; she runs from something that is very secret as well as very frightening to her. The understanding of her present experience through this historical material helped T greatly. She could stop thinking of herself and her reaction as "crazy."

FEELINGS OF UNCANNINESS AROUSED THROUGH A CHILD'S BEHAVIOR

Feelings of uncanniness are sometimes reported by survivors in relation to their children's behavior. Through their children's behavior, the survivor-parent is forced to come into contact with aggression and brutality, and with some split, undifferentiated, and ambiguous aspects of himself which had been repressed.

In the following clinical example, a child of survivors reexperiences or takes over the uncanny experiences of her parents (Gampel, 1982, 1986, 1992a,b; Kestenberg, 1982).

Mrs. N came to see me because of the difficulties she was having with the youngest of her three daughters, who was 16 years old at the time. Her daughter was disregarding previous restraints, both at school and at home; she was not behaving in accordance with the conventions of their home. She was unwilling to come for consultation, sending her mother instead. The mother wanted to meet me in order to later convince her daughter to come.

Mrs. N was 54 years old, very pretty and elegant. She immediately conveyed, in her behavior and conversation, that her family was an important one. She saw rude behavior, crass language, and lack of order and restraint as very unsuited to the family, and that was her daughter's behavior at this time.

The family spent six years abroad, and returned when the youngest was 12. The father then became ill, and died three years ago when the youngest daughter was 14.

The youngest daughter was born when the mother was 38 years old. She was particularly important and special to her mother and was the child who was given "the most time and emotional energy." This child had nightmares almost constantly, wet her bed until the age of 9, and was extremely close to her mother.

The mother related that following her husband's death, she and her daughters went on a trip during which they attended an art exhibition. One of the drawings was a brain with many doors and compartments. The daughter recalled something that her mother had told her during one of the nights when, because of her fears, she had gone to cuddle in her mother's bed. Her mother had told her that she should fill the compartments of her mind and close its doors so that the fear wouldn't come in to fill the empty space.

Her mother suggested that she fill the space with other things, such as pleasant thoughts, so that there wouldn't be room for the fear.

When I asked how they managed with the nightmares and bed-wetting, and what caused the situation to improve when she was a child, Mrs. N said that during the time they were abroad the daughter had a non-Jewish nanny who loved the girl very much. She had helped her to adjust to the new country. Mrs. N said that she was happy for her daughter and wasn't jealous of the love she gave the nanny. The nanny was from the lower class and very simple. The daughter loved spending time with the nanny's family. During their last visit she had spent all her time with these "under-privileged" girls, working with them and helping them, and had spent no time with girls of her own social standing. Mrs. N said that her daughter's sense of justice was keen and that she cannot tolerate society's hypocrisy. Mrs. N also spoke at length about her feelings for her late husband, whom she described as a special man, a patriarchal figure, to whom she had dedicated her life.

It was very difficult to acquire information about her and her husband's place of origin. She strongly denied that there could be any connection between her childhood and her daughter's difficulties. She stated that she and her husband came from a different period of time so there was no connection between her childhood and her children's lives.

Eventually, it became evident that both she and her husband as children had lived in Europe during World War II. Her family was very rich and highly thought of in their community in Germany. She was an only child. When the war began, she was 10 years old. They moved to Poland where there was a rich, powerful grandfather who they hoped could help them. Eventually, they were placed in a ghetto. When I asked about her life there, she said that all the "bullshit" that is written about the war's effects on children is a lie. She told me not to start talking about that with her. "The war had no influence on us," she asserted. She added: "No, it wasn't so terrible. We even played as children in the ghetto. You know what we played? Nazis and Jews, like children today play cops and robbers. But I can only speak about this with those who were there."

In 1942, when Mrs. N was 12, she was placed with a non-Jewish family, who kept her because they had been promised half of her grandfather's property. She met up with her parents at the end of the war, but was unwilling to discuss what happened to them. I asked her to describe what she had experienced during the twenty-six months she had spent with this family. She talked about the striking difference between her rich, orderly home and the home of these village people, who were dirty and uncultured, "Crude people with rude behavior, gross language, and lack of order and restraint." She had been obliged to teach them the basic principles of hygiene. Until that time, she had wanted to be a non-Jew because she didn't see why she should have to carry the burden of being Jewish. After staying with this family, however, she gave up the idea of becoming a Christian.

I asked her about her feelings of abandonment, of yearning. She said that it was not easy for her, that she worked very hard and it was terrible in this house. Her consolation was the 9-month-old baby of the family, who had been born when the mother was 38 years old. She had not wanted this child. Mrs. N had taken this girl under her wing and raised her. Later, she met this girl at the age of 20, and the girl told her that she had never had so much care and affection as during the two years when Mrs. N had taken care of her.

Mrs. N repeated that these events had no influence on her and had left in her no sadness or bitterness. After the war, she was reunited with her parents, resumed her studies, and returned, with her family, to their hometown. She studied an academic subject for four years, although she did not finish her studies. Instead, she came to Israel to marry her husband, who was unwilling to leave Israel. The husband, who had grown up in Poland, had passed through many places and had been sent to Israel with a group of children in 1943.

I spoke of her daughter's suffering: at age 12, returning to Israel, a place unknown to her, the loss of her loved, supportive nanny, her father's subsequent illness, and the family being busy with the illness. The mother stated that her daughter had spent entire days alone at home. I added that at age 14, the girl had also lost her father, and asked Mrs. N if she had thought about her daughter's suffering and feelings of loss. I pointed out that at the same age Mrs. N had also experienced separation, a certain loss of her parents, and the transition from an ideal life to a very difficult situation. Mrs. N became very angry at this comparison, stating that she herself had not suffered at all. She could consider her daughter's suffering, but stated that, in spite of everything, she had been there with her daughter.

She continued discussing her daughter's sensitivity, quest for truth, her intolerance of pretence, and the rude manner in which she exposed any falsity.

I suggested to Mrs. N that she think about her enormous strength and the thick skin she had built for herself since childhood. She had constructed this skin in order not to feel the pain and suffering too deeply, to get through the difficult things that she had experienced during the war, and later with her husband. It was as if these difficult experiences did not touch her.

I suggested that, perhaps, she examine to what extent this daughter, who has been "special" to her since birth, experienced, screamed, and cried for all those aspects of her mother that her mother, herself, never screamed and cried for—"she closed the door in her mind." (Perhaps this also explains the daughter's continuous quest for truth and her intolerance of pretence. She tries hard to break through her mother's thick skin.) I suggested that while her daughter may need psychotherapy, she, herself, needs to try to take back and release her daughter from those aspects of herself which she put, unconsciously, into her daughter. She answered me by saying: "I have never cried, I have always controlled myself, and my daughter talks about what hurts her."

Perhaps, if Mrs. N can begin to talk about her pain and anger, she will be able to reintroject the double of herself which she unconsciously projected into her daughter. By taking responsibility for her own aggressive and angry aspects, her feelings of uncanniness aroused by her daughter's behavior will abate (Gampel, 1986).

ACTUALITY AND THE RADIOACTIVE SOCIAL HISTORICAL IDENTIFICATION

The constant search of the human being for a safe place and a secure identity leads us to question the continuous existence of war that destroys, exiles, divides, and confuses. This struggle for a secure identity and a safe place in which to live was poignantly expressed in a psychoanalytic session with an adult patient.

Case Example

Mrs. A spoke of the lack of security of life in Israel, and expressed her concern about the economic and security situations. She said: "I remember the fifties. I was a child, we had very little, but we were united, we had hopes; today the future threatens us with war and catastrophe." She was referring to a criminal event in which Arabs were involved.

> What is going to happen? In my associations the Arabs are linked with the Germans. I understand that that is an internalized interpretation of the history of my parents who went through the Shoah. From that standpoint I should be in favor of Gush Emunim [a right-wing party that believes in settling Greater Israel], but that is the neurotic approach of the past, that everybody is persecuting us and that everybody is against us. In general, I don't hate Arabs, but toward the murderers in the bus attack I would implement the rule of "an eye for an eye." I grew up with a sick mother and father knowing it was all because of the war; it wasn't talked about but it was clear—their longing for their childhood and their parents. Afterwards came the sixties, with the awareness of the consequences of the atomic bomb. I thought that children should not be brought into the world when danger is so concrete. Who can guarantee that the Shoah won't happen again?

Later, after referring to another event, Mrs. A said: "I asked myself who is more important—me or my children? I do not know. Semadar Haran, the one in Nahariya whose house was broken into by terrorists, was no worse a mother than anyone else, when she had to silence her daughter, when she was so scared that she smothered her to death. My 3-year-old son can't understand what I ask him to do. How do you live with it afterwards?"

The above clinical vignette highlights the need to confront the place of actuality within the personal history and the radioactive social historical identification. It is agreed that every situation of actuality may be linked in a symbolic manner to internalized figures and events of the past. How can we relate to both the past and the present, to the external and the internal without giving up either of them? Winnicott (1951), in speaking of the transitional object, distinguished between its symbolic value and what he called its "actuality": In the same symbolic manner, we can relate to events happening in the external world that cause an eruption in the expected, normal life, when patients and analysts are immersed in the same social context. We, as analysts, have to understand the actual eruption as well as its symbolic value or meaning for the patient (Gampel, 1990).

In 1932 Einstein wrote to Freud asking "What can be done to protect mankind from the curse of war." Today, over sixty years later, we stand before the same question. This century has witnessed numerous self-destructive acts by human beings. Auschwitz and Hiroshima revealed to us that death and violence belong to a most intimate and concealed part of our identity. The scenes they left behind, monstrous and painful, damage our perceptual and representational systems. These systems have been overloaded or destroyed by all too powerful stimuli, leaving behind a heritage that gives rise to cruel and violent forms of identification. At times, these identifications can be likened to the effects of radiation, an external reality that enters the psychic apparatus without the individual having any control over their entry, implantation, and effects. This "radioactive identification" (Gampel, 1993a,b) is comprised of nonrepresentable remnants, remainders of the radioactive influences of the external world which are imbedded within the individual. Occasionally, the effects to these remnants are not felt within the individual, but rather in future generations.

These nonrepresentable remnants of the radioactive influence cannot be spoken about or described in words. Several psychoanalytic models have referred to a zone in which words do not exist. Freud spoke about "thing representations," Lacan referred to "the real," Aulagnier (1975) referred to the "pictogram," Anzieu (1987) referred to the "formal signifiers," Rosalato (1985) speaks of "demarcation signifiers," and Bion (1962) presented his model of preconceptions. The above conceptualizations refer to an inherent potential of human nature which is part of the individual's development. Puget (1988) further developed these ideas, taking into account social violence, through the introduction of the unthinkable and the unthought. The acceptance of this category is for Puget "equivalent to tolerating the existence of an unknowable mental space whose transformation into words would produce madness and death. It also means tolerating the existence of a world outside the ego, in which the subject is immersed but without being able to know that this is so. It also suggests recognition of the unknowable-unshareable, of sensorial knowledge" (p. 123).

Similarly, the concept of radioactive identification attempts to serve as a conceptual and metaphoric representation of the penetrations of terrible, violent, and destructive aspects of the external reality, against which the individual is defenseless. The individual internalizes the radioactive remnants of which he is unaware, and identifies with them and their dehumanizing aspects. Later, the individual acts out these identifications which are alien to him, or they are acted out by his children through the process of transgenerational transmission (Gampel, 1992a,b).

Survivors' children do not have their personal memories of the Shoah, but an internal reality bearing family themes of past loss, suffering, and humiliation that have been deposited in them by intergenerational transmission. For these children, the purpose of analysis is to work through these deposits so that they can distinguish between internal and external reality and thus gain some control of their lives (Kestenberg, 1982).

In the intergenerational associative group chain, the missing links are represented by fantasies that tell us about the "forgotten." Yerushalmi (1982) tells us that what is called "forgotten" occurs when historical catastrophe that violently interrupts the occurrence of events, a human group will not be able to transmit in words. In this sense, the commandment to remember and not to forget that is directed at the Jewish people became efficient, when history became a canon of the Torah that signifies teaching in the broadest sense of the word.

Freud in 1938 wrote to the International Congress of Psychoanalysis: "political misfortunes that have been suffered by the Jewish people have taught them to treasure the only valuable thing left to them—the written word." The way to retrieve history is to put into thought and words all the misfortunes suffered. Yerushalmi points out that for the sages of the Torah, the anxiety was not that history will be forgotten but that the word, the law, the way of life will be forgotten. That is to say, history is integrated into a system of values. In this way, the antonym of forgetting is not memory. The opposite of forgetting is justice.

For the generations that follow, in order to rescue themselves from the heritage of social violence suffered by their parents who were victims or inflicted by their parents who were perpetrators, they have to discover, disclose, and confront the radioactive identification as the metaphoric representation of the penetrations of terrible, violent, and destructive aspects of the external reality, and in this way to maintain the possibility of searching for causes and meaning. This work can be achieved and we as psychoanalysts can facilitate it without obliterating the past and present effects of the social violence in ourselves and in our patients. We can do so by reconstructing the social network and in this way, jointly make possible its transformation.

REFERENCES

Anzieu, D. (1987), Les significants formels et la moi peau. In: *Les enveloppes psychiques*. Paris: Dunod.

Aulagnier, P. (1975), *La violence de l'interpretation*. Paris: P.U.F.

Bleger, J. (1971), Ambiguedad y sincretismo en "Lo Siniestro" de Freud. In: *Simbiosis y Ambiguedad: Estudio Psicoanalitico*. Buenos Aires, Argentina: Editorial Paidos.

Bion, W. P. (1962), *Learning from Experience*. London: Heinemann Medical.

Freud, S. (1919), The uncanny. *Standard Edition*, 17:21–25. London: Hogarth Press, 1955.

Gampel, Y. (1982), A daughter of silence. In: *Generations of the Holocaust*, ed. M. S. Bergmann & M. E. Jucovy. New York: Basic Books, pp. 120–136.

——— (1986), L'effrayant et le menacant: De la transmission à la repetition. *Psychoanalyse à L'université*, 11:87–102.

——— (1990), Some reflections on counter-transference in psychoanalytical work with Shoah survivors. Paper presented at "Children in War" Conference of the Sigmund Freud Center, Jerusalem.

——— (1992a), Thoughts about the transmission of conscious and unconscious knowledge to the generation born after the Shoah. *J. Soc. Work & Policy in Israel* (Spec. Issue), 5:43–50.

——— (1992b), Taking leave of one's grandparents' past. Paper presented at the Second Scientific Seminar of the Sigmund Freud Stiftung, Emmendingen, Germany, June 18–21.

——— (1993a), From the thing in itself by modeling through transformation by narration in the therapeutic space. *Brit. J. Psychother.*, 9:280–290.

——— (1993b), Between the safety background and the background of the uncanny: Theoretical and technical aspects of working within the context of social violence. In: *Psychoanalytic Theories in Practice: A Festschrift to Joseph Sandler*, ed. P. Fonagy, A. Cooper, & R. Wallerstein, in press.

Kestenberg, J. S. (1982), A metapsychological assessment based on an analysis of a survivor's child. In: *Generations of the Holocaust*, ed. M. S. Bergmann & M. E. Jucovy. New York: Basic Books, pp. 145–155.

Puget, J. (1988), Social violence and psychoanalysis in Argentina: The unthinkable and the unthought. *Free Associations*, 13:84–140.

Rosalato, G. (1985), *Elementes de l'interpretation*. Paris: Gallimard.

Winnicott, D. W. (1951), Transitional objects and transitional phenomena. In: *Playing and Reality*. London: Tavistock, 1971.

Yerushalmi, Z. (1982), *Jewish History and Jewish Memory*. New York: University of Washington Press.

8.

THE NONVERBAL COMMUNICATION OF THE ANALYST TO THE PATIENT

HAROLD STEWART, M.B.B.S., M.R.C.S., L.R.cP., F.R.C. Psych.

From the very beginnings of psychoanalysis, Freud recognized the significance not only of the verbal utterances of patients but also their nonverbal communications during the analytic process. In the Dora paper of 1905, he gave a vivid picture of the situation: "He that has eyes to see and ears to hear may convince himself that no mortal can keep a secret. If his lips are silent, he chatters with his finger-tips; betrayal oozes out of him at every pore" (pp. 77–78). In his writings, he registered the physical postures of his patients, their tones of voice, their silences. He noted the symbolic aspects of communication via parapraxes, via hysterical symptoms and hysterical phenomena arising during the course of an analysis, via obsessional practices, and via the timing of psychosomatic symptoms. He recognized acting out as another form of remembering, although its value as a special means of communication in itself was a much later concept (Limentani, 1966).

Following these basic and fundamental clinical observations by Freud, there have been several subsequent developments in conceptual thinking which bear on this topic of nonverbal communication. It is impossible to deal with these and associated topics in any but a very selective fashion; nevertheless we should note the concepts concerning projective identificatory mechanisms together with those of containment; of externalization of parts of the self together with unconscious enactments; of the maintenance of a holding environment together with therapeutic regression in its benign and malignant forms. The importance of all these forms of nonverbal communication for the purpose of this paper concerns the effect they have on the analyst and of the ways he or she attempts to deal with them. We shall try to examine his nonverbal communications and their effect on the patient, whilst taking the verbal communications for granted. The importance of such communications in the form of verbal interpretative techniques is, of course, paramount in effecting permanent psychic changes in patients, although even here, controversy exists between those analysts who believe that only mutative transference interpretations give rise to permanent change, and those who believe on the basis of their clinical experience that this is only one of the therapeutic agents that can give rise to such change (Stewart, 1990).

In trying to examine this topic, or in fact any other topic in our clinical work, we must recognize the difficulty that we are dealing with multiple complex clinical phenomena which are often taking place simultaneously. In these circumstances, distinctions in the interest of clarification and understanding will tend to create a certain artificiality, but as this is inevitable, we must bear with it. Let us start from the beginning of an analysis where the analyst in his first nonverbal communication to his disturbed and suffering patient provides a setting in which therapy can take place. To quote Charles Rycroft (1956):

> The analyst's various technical procedures are designed to establish a [special form of] relationship between himself and the patient. The first thing he does is to provide a setting within which this relationship can develop. This comprises, among other things, a quiet room with a couch and a chair behind it, a closed door, regular and frequent appointments—and himself. This setting itself is a communication to the patient, since its details are all signs that the analyst intends taking up a certain attitude towards the patient, that he intends to listen to him, to concern himself with him without requiring the patient to be concerned with him, and to protect the contact between them from external interruption or distraction. He does this, then, in the first instance by means of *signs*—I am here using the word "sign" as a technical, semantic term—which indicate the existence of a particular psychological situation. . . . These details are all primarily signs of the analyst's contribution to the establishment of a relationship between himself and the patient, this notwithstanding the fact that the patient may also use any particular

> detail as a symbol with which to represent specific ideas within his own mind. I have here made use of the distinction drawn by logicians between signs and symbols. Signs indicate the existence or presence of some process, object, or condition, while symbols refer to or represent conceptions of processes, objects, or conditions. . . . Signs seem to play a fundamental part in communication of affects since most forms of emotional expression are innate and are immediately comprehensible without recourse to symbolic interpretation. Dreams and symptoms, on the other hand, are symbols, since they refer to, and are only comprehensible in relation to, conceptions arising in the patient's mind. The words used in analysis are also symbols, since they refer to ideas in the patient's and analyst's mind, but the inflections and tones of speech are signs, since they indicate the speaker's affective state [pp. 64–65].

I have given this extensive quotation of Rycroft's not only for the purpose of clarifying the nature of the setting but also, more importantly, for his clear explanation of nonverbal communication in terms of the existence of signs which are in themselves direct conveyors of affective states. It is in this direct communication of psychological affective states that the nonverbal attains to importance, since psychoanalysis has the experiencing and understanding of affective states at its very heart. Without it, there is only intellectual understanding and a sterile therapy.

We should also notice here that the nature of the setting also conveys a great deal of more specific nonverbal communications from the analyst. What the analyst's premises and consulting room actually look like, the way they are decorated and furnished, gives them an ambience that suggests a great deal about what the analyst is like as a person. Balint, in one of the earlier papers on the subject, called "On Transference and Counter-transference" (1939), written in collaboration with his wife, Alice Balint, was one of the first to recognize the importance to the patient of these formal aspects of the analyst's behavior and setting. This must also be true of the analyst's actual physical appearance and personality, although this is a topic that is rarely commented on in analytic papers and discussions.

The setting also forms an essential component of Winnicott's concept of the holding environment (1960). For him, the term *holding* is used to denote one aspect of the care that the dependent infant needs from the parents in order to achieve its developmental potential to move toward future independence. The analytic relationship is conceptualized in similar terms. "Holding" denotes not only the actual physical holding of the infant, but also the total environmental provision, including a three-dimensional spatial relationship and the necessary time to allow development and growth to occur. He thought that holding allowed the initiation of processes for the ego or self to change over from an unintegrated state to a structured integration, to gradually emerge from the merger with the mother, and to change its object relationships from those with a subjectively conceived object to those with an objectively perceived object: in fact, the separation of "me" from "not-me." For the analyst, Winnicott's actual physical holding would be represented by the role of the couch and not, as he occasionally recommended in the analysis of borderline or psychotic patients, the actual physical handling of the patient by the analyst.

Masud Khan (1969) has suggested that the result of this holding as described in space and time is to establish within the patient the sense of "being," and he differentiated this state of "being" from those of "knowing" and "experiencing." In most patients, the sense of being can be taken for granted, but in borderline and psychotic patients this is not necessarily the case. Under these circumstances, the communication from the nonverbal holding and the setting constitutes an essential and vital aspect of therapy. It is a common clinical observation that in the analysis of such patients, intrusions into the consulting room from outside, such as by extraneous noises or from the mistaken entry of another person, can so invade the patient's space that regressive disintegration can easily occur. Similarly, with any disruptions of the regular time of the patient's scheduled appointments, the same phenomena can be observed.

In 1963, Winnicott extended the notion of "holding" the patient. He said:

> It is very painful to the patient to be dependent unless one is actually an infant, and the risks that have to be taken in regression to dependence are very great indeed. The risk is not that the analyst will die so much as that the analyst will suddenly be unable to believe in the reality and the intensity of the patient's primitive anxiety, a fear

> of disintegration, or of annihilation, or of falling for ever and ever. You will see that the analyst is *holding* the patient, and this often takes the form of conveying in words at the appropriate moment something that shows the analyst knows and understands the deepest anxiety that is being experienced, or that is waiting to be experienced. Occasionally, holding must take a physical form, but I think this is only because there is a delay in the analyst's understanding which he can use for verbalizing what is afoot [p. 240].

Here we are dealing with the holding function in terms of verbal communication of understanding and this will take us to the topics of empathy and identification. But we should first notice Winnicott's comment about the physical form of holding. He is here relating it to a delay of understanding and it is difficult to see any reasoning as to why a lack of understanding at a particular point in time should be dealt with by physical contact. One might have thought that a delay in understanding should be dealt with by waiting until such understanding does start to glimmer and allowing more space and time to occur as in the earlier version of holding.

In order to be able to convey in words the analyst's understanding of the patient's anxieties, or indeed any other state, the analyst must have a close empathy with the patient, the capacity to identify with him or her. The ability to empathize is dependent on the capacity for making both temporary and partial identifications with the patient and constitutes an intimate and nonverbal form of establishing contact (Greenson, 1960) which originates in the earliest mother-child relationship. Empathy is one of the forms of the projective identificatory mechanisms, which originate in this relationship (Klein, 1955), and consist of putting oneself into the other person's shoes. This ability for empathic, intuitive, nonverbal emotional closeness and awareness is an essential factor for the analyst in being able to make verbal and emotional contact with the patient. The verbal contact consists of the interpretation or other utterance that the analyst considers most appropriate at that moment. In some instances, patients experience a correct interpretation not simply as mental understanding but also as a feeling of being closely held physically by the analyst, a feeling which most probably arises from the nonverbal implications of a good interpretation, of being closely and attentively listened to, and of being understood.

The tone of voice of the analyst is clearly an important nonverbal aspect of the verbal communication. No matter what the tone of voice happens to be, it must always convey something of the emotional state existing in the analyst, whether it be excitement, pleasure, anger, boredom, or whatever. Even a neutral tone conveys the state of neutrality to the patient and the changes in tone that go on throughout any session provide a vivid commentary on the analyst's inner emotions. In addition to the tone of voice, we also have the mood of the analyst and the emotional atmosphere created in the session as powerful nonverbal conveyors of these inner states. The analyst may often not be aware of his or her own mood in the session until the *patient* communicates it either in so many words or indirectly in associations or behavior. How often we, as analysts, get out of bed on the wrong side or else bring in to the next patient's session the mood state engendered by the previous patient.

We must also include the condition of our physical bodies in these nonverbal considerations. I have already mentioned the appearance and personality of the analyst when we considered the setting, but here I am thinking of the analyst in the chair behind the patient. The analyst may be quite still and relaxed, or tense and alert, or fidgety and perhaps bored. All of these may be communicated directly to the patient. Occasionally, the analyst's stomach rumbles or his guts gurgle; there may even be this sort of visceral dialogue going on for a time between both analyst and patient whilst they are silent. All of these convey emotional state messages to the patient.

Finally, there are the analyst's silences. As with the patient, silence can be a most powerful conveyor of many different emotional states, and we need to be aware of what we are communicating in this state. We may be temporarily withdrawn and preoccupied with our own thoughts; we may be temporarily sulking or depressively silent; or we may just be in a relaxed silent state but attentive and receptive to the patient. Sometimes the analyst's silence may be, paradoxically, the most important form of interpretation to be made to the patient. By this, I mean the importance of not interpreting at this particular moment. The mood and feeling contained with the analyst's silence is the operative nonverbal communication.

Joseph (1985) wrote that:

> Much of our understanding of the transference comes through our understanding of how our patients act on us to feel things for many varied reasons; how they try to draw us into their defensive systems; how they unconsciously act out with us in the transference, trying to get us to act out with them; how they convey aspects of their living world built up from infancy—elaborated in childhood and adulthood, experiences often beyond the use of words, which we can often only capture through the feelings aroused in us, through our countertransference, used in the broad sense of the word [p. 447].

These views on the transference are similar to those expressed by Sandler, Dare, and Holder (1973), particularly with regard to the unconscious, or not so unconscious, subtle attempts to manipulate or provoke situations with the analyst which are a concealed repetition of earlier experiences and relationships. It is the subtlety of these projective identificatory mechanisms, or externalizations, to use Anna Freud's phrase (1936), to produce actualization of these relationships, that creates the problems in handling and understanding them.

Let me give a clinical example, not from a patient of mine, but from an unpublished paper given by my colleague, Maurice Whelan (1992), to the Independent Group of the British Society. He presented some material from the analysis of a depressed, psychosomatically ill woman. It is from a Friday session following an unusual two-week break that the analyst had initiated. The patient had been speaking of her various symptoms, of tensions in the lives of certain members of her family, and of her feeling of being boring to the analyst. He decided to say:

> [T]hat maybe she is still upset with me about the two-week break, and the effect it had on her, because she might have been saved that attack if I had behaved differently and taken breaks in the usual way. She did not respond. After a while she says "and Bruno Bettelheim has killed himself. How awful. I wonder why? Primo Levi too. What is it about someone who survives a concentration camp and then takes his own life. Bettelheim was a real hero of mine. I loved his writing. The way he died seems awful . . . a plastic

bag over his head—did it all get to him—did the experience of the camps eventually get to him and destroy him?" My next response is the one I want to draw attention to. I am here going to tell you the words I spoke. My emotional state when I said them is perhaps as (if not more) relevant and I will soon describe my state of mind.

The patient is upset and crying very audibly. I waited for her weeping to subside a little and then I said, "It is quite a puzzle about Bettelheim. I had heard a while ago that he had a serious illness, a stroke I think, and that he was very disabled. I don't know why he took his life. I think though that what is concerning you at the moment about him is whether he felt everything was useless and he despaired." After a pause she replied, "When you were speaking my hands were so fiercely held together, so tight, that they were white." I then said, "Earlier you said that when you feel bored and tedious, you are convinced that I feel the same. If that is the case then you believe that you can induce in me a state of mind. You can make my mind have in it what is in your mind. So like the experience of Bettelheim, you have then done something to me to destroy the life in my mind, so that you are left, not only alone and stranded, but with a sense of your own destructiveness and capacity to cause isolation."

The session then continued until the end. The analyst commented that he had found himself shocked, surprised and shaken by the reference to the plastic bag. However, instead of waiting to calm down and recover his balance, he had spoken to her while he was still feeling unsteady and had included in his interpretation some of his own thoughts about Bettelheim's suicide. He remarked that it was unusual for him to respond to a patient in this particular way, which could well be called acting out in the countertransference. But even though aware of this dilemma, his inclination to respond in this way persisted, and so he decided to go ahead and speak. This and other thoughts went rapidly through his mind at this moment. He thought that if he had not responded in this direct way but had taken deep breaths and waited, he would have been talking from a false self position; the patient often took deep breaths to wait and enable emotional moments to pass and so distance herself from the analysis. He thought that if he had reacted in his more usual way by calming and distancing himself emotionally and then giving the more usual interpretation, it would have most likely met the same fate as previous comments, no response, a groan, or an asthmatic wheeze. He thought that by showing her that he could actually have his own thoughts and not simply be in the usual interpretative mode, he could demonstrate that he was not simply bored with her. He thought that the specific content of what he was saying was not of primary importance; it was more his capacity to risk saying something unusual and in an unusual mode that was making a declaration of independence of thought. His final thought was that he knew of another analyst, Neville Symington (1983), who had written of acts of freedom and unconventionality, and thus encouraged him to act against the dictates of his own internal analytic supervisor-superego. After all these considerations, it is interesting to note that the outcome of the interpretative and the nonverbal communicative aspects of the analyst resulted in a significant therapeutic effect on the patient, who was able to really confront her dominant mother for the first time in her life—another declaration of independence.

One of the problems that concerns us is how the analyst manages to tolerate and deal with the often very powerful feelings that are evoked in him or her by the verbal and nonverbal projections of the patient. In the material that I have just presented, the analyst described the traumatic effect that was produced in him by the patient. The analyst has to try to understand whether the feelings that are induced in him are primarily a direct result of the patient's projections, that is, a consequence of the patient's psychopathology, or else the direct result of the analyst's own personal response to them, a consequence of his pathology. This is essentially the difference between countertransference as defined by Heimann (1950) and as defined by Freud (1910). From his understanding of this, the analyst will attempt to decide an appropriate response in the transference relationship at that moment, a more daunting task than it seems, particularly as the Freudian countertransference is so often unconscious and hence not recognized until long after the event. Bion (1962) introduced the concept of the analyst acting as the container for the patient's unacceptable projections and allowing them to be reflected on within the analyst's mind over a period and then offered back later to the patient in an acceptable "detoxified" state in the form of an interpretation. This should mean that the analyst accepts and contains whatever thoughts and feelings the patient projects into him, does not attempt to formulate immediate meaning or understanding of these projections for the patient, but waits until he feels he does have some proper understanding of the analytic situation before doing so. Of course, this does not mean that the analyst should remain silent during this period, since empathic emotional understanding of the situation is essential at these times.

Brenman Pick (1985), in a paper on working through in the countertransference, talks of these difficulties. She rightly says that the analyst being human is as likely as the patient to wish to avoid the pain and distress of the projected experience but then having wished this, the analyst uses his feelings to attempt to understand the countertransference situation. My clinical illustration demonstrates this. Pick also suggests that the patient watches, consciously and unconsciously, to determine if the analyst is evading or meeting the difficult aspects of the projective phases of this interaction. Carpy (1989), in a paper on tolerating the countertransference, extends this view and suggests that he believes that the inevitable partial acting out of the countertransference allows the patient to see that the analyst is being affected by what is projected and that he is struggling to try to tolerate his feelings and is managing sufficiently to maintain his analytic stance without grossly acting out. This partial acting out is indicated in the choice of the type of interpretation, its wording, and the tone in which it is delivered. It is through this process, a verbal and nonverbal communication, that the patient is able gradually to reintroject the previously intolerable aspects of himself that had been projected. The patient is also able to introject the capacity to tolerate them which he has observed in the analyst.

Grinberg (1962), and in subsequent papers, has put forward the concept of projective counteridentification, where the main danger is that the analyst has failed to assimilate the projective identifications, which resulted in antitherapeutic acting out responses by the analyst. It is important to recognize that not all acting out in the countertransference is antitherapeutic. The spontaneous gesture and act of freedom are often therapeutic, as is also the partial acting out of the countertransference as described above. Perhaps the Freudian countertransference and the lack of understanding of the analytic transference relationship are the main antitherapeutic agents.

This topic of the analyst's tolerance and ways of dealing with the patient's projections leads us on to consider the importance of the nonverbal aspects of interpretations, and particularly of transference interpretations, in initiating the processes of psychic change in the patient. James Strachey (1934), in his important paper, postulated that for a transference interpretation to be effective, the patient must be able to recognize the difference between his phantasy of the analyst's behavior and the analyst's actual behavior as he has experienced it both at that moment and over the course of the analysis. To quote him: "in the second phase of a complete interpretation, therefore, a crucial part is played by the patient's sense of reality: for the successful outcome of that phase depends upon his ability, at the critical moment of the emergence into consciousness of the released quantity of id-energy, to distinguish between his phantasy object and the real analyst" (p. 147).

Winnicott (1969) in his paper "The Use of an Object" suggested that the very intensity of the projective identifications of the unacceptable destructive parts of the patient's self together with the survival of these attacks by the analyst in his analytic functioning, is the factor that helps to create the quality of externality of the object. Instead of being projected and subjective the object becomes objective, real, and separate. Similarly, Carpy as I have described suggested that it is the patient's observations and experiences of the partial acting out of the analyst under the onslaught of the patient's attacks that allows the patient to reintroject the previously intolerable aspects of himself and also to introject the capacity to tolerate them as he has observed in the analyst. In these ways, all three authors have suggested that it is the actual handling of the nonverbal aspects of the relationship as manifested by the analyst's actual behavior toward the patient, as well as the understanding shown by the verbal interpretation, that is of essential and crucial importance in these processes of psychic change.

As I have already mentioned, these processes for psychic change depend on the patient having a reasonable sense of reality, and further difficult problems will arise when this reality sense is poor or hardly functioning. Here the patient will have regressed to the stage of a transference borderline or full psychosis. In these states, interpretations are no longer heard and experienced as such by the patient but tend to be felt concretely as persecuting or seductive utterances of the analyst. Sometimes the patient is quite withdrawn during sessions. The reality-testing of the analyst's actual behavior as against his phantasied behavior no longer exists. Usually the problems that are encountered in this state are considered in terms of how to try to reach the nonpsychotic aspects of the patient by verbal means of empathic understanding and of correct transference interpretations. These verbal measures are essential in the analysis but some authors have also considered additional aspects of the analytic relationship which they consider to be of fundamental importance. Perhaps the best known of these are Michael Balint (1968) in his book *The Basic Fault*, and Donald Winnicott (1954) in his paper on "Metapsychological and Clinical Aspects of Regression." Both discussed these issues in the context of the therapeutic aspects of regression and both stressed the therapeutic value of the actual object relationships of the situation as distinct from the therapeutic value of interpretation. To quote Balint:

> In some cases in which words, that is associations followed by interpretations, do not seem able to induce or maintain the necessary changes, additional therapeutic agents should be considered. In my opinion, the most important of these is to help the patient to develop a primitive relationship in the analytic situation corresponding to his compulsive pattern and maintain it in undisturbed peace till he can discover the possibility of new forms of object relationship, experience them, and experiment with them [p. 166].

To quote Winnicott (1963):

> In treatment of schizoid persons the analyst needs to know all about the interpretations that might be made on the material presented, but he must be able to refrain from being sidetracked into doing this work that is inappropriate because the main need is for an unclever ego-support, or a holding. This "holding," like the task of the mother in infant-care, acknowledges tacitly the tendency of the patient to disintegrate, to cease to exist, to fall for ever [p. 241].

Winnicott and Balint differed, however, in their ways of dealing with regressed patients, particularly from the viewpoint of nonverbal communication. Winnicott (1954) regarded regression as regression to dependence, based on the mother–infant relationship, and he would vary his normal analytic technique if he thought it was necessary to unfreeze an environmental failure situation, which the patient was thought to have internalized in early life, leading to the development of a false self organization. These variations he described as management, and they might consist of an increase in the length of sessions on a regular basis, of holding the patient's hands or head for prolonged periods if he thought it appropriate, as described by Margaret Little (1985) in her account of her analysis with him. She experienced these extensions of nonverbal communication as therapeutic, yet Winnicott described these procedures, according to Little, as being very taxing on the analyst. This could well be because of the countertransference feelings aroused, particularly with the physical contact. It was Winnicott (1949) who had written on hate in the countertransference and had indicated that in the maintenance of the analytic setting by such things as having beginnings and endings to sessions, by charging fees, and by not gratifying the patient's wishes, the analyst's hate is expressed. The altered circumstances of some aspects of this management of regressed patients must, no doubt, impair these opportunities for hate's expression by the analyst.

Balint, on the basis of his and Ferenczi's experiences of the treatment of regressed patients, believed that any such gratification of the patient's instinctual wishes and demands could often lead to fresh demands, eventually leading to a breakdown of the analysis. He thought that "possibly it is because the instinctual needs of any adult, no matter how far regressed, are to an extent more complex than an infant's, that it is as a rule beyond the possibilities of even a more sensitive and sympathetic analyst to achieve a faultless identification with all of them" (1968, p. 112). For him, the management of a regressed patient was a delicate and precarious task and difficult to perform satisfactorily. He distinguished two forms of regression, benign and malignant. The benign form, as its name implies, was essentially harmless, with the regression being in the interest of the patient trying to reach something within himself, some early experience or phantasy-experience of which the patient had not previously been consciously aware. The malignant form was the opposite of this, with the patient not trying to reach something in himself, but wanting and demanding active gratification of his wishes by the analyst. Acceding to these demands would constitute a major nonverbal communication from the analyst. The short-term therapeutic outcome may well be of improvement, but the long-term prospect is often of disaster. This form of regression is often characterized by intense envious and destructive attacks on the analyst's mind, and sometimes his body, either in the subtle, or not so subtle, form of manipulatory gratification, or occasionally by reaching the level of physical violence. It is in this regressed state that one particularly experiences the difficult but essential analytical task of maintaining and preserving the analytic setting while surviving the attacks in a nonretaliatory way as described earlier.

In a previous paper (1977), I described my experiences of having to physically contain and restrain a borderline hysterical female patient who was determined to feel if I had an erection or not. The essential nonverbal communication by me was in terms of this physical containment of her attacks in order to maintain the analytic limits that I considered to be essential both for myself and the analysis. The firmness and determination of the analyst in maintaining the limits and boundaries of the analytic setting are essential in the nonverbal communication regarding the analyst's own psychic and physical boundaries, ego strength and indestructibility. These are vital factors in helping the establishment and differentiation of the "me" from the "not-me" of the patient, and goes together with the internalization by the patient of the analyst's real capacity for maintaining this psychic process. It is in this respect as well as others that Balint likened the analytic state to those of the four primary substances, earth, air, fire, and water, in being indestructible.

The situation is very different in the benign regression, where the patient is reaching something within. Here the emotional atmosphere and mood is accepted and contained by the analyst, who does not try to understand it too rigorously at that moment, particularly in its transferential aspects. This state of quiet receptivity, of simply being with the patient, and sharing his or her experience, is a crucial requirement, a crucial nonverbal communication, at these times. It is akin to Bion's notion of Keat's negative capability, of tolerating nonunderstanding for the time being.

At this point, we need to take up the issue of physical contact, of holding or touching, as an ingredient of analytic technique, an obvious form of nonverbal communication. Freud, and following him most analysts, were not in favor of such contact since it could easily lead to addictive demands for further contact with potentially disastrous results for the analysis. Ferenczi, and following him, Balint and Winnicott to differing extents, did report finding it therapeutically helpful if such contact were made, although critical criteria as defined in their writings, were uncertain. However, this issue has been further examined and discussed by Stewart (1989) in which it was pointed out that although such contact may be helpful, it may well conceal more than it discloses. Balint, for example, suggested that if the emotional atmosphere was *arglos,* to use his term, meaning innocent and guileless, and in a late period of the analysis, finger or hand holding could be allowed. However, this physical contact is often followed by a dream or parapraxis suggesting rape or physical assault, with the inference that the unconscious experience of the patient had been anything but innocent or guileless. The atmosphere had this quality since the psychic realities of persecutory traumatic and sexual anxieties had been split-off and denied, leaving the opposite state of innocence and guilelessness in a hysterical-type idealized defensive maneuver. Since the analyst cannot easily differentiate the real arglos state from the fraudulent, it seems therapeutically more advantageous to forgo this form of nonverbal communication rather than risk colluding with the patient's denials.

I will conclude by briefly mentioning the most esoteric form of nonverbal communication in analysis, the parapsychological. Freud and later analysts have been interested in the phenomenon where the patient is apparently able to see into the analyst's mind and observe something factual but unexpected and startling to the analyst. For example, a patient one day told me, correctly, that it was my birthday. She had no possible means of obtaining this fact without extensive investigations into birth records and I knew this not to be so. Another patient knew I had been left a legacy, even to the extent of being almost correct about the amount. Both patients may have been aware, as Balint suggested in his paper on the subject (1955), that my emotional state was elsewhere, other than with the patient, and so produced these phenomena in order to startle me and ensure my emotional return to them. However, my emotional state has often been elsewhere and no such phenomena were produced, and furthermore, how does the patient know the details of my state of mind? Unless one believes that the patient is actually able by some means to enter my mind, the only alternative seems to be that the analyst has, by some nonverbal means, communicated these details of states of mind to the patient, perhaps in some way akin to the sign language of deaf people. The often observed fact that patients will produce appropriate material on specific topics to help students in clinical sessions is perhaps another example, here of a need being conveyed from analyst to patient in nonverbal form. It seems to be the fact that "there are more things in heaven and earth, . . . than are dreamt of in your philosophy."

REFERENCES

Balint, M. (1955), Notes on parapsychology and parapsychological healing. In: *Problems of Human Pleasure and Behaviour*. London: Hogarth Press, 1957.

——— (1968), *The Basic Fault*. London: Tavistock Publications.

——— Balint, A. (1939), On transference and countertransference. In: *Primary Love and Psychoanalytic Technique*. London: Hogarth Press, 1952.

Bion, W. (1962), A theory of thinking. *Internat. J. Psycho-Anal.*, 43:306–310.

Carpy, D. V. (1989), Tolerating the countertransference: A mutative process. *Internat. J. Psycho-Anal.*, 70:287–294.

Freud, A. (1936), *The Ego and the Mechanisms of Defense*. New York: International Universities Press, 1966.

Freud, S. (1905), Fragment of an analysis of a case of hysteria. *Standard Edition*, 7:3–132. London: Hogarth Press, 1953.

——— (1910), The future prospects of psychoanalytic therapy. *Standard Edition*, 11:139–151. London: Hogarth Press, 1957.

Greenson, R. R. (1960), Empathy and its vicissitudes. *Internat. J. Psycho-Anal.*, 41:418–424.

Grinberg, L. (1962), On a specific aspect of the countertransference due to the patient's projective identification. *Internat. J. Psycho-Anal.*, 43:436–440.

Heimann, P. (1950), On countertransference. *Internat. J. Psycho-Anal.*, 31:81–84.

Joseph, B. (1985), Transference: The total situation. *Internat. J. Psycho-Anal.*, 666:447–454.
Khan, M. M. R. (1985), Vicissitudes of being, knowing and experiencing in the therapeutic situation. *Brit. J. Med. Psych.*, 42:383–393.
Klein, M. (1955), On identification. In: *The Writings of Melanie Klein*, Vol. 3. London: Hogarth Press, 1981, pp. 141–175.
Limentani, A. (1966), A re-evaluation of acting out in relation to working through. *Internat. J. Psycho-Anal.*, 47:274–282.
Little, M. I. (1985), Winnicott working in areas where psychotic anxieties predominate: A personal record. *Free Associations*, 3:9–42.
Pick, I. B. (1985), Working through in the countertransference. *Internat. J. Psycho-Anal.*, 66:157–166.
Rycroft, C. (1956), The nature and function of the analyst's communication to the patient. In: *Imagination and Reality*. London: Hogarth Press, 1968.
Sandler, J., Dare, C., & Holder, A. (1973), Transference. In: *The Patient and the Analyst*. New York: International Universities Press.
Stewart, H. (1977), Problems of management and communication. In: *Psychic Experience and Problems of Technique*. London: Routledge, 1992, pp. 82–100.
——— (1989), Technique at the basic fault and regression. In: *Psychic Experience and Problems of Technique*. London: Routledge, 1992, pp. 111–126.
——— (1990), Interpretation and other agents for psychic change. In: *Psychic Experience and Problems of Technique*. London: Routledge, 1992, pp. 127–140.
Strachey, J. (1934), The nature of the therapeutic action of psychoanalysis. *Internat. J. Psycho-Anal.*, 50:275–292.
Symington, N. (1983), The analyst's act of freedom as agent of therapeutic change. In: *The British School of Psychoanalysis: The Independent Tradition*, ed. G. Kohon. London: Free Association Books, 1986.
Whelan, M. (1992), Beyond words—beyond analytic neutrality? A countertransference dilemma with a psychosomatically ill patient. *Brit. Psychoanal. Soc. Bull.*, 27:11–18.
Winnicott, D. W. (1949), Hate in the countertransference. In: *Collected Papers: Through Paediatrics to Psychoanalysis*. London: Tavistock Publications, 1958, pp. 194–203.
——— (1954), Metapsychological and clinical aspects of regression within the psychoanalytical set-up. In: *Collected Papers: Through Paediatrics to Psychoanalysis*. London: Tavistock Publications, 1958, pp. 278–294.
——— (1960), The theory of the parent-infant relationship. In: *The Maturational Processes and the Facilitating Environment*. New York: International Universities Press, 1965, pp. 37–55.

——— (1963), Psychiatric disorder in terms of infantile maturational processes. In: *The Maturational Processes and the Facilitating Environment.* New York: International Universities Press, 1965, pp. 230–241.
——— (1969), The use of an object and relating through identifications. In: *Playing and Reality.* London: Tavistock Publications, 1971, pp. 86–94.

9.

ENDINGS

NINA E. C. COLTART, M.A., M.B.

My own very first association with the title of this paper was an image with no people in it, of wintry fields, not snow-covered or sunlit, but grayish and rather wet. It was accompanied by a very faint bodily sensation, a slight chill, and this was followed rapidly by an emotion which was distinctly bleak, and, I suppose, lonely. All this happened very fast, of course, and is even difficult to break down into elements. At this point, there were no words. Then things speeded up, the grayish fields flooded and froze over, some people were skating, and the ice cracked. The water was not deep, so I can deduce that at this point it was not a particularly aggressive fantasy. It was more bleak and desolate than dangerous, but at least there were now some people. A kind of self-consciousness intruded, and with it came more thoughts. I did think about endings of treatments, but the first and stronger thought was about death.

Ending is one of the greatest of all human concerns, the only one that none can escape. I was not aware that I myself thought about death as particularly bleak or desolate, though I know there are those who do. Sometimes I think, like Peter Pan, that it could be a big adventure. Mostly I think it will be extremely *interesting*, and it seems to me as if almost the greatest blessing that life can grant is to go consciously into one's own death. It would be maddening not to be able to write a paper about it afterwards; but to

This paper was first given as an Arbours Public Lecture on November 17, 1993, in London.

greet one's death, to observe and inspect it, would feel like a fitting ending—particularly to a psychotherapist's life.

A brief discussion of the word *concern* is appropriate here, not, of course, meaning worry—a misuse of the word—it is a far greater word than that. Concern is not delusional or shallow, as worry can be. Worries can be real and frightening, but more often they are transient, invented, silly, or imaginary. When worries get serious they are more properly called anxiety.

When I was a medical student one of my professors said: "Try not to *worry* about patients, and certainly don't ever take worry home with you overnight. Be concerned for the patients, always—you will find that with true concern, you can leave them behind when you aren't with them. Work out the difference." This repays reflection, especially in the analytic profession.

In life itself, apart from the strange lives lived out in the consulting room, a lot of people are worried about death; at least, they are often not sure if it is death or dying they are worried about. I think it is more likely to be dying. At any rate, they are worried, and could be said to be in a chronic state of anxiety about the prospect of their own death. Such people often give little conscious thought to the deaths of others: though there is another group of people, usually those who have experienced severe traumatic loss in their lives, who are deeply anxious some of the time about the prospect of a loved person's death, and fear little for themselves. From being within relatively normal limits, both these sorts of worry about ending can grow to monstrous proportions.

I once analyzed a man whose anxiety about his own death was pathologically severe. He was only ever free of it for a few hours, then it came creeping or crashing back. He would wake up in the night and lie there in a panic about the fact that he was going to die. He had brought this monosymptomatic anxiety to analysis several years before, and as luck would have it, first one, and then a second, analyst had died on him, not during a session, but in the middle of an active working treatment. It was almost as if a malignant fate had got it in for him, and naturally he had a paranoid feeling about that. However, although he often bewailed his misfortune in losing two apparently healthy though aging analysts, one had to steer back past them, because strictly speaking they were irrelevant to his psychopathology. I was rather flattered, ignorant young ass that I was, to be asked by a little group of senior analysts to take him on, soon after I qualified. Looking back, I think everyone had become magically superstitious and they were saving their own faces by being flattering to me. Of course, it was my youth and vigor they were after, not my precocious talent.

He was in every way a most unsuitable patient for psychoanalysis, and I say this well aware that at least three analysts had taken him into treatment five times a week. He was exceedingly difficult to work with. He was a cold, cruel, sentimental and deeply narcissistic man, and for quite a long time I was of the opinion that his fear of death was a crippling fear of his superego which would finally punish him for his emotional and character defects. In fact, I still think this may have been so although the narcissistic horror was deeper than that; but he was completely nonresponsive to interpretations of any sort. He was not even compliant or courteous about them, the way many frightened people are; things had gone too far for that. He did not at all like me, and he tended to despise women generally. Occasionally, he would consider something I said for a short while, then dismiss it, and plunge back into his solipsistic ruminations.

It took me about eighteen months to come to the supremely simple formulation, which eventually I interpreted, that in his view, and intention, we were locked in a fight to the death. This connected with his early history, as well as with the deaths of his previous analysts. He did listen to this, and his ultimate reaction to it, about a year later, was to leave. Contrary to what my colleagues had thought, my comparative youth and health was not a mark in my favor at all so far as the patient was concerned. I was quite a lot younger than he, which was not the case with the other people he had outlived and triumphed over. As some profoundly narcissistic characters do, he merged with me to a considerable extent, rather than forming an ordinary neurotic transference. The fusion produced pseudo-projective identifications, so he became convinced that *I* would suddenly die, and he never could tell whether he most feared, or wished for, this event. He envied me, he hated me, but worse, he feared defeat in the life-or-death battle. Yet, really, that was the only prospect; the ending, or death, of either of us would have spelled defeat. The continuing analytic work, such as it was, was a dreadful sort of "Pass-time," such as one might do in the anteroom to hell. Although he was desperate to get away from me, he held on grimly and forced *me* to bring up the subject of ending the analysis. Eventually, I admitted defeat, whatever he feared, and said I was not prepared to go on. It was not by any means an exemplary ending, as he spent most of the intervening weeks, before he finally stopped, screaming with rage, or sobbing, also with rage. His behavior served only to strengthen my resolve. I am afraid he aroused only the most marginal sympathy in me. He demanded another analyst, but could not begin to describe the person he now thought would be right for him. I anyway refused because of my decision about his unanalyzability, and also out of compassion for whoever might land him next. What I did do was offer to refer him to a good behavioral therapist; the grinding, addictive monotony of his symptom, and other features, struck me as being obsessional in quality. He accepted this offer, and then could hardly wait to be off. I did not hear from him again.

What I learned from that experience I suppose was to withstand chronic hatred and contempt. Also I realized how difficult it is to be heard as a valued interpreter when one is the object of true hatred and envy. I learned about certain narcissistic features, and how resistant to analysis they are. I really became convinced that, in spite of what some people say, including analysts, analysis can*not* treat "anything," given time and the "correct" interpretations. This idea is one of omnipotent lunacy. Freud certainly did not think so. He has a wonderful phrase somewhere about "low and repellent characters who are good for nothing in this world." I never discovered if anything else underlay that patient's choice of death as his object of dread; or perhaps I should say, if it was truly an existential dread, or was primarily about something else. I also learned that the prospect of inevitable death can make life itself a living death for some few unfortunates. Had I known about the theory and techniques of self psychology then, I might have treated him differently from the beginning. But it had not yet appeared on the scene.

Death should be a "concern" of all human beings; it crops up in various guises often in our work, and therefore should be reflected upon by analytical psychotherapists, apart from the fact that it is not going to spare us. The opposite extreme to the man

I have described is met with more often; the variations of denial. There is actually a society in America about which I read a long article a few months ago; it is composed of people who are going to live forever. The Live Forevers believe that they have, if I remember it aright, a mutated gene which has only recently appeared in mankind, and which ensures this eternal journey. I am not at all sure how one knew if one had it, or what, besides living forever, it was said to promise. All the members of the Society, about sixty in all, are less than 45 years of age and presumably had not thought through the horror-filled possibilities of continuing to show ever-increasing signs of aging, without the often-welcomed rescue of death.

I believe that there is another way of approaching death, a strong and resilient middle way between denial and terror. Eschatology, or the study of last things, is not fashionable at present, at least not under this, its old name, and has not been for a century or more. Nevertheless, death is not quite the forbidden subject that it was even a few years ago. Bereavement counseling can almost be said to be one of the fashionable bandwagons, and this is on the whole a good sign, although unfortunately a rather mechanical quality inheres in the developing technique. In the heyday of Western religion, from about the twelfth century to the midnineteenth, death, and particularly what was referred to as "a good death," was one of the most important subjects of study and attention. Islam and Christianity offered a confident belief in eternal life, of peace and happiness, as a reward for a courageous good life on earth. It was seen as compensation for the widespread suffering that was accepted as part of most people's lot here below, in what Gray, in his Elegy, called "the short and simple annals of the poor." Eternal life was to be spent in the presence of God, and it was the encounters with God, Jesus, the Blessed Virgin, and the Communion of Saints that were faithfully anticipated, in a metaphysically vague place called Heaven. Jesus himself concentrated more on living this life, and it is only in the Revelation of St. John the Divine that there is anything descriptive about heaven. This is so extraordinary, with its jeweled floors and strange mythical creatures, that one is left with the feeling that it would be extremely uncomfortable. Cultural themes have changed radically in this century and people tend to be more self-conscious, atheistic, agnostic, and conditioned to thinking about notions such as time; an earth-bound awareness of time can give the impression that an afterlife, were such a thing possible, would be one of intolerable and endless boredom.

However, this idea of dreadful boredom in the believer's heaven may in itself contribute to something positive about the nonbeliever's view of death. What I mean by a "positive" contribution is that there is something appealing in the idea of simply stopping, as opposed to an unimaginable change of circumstances in which nevertheless consciousness, as we know it, always seems to persist. A strong and resilient middle way, of which I spoke, consists at least in part of a regular contemplation of the very fact of death, so that we familiarize ourselves with it. A discipline of simple meditation as part of one's life makes this sort of approach unalarming, partly because it increases calmness and detachment from the importance of the self.

Many people who are ignorant of Buddhism think that they know at least one thing about it, and bring up the subject of reincarnation: as a matter of fact, as with most views and opinions on anything requiring blind faith, which is not a feature of Buddhist teaching, an open mind is maintained. Fanciful ideas of many lives with a clearly defined self, or coming back as an insect if one has not been good, are either fantasies projected into Buddhism by the uninstructed, or derivations from some of the mythology which grows up around any religion. There is a central, and somewhat esoteric, teaching which is very much at the heart of Buddhist understanding of life, which is to do with egolessness; this, as no self, is said to be one of the three signs of being, the other two being impermanence and suffering. Where ego does not exist, and is fundamentally only the result of conditioning, the notion of dying would of necessity be different, to say the least. Briefly, the teaching on death tells us that life itself is an energy, which is inextinguishable; but the metamorphosis of personality and of the self is embroidery. Of course, understanding that the ego is a delusion adds a certain humor to practicing Western psychological disciplines in which we try to strengthen the ego. But I do also believe that one has to have a stronger "conceptual ego" before one can confidently set about losing it!

The simple act of contemplating one's own death does much to contribute to peace of mind in the here and now; and when you come to think about it, the here and now is all there ever is for anyone. There is nothing more liable to banish anxiety than to accept the inevitable with one's whole heart, and to practice living only in the here and now.

I will discuss now the termination of a long and complex treatment by analytical psychotherapy, which may in some ways be compared to death. I wonder if perhaps this idea has occurred to some (it has certainly cropped up in more than one analysis which is working toward an ending) but that they may have held back from exploring it because of some anxiety about being accused of extremeness or even grandiosity. Even a mature, level-headed, and commonsensical person may have an almost superstitious fear of talking about death, and this would certainly include any comparative reference to death in connection with such a frequent phenomenon as ending a treatment in our own professional lives. Endings are a regular part of these lives, and they can present a wide range of problems. It is just as well to have an idea of what some of these can be; there is little advantage during the termination stage in being taken by surprise, and a happening which might otherwise induce alarm and despair can be calmly surveyed if anticipated, or at least, made familiar in outline and expectation.

Some of the things we do in analysis are very *odd*. I think this applies to ending the treatment. We have clothed the oddness in theory, technique, and familiarity; we discuss the interesting clinical phenomena of the termination phase in matter-of-fact voices; there are symposia on criteria for termination, and so on. All this material tends to disguise the oddity to which I refer, which is the fact of ending at all. Consider: analysts join with their prospective patients, after a careful and searching preliminary interview (itself probably following a long assessment by someone else), and between them they agree on a treatment contract. The treatment is usually prolonged, and is said, quite justifiably, to be one of the most important relationships of one's life. The patient will, under good-enough circumstances, become deeply, if ambivalently, attached to the therapist, both through the transference and through the real relationship, which by the time termination is decided upon, will be quite extensive, and will occupy some of the sublimated libidinal energy freed up by the preceding work. This complex attachment to the therapist is welcomed, and, up to a point, reciprocated. Indeed, although the therapist's personal involvement is more shadowy and delicate, it has to be authentic, in my view, or else the therapy does not truly "take" at the deepest levels. False selves and phoniness are part of psychopathology, and the patient does not need to encounter them in his therapist as he works away at the painful business of outgrowing his own, and becoming responsible for genuine human intercourse. All levels of object relating, closeness, and intimacy, are at the very heart of analytical therapy. The patient often ceases to suffer in his way of relating and the acute, but passing, pains of insight take over from the personality problems presented at the beginning. Defenses, of course, may have taken years to build up, and are only slowly dismantled where unnecessary, to be supplanted by ego itself and by defenses which are more resilient and healthy. Profound, moving, and significant conversations take place. The most casual observer would have no difficulty in noting that here is a relationship of great richness and importance. Such an observer might come to understand that this absorbing relationship is often experienced as the central feature of the patient's *life*. Emotions are withdrawn from other cathected object relations as if to feed the analysis, and it is an utterly serious statement if patients say, as they sometimes do, something on the lines of: "For the moment, my analysis is my life." So what do we do? We bring it to an absolute end. And it is not an exaggeration to say that although they *know* that this will happen, some patients experience the agreement to end as a death sentence.

The untutored observer might react with shock. He would watch as a period of considerable disturbance ensues, but he would observe also, at one and the same time, that both therapist and patient take something about the situation for granted. Of course, there may be massive protest, that is what the disturbance is all about, but curiously it seems to be contained within a framework of not exactly acceptance, but something which is acutely paradoxical, resigned yet fighting, striving for freedom yet arguing against the agreement to stop, pleased yet anguished. The therapist, overall, can be observed to be constantly restoring and rerestoring a negotiated equilibrium, driving steadily toward a shared, whole-hearted point in time, consciously agreed upon by both parties, when this complex, deeply related couple splits apart forever. It is the ultimate paradox. Yet what else can happen? What options are there? The natural, expectable progress of such a deep relationship, in what we call "real life," would be for it to continue to enrich the participants. But although the patient spends part of the last few months elaborating fantasies around this prospect, he mostly knows they are fantasies. The therapist's time is not infinitely elastic. By now, over a period of thirty years, I suppose someone like myself, who has always run a full-time mixed analytic and psychotherapy practice, has probably treated at some depth several hundred people. Life admits of the continuity of such a phenomenon only in limited sequences, certainly not in parallel.

The totality of the ending, which seems to go against the grain of all our work on love, loyalty, object constancy, and intimacy, is reinforced by the austere prescription of no social contact thereafter. Thus we create an arbitrary situation which has much in common with a death. I am very much in favor of strict adherence to this rule, and am quite willing to explore it with anyone who feels doubtful, or confused as to its rationale. Features which recommend it include the reinforcement of the strength of internal objects; a refusal to expose, and perhaps *im*pose, too much of the therapist's real self on vulnerable ex-patients; and granting them a freedom to work through and resolve final transferences, in fact, all remaining problems, on their own. It also allows patients to be sad and manage their own mourning for the loss.

I stand by this rule strongly myself, partly because, having experienced death in my early life and worked on it extensively during my analysis, I needed to handle this mourning alone, which is the only authentic way. This finally achieved a resolution that had never come about in my early adolescence, and could not now have come about in the presence of the "lost object," that is, my analyst. But also I have seen a number of badly fumbled attempts by analysts or therapists who attempt to establish a post-therapy relationship with the patient, of whatever sort. The work of the therapy itself may be grossly undermined, and there can be no experience of completeness. There is an unsatisfactory lack of distinction in the ex-patient's mind between the absolute ending to the unique professional relationship, and residual transferences which may never be fully recognized as such if the analyst subsequently presents wholly as a real person. This presentation puts a ban on the sort of patient-oriented exploratory talk that he or she has been accustomed to, and frequently disastrous regressive states set in. The commonest of these is a bitter vengefulness on the part of the patient. This is often suppressed, out of shame, yet I truly believe it could have been avoided. If one comes across this, one can be sure that either the therapy was not an overall success, or, more likely, that there have been botched attempts at what the therapist may well have thought of as a more "human" relationship after the treatment. I believe that this idea is a fallacy, and is always doomed to fail. It is unreal and injurious to the ex-patient insofar as the ending is wrenched away by the therapist from the necessary similarity to death.

The signs and symptoms of the termination period, which should ideally be, like gestation, about nine months, make a lot more sense immediately when we see that often the patient is protesting at the very point I have been making; that is, the existential and human irrationality of what we are doing in bringing the relationship to an end. Because certainly, even if the patient has been in full control of the date, the timing, the very fact of ending, there is a phase when it feels as though it is the therapist's doing. Projection can undermine intention. However, it is as well to pay the closest attention to the ending of one's own therapy. It sounds rather cold blooded, but by then one should be in a position to study, as well as experience it. One should have learned enough detachment.

During termination, there is a particular set of phenomena that may come about and to a young therapist experiencing them for the first time, they can be extremely unnerving. It is as if all the hard-won ground is lost. Suddenly, in place of the open, mature, balanced individual with whom we are able to discuss ending, there is a weeping, angry, bitter, scathing, jealous child, who may in addition be wheezing, or scratching, or shitting, or threatening suicide from black incomprehensible depression. I have lumped together here a number of symptoms which may have presented at the start of treatment, in different individuals, particularly those with psychosomatic symptoms, all long in abeyance by the end, mastered by insight and work and the facilitating environment.

They sound monstrous when lumped together like this, but any previous, long-forgotten symptom can be pretty horrifying when unexpectedly cropping up alone. Our hearts may faint within us, especially near the beginning of our professional lives, but it is now that a cool head and endurance are called for, alongside the mustering of our analytical skills to their uttermost. Last but not least, hanging onto that faith in the *process* of analysis, and in ourselves, that I so often speak of.

This display of acute regression into a symptom-laden state, a repetition of the early days of their own history in analysis, is complicated, but, nevertheless, it is similar in presentation from one patient to the next, and tells us a number of similar things. It is as if there is a sort of secret sharing of knowledge, among patients, of a final common pathway. There is often fear, rather suddenly, of being abandoned into aloneness, in other words, fear of the bereavement which lies ahead. There may be a punishing wish to frighten the analyst, to show him or her up, to demonstrate that the analyst has been fooled, as well as inept. This often occurs in patients who have never quite resolved an infantile ambivalence. It is a final kick in the direction of a bad internal object from childhood or youth, as if recognizing that this is a last permitted opportunity to take a bit of revenge. This particular interpretation is of considerable value at this point, and may finally resolve the primitive ambivalence. There is also, rather strangely, a deep reluctance to bid farewell to these wild and childish parts of the self. At the same time, these demonstrations are a kind of leave-taking ceremony, in the presence of the only person who is likely to tolerate them, let alone understand them. For better or for worse, this, too, is the patient's self, though a self that is usually now carefully stored away in the archives.

It is an exhilarating time; the therapist must have all his wits about him and use them as never before, especially, I believe, in strengthening the resolve not to extend the duration of therapy. Often, in the midst of regression, there is a pitiful pleading, "Couldn't we extend, just till Christmas?" or "I know I'd be able to work it all out properly, if I had another six months." On the ultimate level, this is all baloney; if one gives in, six minutes would be about as valuable as six months; one has to sit it out, and continue to work. Nor do I think anything advantageous occurs if one yields to the much rarer request to end sooner than planned. Unless a realistic and practical need is obvious, there is something going on which needs analyzing rather than collusion. I have recently wondered if there is any comparison to be drawn with euthanasia, and have not yet come to a conclusion. I would be concerned about a patient who suddenly got up and went off, thus trying to preempt the ending, illusorily snatching away control. Most patients by this time will in fact be sufficiently analyzed to express the impulse verbally rather than act on it. However, the odd one who enacts it provides an opportunity for discovering how vital it is to have faith in the work oneself before, and during, the termination period. Patients are extremely perceptive about us, both consciously and unconsciously, and will spot and exploit a wavering of confidence and a readiness for anxiety. I believe that no effort should be spared to get a patient *back* at this point. Forget your dignity and analytic persona, and work at the primary task, before the patient's pride gets him or her stuck in an irredeemably damaging position.

The only concession I make to pleas for extra time, or brilliant ideas for friendship, or meeting socially or even having an affair, when therapy is over, is to make it clear that if ever people are in real trouble, or have a problem patch in their lives, the door will be ajar for them to come back and do a piece of work, providing I can offer some space; say, one or two sessions or half a dozen or so. Once a terminating patient, in a receptive, nonregressed mood, has taken this in thoroughly, it is surprising how rarely it needs to be used. And if the offer is taken up, then the time is always fruitfully used, taking advantage of all the mutual deep understanding and the shorthand developed during the treatment. Repair can usually very soon be achieved. Similarly, I have observed more than one example of a person with a terminal illness, who has been clearly told by an experienced physician that he has only a short but well-defined period of life left to him, who rather suddenly carries out some searching introspection, usually in conjunction with talking to a close friend. Very often, quite unexpectedly, someone who has never practiced a religious discipline, or developed any particular philosophy of life or death for himself, may reach a thought-through position of calm acceptance and peace of mind, which will then sustain him and those around him to the end, without anxiety or denial. This is very impressive, as is also a patient who moves toward termination with appropriate affect and full use of all the preceding therapeutic work.

Part III

Toward the Group

10.

AMBIVALENT SIBLING RIVALRY: LATENT CONCERNS IN ANNA FREUD'S CANDIDACY PAPER

Rivka R. Eifermann, Ph.D.

DIALOGUES WITH AUDIENCES AND WITH READERS

In the course of writing for publication or public presentation, members of an audience or readers are presences, whether in awareness or not. Such real and fantasized participants in writing are traceable in the published text. For they affect what is said, how it is said, as well as what remains unsaid. They may be highly complex, and may serve as transference objects to the writer (Eifermann, 1987b, 1993). The process of writing involves dialogues with these inner representations, which also find expression in the completed text.

I propose to explore Anna Freud's earliest paper (1922), with the aim of focusing on such a dialogue with her analytic "siblings." The paper, *Schlagephantasie und Tagtraum* (Beating Fantasies and Daydreams), was her membership presentation to the Vienna Society; "a test presentation" as Freud called it in a letter to Eitingon, commenting, "Perhaps she is going to make a decisive step" (Young-Bruehl, 1988, p. 108). It was indeed a decisive step in a life-long commitment to psychoanalysis, and herein lies its special interest.

While the "siblings" nature of Anna Freud's relationship with her analytic colleagues is well documented (Young-Bruehl, 1988), in this paper I show how latent and delicate aspects of this relationship may be learned of through a close reading of a text that aims to discuss clinical and theoretical material in an impersonal style.

The present paper comes as a sequel to Blass' (1993) definitive investigation of Anna Freud's article. Central to her analysis is a close inquiry into the extensive dialogue with Freud embedded in her presentation. Blass explores this dialogue in great detail, demonstrating through it how Anna Freud's transformation of her analysis by her father to an analysis of herself may be viewed as an instantiation of her powerful struggle with her wish to create on her own. Blass has pointed out in detail the discrepancies between Anna Freud's explicit statements in her text regarding the foundations and sources of the ideas on beating fantasies and on daydreams, and those that become apparent from a careful comparison of the respective writings of Anna and Sigmund Freud.

In unfolding herein the dialogue with her "siblings," in reviving the presence of these "siblings," it is my objective to allow immediate access to the scene of enmeshment of rivalry and theory, access that I gained in reading Anna Freud's text in its three extant versions (1922, 1923, 1974). Reading Anna Freud's text carefully, being attuned to its veiled expression, allows the reader a close, perhaps immediate understanding, even involvement, in the personal wishes and fears with which Anna Freud was struggling in the course of her early development as a psychoanalyst, and specifically how these were influenced by her complex relationships with her prospective colleagues. Further exploration may lead to an understanding of ways in which this early development affected her later work and the controversies in which she was later involved.

In a sense, in addressing her father in the presence of these "siblings" Anna Freud was making them indirect partners to that dialogue as well. Moreover, as will be seen, the "siblings' " dialogue sometimes runs parallel, at others it intertwines with the dialogue with Freud. Hence also, while my subject is her "siblings" primarily when I refer in this paper to Anna Freud's *audience*, Freud nevertheless remains an unfocused presence within that audience.

ANNA FREUD'S PRESENTATION: THE CIRCUMSTANCES

Imagine the setting and atmosphere: Vienna, May 31, 1921, a meeting of the Vienna Psychoanalytic Society. Anna Freud, aged 26, presents her candidacy paper. There are members and some guests attending, as well as, of course, her father, Sigmund Freud. Many in the audience have been or still are in analysis with Freud, who has also analyzed his daughter. From the vantage point of over seventy years after the event, its extraordinary, even dramatic circumstances may be more apparent than they were at the time this scientific meeting took place. Anna Freud's paper contains a reflection of her experience of that drama.

Her inner drama is even greater than is evident. For, as is suggested by the original title of her paper (1922)—*Schlagephantasie und Tagtraum(.) von Anna Freud(.)*, meaning literally, *Beating Fantasy and Daydream(.) of Anna Freud*—it is herself, her own analysis that she discusses in her paper. Her presentation centers on a case illustration of a patient whom she refers to as the "little girl" or "the girl" (*Mädchen*). As has recently been demonstrated by Blass (1993) and supported by biographical research (Young-Bruehl, 1988) this little girl is none other than Anna Freud herself. It was her personal material and fragments from her first analysis and further self-analysis that she presented to her audience.

AMBIVALENT SIBLING RIVALRY CONCEALED AND REVEALED

In the introductory remarks to her paper Anna Freud makes quite explicit how she feels about the task before her. These remarks have been edited out of the two English versions of the paper (1923, 1974),[1] appearing only in the original version in German. On the face of it they are just a few introductory comments addressed to her specific audience, and therefore superfluous except in the presentation itself. Yet for an understanding of latent aspects of the paper as directly addressed to her live audience (and the true siblings represented by them), this excluded first section is its essential introduction.

Anna Freud opens as follows:

---

[1]It is likely that Anna Freud was her own translator of the 1923 version published in the *International Journal of Psycho-Analysis*. She had already translated a whole book from English before writing her paper and at the time of the publication of the English version was working on the staff of the *International Journal*. The 1974 version was expressedly her own revision, apparently carried out with both the German version and the first English translation before her.

> Gentlemen and Ladies! I have been taking advantage of (using / have accepted / laid claim to [*nehme in Anspruch*]) your hospitality for a number of years, but until now without making myself noticeable by any form of active participation [*Mitarbeit*]. Indeed I do know from a good source that the Association does not generally tolerate such onlooking among its guests. But, I believe I would have persisted in my behaviour if it were not for your strict rule that anyone who applies for membership first present something to you; [and she further makes explicit that it is] my seeking of acceptance [*Ansuchen um Aufnahme*] at the Vienna Association that is the motive and at the same time the excuse for my lecture today [1922, p. 317].

In this brief, informal introduction Anna Freud emphasizes her great reluctance, past and present, to "let something be heard" from her. While acknowledging that she finally must follow "your strict rule" applied to everyone, she thereby also says that she has been an exception, having passively attended their meetings for a number of years already. And in referring to her "good source" the special accessibility of her father is implied.

It is her desire to be accepted as a member that is the "motive" for her lecture, but why is it also the "excuse"? I propose that she needed this "excuse" to present herself in disguise, and more especially because of the underlying theme of her presentation to her "siblings." In her further remarks, Anna Freud introduces this theme, saying, "In the communication [*Mitteilung*] which I bring forth, a small illustration is given to the essay [*Aufsatz*] of Professor Freud, 'A Child is Being Beaten' " (1922, p. 317). The leitmotif of that essay is, "Father loves only me."

Many years later Anna Freud wrote regarding sibling rivalries amongst candidates:

> In every analysis, sibling rivalries are reawakened in the transference. . . . Candidates of one and the same training analyst behave in the transference as if they were real siblings; they compare themselves with each other; they compete, they envy each other in view of alleged parental preference; they combine forces occasionally to fight the parent, etc. [1965, pp. 417–418].

This complexity of motives, of intense rivalry with the "siblings," yet at the same time a display of independence from her father expressed in gestures toward the siblings in some opposition to the father, can be discerned at various points in her essay.

Taking into consideration that the case Anna Freud presents is her own, her allusion to her own extensive presentation as being "a small illustration" to Freud's essay is significant. Freud's (1919) paper "A Child is Being Beaten," to which Anna Freud refers in her title, is based on four female and two male patients. Freud gives brief notes about five of these patients but omits any direct reference to the sixth. Young-Bruehl (1988) suggests that he may have thus protected his daughter's privacy, but she also points to the possibility that the fifth patient described is his Anna since the description sounds very much like her. Either way Young-Bruehl offers convincing, extensive evidence to the effect that Anna Freud is in all likelihood one of the cases included in Freud's schematic description. Hence it may be said that in point of fact it is she who had served as merely "a small illustration" in Freud's paper, undifferentiated from his other female patients in what he presents as an "average case" (1919, p. 184). By presenting her case extensively in her own paper Anna Freud brings herself back to full size. Indeed, even more so, in the unlikely possibility that Young-Bruehl is mistaken after all and that Freud had altogether excluded her in his considerations. But in particular, she also recovers her individuality and, specifically in relation to his other analysands, her position of exclusiveness since, contrary to her declaration in her introductory remarks, she presents a case that varies considerably and significantly from Freud's "average case."

But in doing so she does something else as well: She reveals to her audience (albeit in disguise, as belonging to "the girl") details (secrets) which Freud failed to uncover[2] or chose not to discuss. Indeed, when going beyond Freud's interpretation of her own material, as well as in adding new material to that discussed by Freud, she discloses to her audience a disguised piece of self-analysis. In

[2]There is some evidence indicating that Anna Freud reveals to her audience (in disguise) some matters that she had failed to reveal privately to Freud. Curiously, only he himself could have been aware of such (concealed) new revelations. Thus, for example, she comments on the dullness of "the girl's" reporting in analysis on her early beating fantasies: "We can assume that the various scenes were quite vivid in the child's imagination, but her references to them during analysis were quite scanty and vague" (1974, p. 139). It is as if Anna Freud had at least recalled such vividness, if not the details of the fantasies, but remained scanty and vague in her reporting. Otherwise why make the assumption?

so doing she turns away from their common "father" and toward her "siblings." Though ambivalently and in disguise, she reveals disagreements with her father-analyst, as well as revealing more than she had either shared with Freud in the privacy of her analysis, or that he had chosen to report from that source in his essay.[3]

Her claim to being an exception, especially loved and preferred by her father, thus finds expression in her introductory remarks, alongside conflicting wishes to find favor with her "siblings." This dilemma is also traceable in her presentation of "the girl's" daydreams.

FANTASIES OF SIBLINGS BEING BEATEN

Following the introductory remarks Anna Freud says that she will take for granted that her audience is familiar with the content of Freud's (1919) paper on beating fantasies. Such familiarity makes it possible to see not only to what she highlights in Freud's paper, but also those aspects that are underplayed or left unmentioned. Indeed it can be assumed that her listeners could follow her closely; that they were able to fill in the gaps in her resumé of Freud and may at points have been sensitized to their personal significance at least in part, in directions illustrated in the following discussion.

Her brief description of the beating fantasies covers the three phases presented by Freud. Only the third phase is elaborated on and discussed in her paper directly with reference to her own case. The fantasy of the first phase is anchored in sibling rivalry. She specifies that the person who beats in this fantasy (as in all others) is the father, "while the child who was being beaten was not the fantasying child but other children, brothers or sisters [siblings, in the German original], i.e., rivals for the father's love. In this first

---

[3]This nonexclusiveness of father also finds expression in the final sentence of her personal introduction to the German version. Anna Freud emphasizes the essential role in the creation of her communication of "a series of joint [*gemeinsamen*] talks with Mrs. Lou Andreas Salomé. For her interest and participation [*Anteil*] in this I have a great deal to give thanks for" (1922, p. 317). This fact is also acknowledged in footnotes in both translations, which say that the paper was written "on the basis of [1923] / following [1974] several discussions" with Lou Andreas-Salomé. In her grateful acknowlegment of a "joint" "participation," Anna Freud tells her audience about a meaningful and important influence on her work and self-analysis, in addition to that of Freud. At the time Lou Andreas Salomé was not yet a Society member.

phase, therefore, the child claimed all the love for himself and left all the punishment and castigation to the others" (1974, pp. 139–140). Freud's description is more extensive than Anna Freud's summary, and in particular, it involves a number of points explaining the evolution of the fantasy and its meaning.

Freud says not only that in its first phase (occurring in very young girls), the child being beaten is most often a brother or a sister; he paraphrases the content of the fantasy: "My father is beating the child *whom I hate*" (1919, p. 185), hence "My father does not love this other child, *he loves only me*" (p. 187). This direct expression of hate toward the sibling, the rival, is missing in Anna Freud's summary of Freud. Actual hatred of the siblings is more difficult to face and admit to than the thought that they deserve the fantasized "punishment and castigation." Freud explains that the hatred is rooted in the fact that siblings must share their parents' love. But it is on the special position of the "youngest child," "the newcomer"—a persona omitted from Anna Freud's summary—that Freud elaborates in particular. That "newcomer," according to Freud, "is despised as well as hated; yet it attracts itself a share of affection which blinded parents are always ready to give the youngest child, and this is a spectacle that cannot be avoided" (1919, p. 187). For Freud, therefore, the youngest child has the exceptional position of being the favorite; but with the consequence of being especially hated by its siblings. Anna Freud, on the other hand, while overtly downplaying, relative to Freud, the intensity and importance of the rivalry for the parents' attention, mentions no such exception. It will be noted that Anna Freud was both the youngest of her siblings as well as being the newcomer to the Society. The girl's family, or its position relative to siblings, is not presented in the paper.

The mother is also markedly absent from Anna Freud's resumé. True, Freud specifically says that it is with her siblings and "not with the girl's relation to her mother that the beating-phantasy is concerned" (p. 186). Yet he goes to considerable length to describe the complex attitude of the little girl to her mother in this first phase, an attitude which combines affectionate dependence with the seeds of hatred and rivalry sown by the father "who has probably done all he could to win her [the girl's] love" (p. 186). It is thus that "The affections of the little girl are fixed on her father"

(p. 186). In omitting mention of the mother Anna Freud continues the trend of downplaying rivalry; yet she evokes rivalrous feelings in dealing with a paper in which Freud so explicitly expresses his understanding of the central role of the affectionate father in creating his daughter's special claim to him. One of the fathers of whom Freud writes—the one best known to him—is himself, while one of the "little girls" is his youngest (hence "favorite") daughter, Anna.

Transference takes place not only in relation to the analyst or even not only in relation to individuals outside the analytic setting. Audiences may constitute important transference objects as well (Eifermann, 1987b, 1993). In the special circumstances of Anna Freud's presentation her audience was particularly fitted to serve as the "transference object." The audience could well evoke emotional reactions of the kind experienced earlier in life toward significant objects in her familial "nursery." Sigmund Freud's presence could not but contribute to this evocation. Anna Freud was competing with her soon to be colleagues for her place in relation to them and her place relative to them in the eyes of her father. Perhaps she could not fully acknowledge even to herself, but in any case it was far from her conscious intention to express publicly any of the underlying intense feelings that the circumstances of her presentation could, or did reawaken. These complex feelings nevertheless found latent expression in her presentation.

THE DAYDREAMS

Anna Freud devotes the largest section of her paper to the daydreams. Once again she offers to her audience material not available in Freud's own reporting in his essay on beating fantasies. There Freud refers only briefly to "an elaborate superstructure of day-dreams," which two of his female patients had built over their masochistic beating fantasies, and that this superstructure "was of great significance to the life of the person concerned" (1919, p. 190).

Anna Freud explains that in contrast to the "ugly" beating fantasies, the daydreams were "nice stories" of pleasant scenes and affectionate behavior. All figures in these "stories" had names and precise individual identities as well as extensive personal histories; details of family circumstances, friendships, and acquaintances as well as incidents from daily life were all specified. The setting of the daydreams, moreover, readily changed with every change in the life of the daydreamer. They were loose in structure, consisting of episodes as in "continued stories," neither self-contained nor complete in themselves. Considering that Anna Freud refers to her own daydreams she could not do otherwise than refrain from revealing the content of these associatively linked "typical stories" to which, by her account, the abundance of personal details was so central. Instead she describes in some detail a daydream of another type, to which she refers as the "knight story." She elaborately explains that the material of this daydream was derived in part from a story "the girl" had read in an "unknown book" when she was 15, and that it is impossible to differentiate the material taken from the book from the girl's own. In listening to her, this comment could sound as an (unconscious) invitation, almost as a challenge (at least for her immediate audience, familiar with the same stock of adolescent books as she herself was), to pick up her "clues" and identify her "unidentifiable" source; at the same time, as though to discourage such interest, she also declares that any such attempt to distinguish elements of the daydream originating in the (unknown!) book, from "the girl's" own creation, would fail (how could she have made that judgment without being aware of the identity of the book?), and furthermore, that in any case such a distinction was of "no practical significance" (p. 145).

Anna Freud's decision to focus her discussion on the (atypical) "knight story" rather than on "the girl's" "typical stories," introduces a bias into her account, of which she is well aware. She explains that she has chosen to elaborate on the former story rather than on the more typical stories, "because of its clarity and completeness" (1974, p. 144). While neatness and compactness no doubt facilitate presentation, Anna Freud, in offering this explanation, states her difficulty in presenting material that is associative and open ended—and hence less controlled in what it reveals. From the perspective of our knowledge that Anna Freud was reporting about her own daydreams, it becomes evident why she could not share the (self-disclosing) associative material with her "siblings," as she may have shared it with Freud in her analysis. It is remarkable, therefore, that the "knight story," on which she focuses, is a daydream that may be described as a test of fortitude of a youth under duress to betray his family secrets.

The background to the main events of the "knight story" on which she focuses is a feud between a medieval knight and noblemen. In the course of one of their battles a noble youth is captured and taken as prisoner of the knight for a long time until at last he gains his freedom. In introducing the daydream Anna Freud describes the relationship between the two as "apparently irreconcilable antagonism between one who is strong and mighty and another who is weak and in the power of the former" (p. 146). She goes on to explain that "The opposition between the two is further intensified by the addition of several incidents from their past family histories—so that the whole setting is one of apparent irreconcilable antagonism" (p. 146). This description not only repeats the emphasis that the antagonism is merely apparently irreconcilable; it also refers to its most sensitive, familial source, yet without disclosing any detail.[4]

The daydream may be described as a test of the fortitude of a youth under duress to betray his family secrets. It centers on the relationship between the knight and the captive youth. Anna Freud describes "the great introductory scene" in which the two meet for the first time. The knight "reveals his decision to threaten to put the prisoner in a torture apparatus in order to induce him to betray his secrets" (1922, p. 324). Thus the original German version says that the knight discloses his intention; and that this intention is to *threaten* physical torture (not carry it out). The two English versions are corrected to simply say, "the knight threatens to put the prisoner on the rack" (1923, p. 95; 1974, p. 146). In the original version the idea of disclosure is repeated twice over: The knight

[4]A comparison with the original German text reveals that in the 1974 revision (as well as in the earlier 1923 translation) a slight correction was introduced, significant in its resultant change in meaning. According to the original, which appears to be a slip, the knight and the youth had a common "past and family history" (*Vergangenheit und Familiengeschichte*) (1922, p. 324). This has been altered to read "past (and) family histo*ries*" in the later versions. One may wonder whether the error had revealed Anna Freud's background preoccupation with her own family histor*y*, shared with her father, and hence sensitive to such a disclosing slip, she noticed the subtle but meaningful difference, or in any event confirmed the correction. The possibility thus suggests itself that her special position, due to sharing family secrets with her father relating to their family history, combined in the slip with a need to remain sole possessor of such secrets while at the same time revealing their existence. This possibility gains support from the contents of the knight story itself.

"*reveals* his intention," so that the youth "betrays" his secrets; it also clearly emphasizes the centrality of the intended repeated psychological trial. Indeed, threat is a form of psychological torture which the knight applies repeatedly, withdrawing it in the youth's favor. "He grants him one favor after another apparently with the idea of harming him" (1974, p. 146). Nonetheless the knight does expose the youth to "all sorts of deprivations" (even to long imprisonment which nearly kills him), but in response to the youth's constancy in not betraying his secrets "nurses" him and grants him "delights." Anna Freud reports that these repeatedly fantasized trials of fortitude evoked excitement in "the girl," which resolved into a feeling of happiness when the knight's pressure (to reveal) was replaced with a kind and loving attitude, which eventually evolved into a lasting, loving friendship.

A central theme in the daydream that Anna Freud has chosen to present to her audience thus revolves around the issue of betrayal of family secrets. While the "apparent" enemy demands their disclosure, he seems no less and perhaps even more interested in the youth and in his fortitude in not betraying, than in his own declared intention of obtaining his secrets.

The material of the daydream seems to contain veiled revelations concerning her analysis with Freud. One of these revelations relates to the exceptional burdens and costs of this analysis. We know that Freud at times exercised pressure in conducting his analyses. As a matter of fact, a case in point is his essay on beating fantasies, in which he says that he obtained certain information from his patients (regarding their role as onlookers) only "in reply to pressing enquiries" (1919, p. 186). The "knight story" suggests that Anna Freud had felt pressured to disclose her secrets, specifically secrets involving "betrayal" of their common family members. The other veiled revelation concerns a fantasy expressed through the daydream: that she will be rewarded with a special, life-long friendship for her steadfastness in preserving the secrets she shares with her father. It is these complexities and the conflicting loyalties inherent to them, that she has a need both to share and to conceal from her audience.

Analytic reading of her membership paper suggests that in and through it Anna Freud expresses what becoming a member means to her. The underlying concerns of her paper, with her ability to create independently yet in closeness to her father, and related concerns discussed herein regarding the implications of claiming and maintaining that special closeness for her relationships with others, and specifically with her "siblings," can be viewed in the context of her growth into full membership.

It is noteworthy that secrets and their revelations have been associated in the literature with processes of maturation. A number of investigators (e.g., Margolis, 1966, 1974; Ekstein and Caruth, 1972; Kahn, 1977) have expressed the view that part of the process of maturation lies in a growing ability to keep one's secrets as well as in an ability not to guard them in an attitude of secretiveness, but rather to share them selectively. Anna Freud in her "matriculation" paper appears to be struggling with the dialectics involved in exclusive sharing with her father, the rewards and costs of such exclusiveness, as against sharing with a wider audience of "siblings," and eventually with her readers as well. Fortunately for us, Anna Freud's struggle with sharing allows for the dialogue to actually take place. She presents her concerns at the Scientific Meeting of the Vienna Society and continues to be in dialogue with the "siblings" amongst her current readers to whom she has offered her text in print.

REFERENCES

Blass, R. B. (1993), Insight into the struggle of creativity—A rereading of Anna Freud's "Beating Fantasies and Daydreams." *The Psychoanalytic Study of the Child*, 48:161–187. New Haven, CT: Yale University Press.

Eifermann, R. R. (1987a), Interactions between textual analysis and related self-analysis. In: *Essential Papers on Literature and Psychoanalysis*, ed. E. Berman. New York: New York University Press, 1993, pp. 439–455.

——— (1987b), "Germany" and "the Germans": Acting out fantasies and their discovery in self-analysis. *Internat. Rev. Psycho-Anal.*, 14:245–262.

——— (1993), The discovery of real and fantasized audiences for self-analysis. In: *Self-Analysis*, ed. J. W. Barron. Hillsdale, NJ: Analytic Press, pp. 171–193.

Ekstein, E., & Caruth, E. (1972), Keeping secrets. In: *Tactics and Techniques in Therapy*, ed. P. Giovachinni. New York: Science House, pp. 200–213.

Freud, A. (1922), Schlagephantasie und Tagtraum. *Imago*, 8:317–332.

——— (1923), The relation of beating-phantasies to a daydream. *Internat. J. Psycho-Anal.*, 4:89–102.

——— (1965), The problem of training analysis. *The Writings*, Vol. 1. New York: International Universities Press, pp. 407–421.

——— (1974), Beating fantasies and daydreams. *The Writings*, Vol. 1. New York: International Universities Press, pp. 137–157.

Freud, S. (1919), A child is being beaten. *Standard Edition*, 17:179–204. London: Hogarth Press, 1955.

Kahn, M. R. (1977), From secretiveness to shared living. In: *The Human Dimension of Psychoanalytic Practice*, ed. K. A. Frank. New York: Grune & Stratton, pp. 115–122.

Margolis, G. J. (1966), Secrecy and identity. *Internat. J. Psycho-Anal.*, 47:514–521.

——— (1974), The psychology of keeping secrets. *Internat. Rev. Psycho-Anal.*, 1:291–296.

Young-Bruehl, E. (1988), *Anna Freud*. New York: Summit.

11.

IDEOLOGY AND PSYCHOANALYSIS

Charles M. T. Hanly, Ph.D.

The term *ideology* has different meanings ranging from the philosophically neutral "science of ideas" to the value laden "visionary theorizing." It is this last use of the term that defines the meaning I have employed in this essay, and includes Platonism, Marxism, Fascism, and Capitalism in some of its forms. All of these examples, however different they may be in certain respects, have in common that they have been systems of ideas that have exerted a powerful influence upon human affairs.

Without denying the multifaceted nature of ideologies, I want to focus upon their psychology. Ideologies have a remarkable capacity to work powerful transformations in the lives of individuals. They can call forth heroic self-sacrifice; they can render drudgery euphoric; they can give meaning, purpose, and direction to the individual's life and his experience of it. Ideologies are no less remarkable for their capacity to unite individuals into organized collectivities and to convert ordinary fellow citizens and neighbors into brothers, sisters, comrades, and, especially, comrades in arms. Ideologies find or create enemies. Adherents of ideologies can easily find in them justifications for the destruction of others, even in the absence of any real threat, or for their subjection to the particular ideology's ideals.

Ideologies are characterized by a dangerous polarity that can sustain a high level of beneficial mutual support and love among those who share the ideals and way of life of the ideology, side by side with an equal and opposite self-righteous hostility toward those who do not. The foundations for an understanding of the psychogenesis of this polarity have been laid down by Freud (1921) in "Group Psychology and the Analysis of the Ego" in his explanation of the formation of groups. Freud defined a primary group as "a number of individuals who have put one and the same object in the place of their ego ideal and have consequently identified themselves with one another in their ego" (p. 116). The members of the group are united by identifications based on similarity. This similarity is the result of each individual's identification with a leader who functions as his ego ideal. Each individual has given over an important component of his autonomous ego functioning to the leader who, henceforth, exercises it on his behalf. Instead of having to discover or create purpose and meaning in his own life, the individual who is a group member finds it in a transcendent form in his dedication and service to the leader. Since the leader of a group may be a person alive or dead or abstract principles, ideologies qualify for the function of group leaders in Freud's theory. Ideologies, the prophets who proclaim them, the warriors who make them historical realities, and the bureaucrats who administer them are, in any case, usually bound closely together by causal and identificatory links.

Let us look more closely at the alterations in ego functioning that accompany adherence to an ideology by contrasting it with superego functioning in its absence. But let me, at the outset, introduce the caveat that the distinctions I shall be drawing are necessarily simplified, although I hope not oversimplified. The autonomous superego functioning on which the comparison is based is a fictitious ideal to which the superego life of real people only approximates in various degrees.

With the formation of the superego through the resolution of the Oedipus complex, a number of ego functions acquire shape, direction, and efficacy. Central among these functions is the capacity to critically observe oneself, to experience a signal of anxiety in the form of guilt in response to hostile aggressive and possessive incestuous wishes, and to exercise an instinct mastery sufficient to prohibit actions aimed at trying to satisfy them. So sensitized to wrongdoing may the individual become that he may feel guilty when he finds that he is better off than others for whose misfortunes he has had no responsibility. From this moral sensibility come the good Samaritans of this world. The omnipotence of primary process thought invests the functioning of the superego—one of the relations between the superego and the id that establishes their "deep connection." In this there is evidence of not only an acceptance of responsibility for who one is and what one does, but even for what one has not done, brought about by the resolution of the Oedipus complex. Such persons are the opposite of those who have a large tolerance for wrongdoing in the service of an idealized object.

The formation of the superego strengthens the reality testing capacities of the ego insofar as self-scrutiny and self-criticism also encompass cognitive activities. The ability to critically scrutinize one's own perceptions of persons, things, and events supplements the ordinary awareness that consciousness of our perceptions provides. It does so by demanding that what is wishfully subjective in our perceptions should be owned by the self in order to allow our experience to be determined as much as possible by things as they are. The postoedipal child can no longer just run in terror from the dark inside the closet to the safety of his parents. He must now look inside to see whether or not the bogey is actually there. William Golding's *Lord of the Flies* (1959) is a modern parable of the loss of reality and regression to group violence guided by a totemic "choirboy" ideology in a group of latency boys. Individual autonomy, responsibility, and testing of reality lose their influence under the onslaught of regressive group identifications.

Rationality depends upon the capacity for a critical scanning of perceptions that enhances and consolidates subject–object differentiation. This critical scanning is aimed against the derivatives of projection and denial and thus contributes to the transition to more mature forms of ego defense which interfere less with reality testing.

Although psychoanalysis, like the examples of ideologies cited above, has exercised a powerful influence upon contemporary culture, it is not itself an ideology in the sense in which that term is being used here. Freud (1933) denied that it could even be considered to be a *weltanschauung*. For Freud, the revolutionary challenge of psychoanalysis to the various forms of ideological, religious, and philosophical beliefs about human nature and destiny lies in the new scientific knowledge gained from the exploration of unconscious processes by means of free association. For as revolutionary, as feared, and ridiculed as it may be, psychoanalysis is a body of empirical knowledge subject to continuous clinical testing by observations and interpretations based on the analyst's evenly suspended attention to the free associations of analysands. The psychological foundations of the struggle for a measure of objectivity in the observation and understanding of human nature are to be found in the portion of ego psychology that I have all too schematically elaborated above.

Yet psychoanalysis cannot be immunized against being transformed into an ideology or from being used ideologically. Moreover, by its very nature, psychoanalysis is always at risk of fostering its own deterioration into an ideology. This risk lies at the heart of psychoanalysis as a profession.

The personal analysis of candidates is the most essential part of psychoanalytic education. If it is to work, the candidate must develop a transference to the training analyst. Inherent in the transference is an ego regression to a repetition of the dependent tie to the oedipal and preoedipal parents. To a greater or lesser extent the analysand substitutes the observing ego of the analyst for his own in his search for self-understanding. This substitution enables the analysand to be affected by the analyst's interpretations of defenses and resistances, and hence it facilitates their reduction and the liberation of the processes of free association that lead to the resolution of conflicts. But this identification with the observing and analyzing function of the analyst is not itself a cognitively pure culture of an unconflicted working alliance. Its formation is involuntary; it is bound to the transference; it involves a formal regression of the ego; it has unconscious childhood roots; it is subtle and powerful. Thus while it facilitates reality testing and ego maturation everywhere else, it compromises the analysand's ability to be objective about his analyst and it perpetuates a regressed dependency on him. Idealization is the typical form of this compromise of reality testing.

Shortly after completing his training analysis and graduation, a gifted, highly regarded university historian and psychoanalyst was invited by the organizers of an international conference on history to arrange a panel discussion on psychoanalysis and history. He invited his training analyst to be a panelist, although he could not have helped knowing that his former analyst had no expertise in the subject to be discussed. What is even more surprising is that his analyst accepted the invitation. The training analyst gave a rambling and confused presentation the burden of which was to cast doubt on his former analysand's work in the field because of his lack of analytic experience. The ingenue analyst had the insight, after the event, to be astonished at the force and persistence of the idealizing transference that had caused an unconscious phantasy concerning his analyst's brilliance and knowledge to override his mature, critical, academic judgment. He was less aware of his need to break his dependent identification with his analyst or of the hostile wish to embarrass his analyst by drawing him into a situation in which his analyst would appear inadequate and out of his depth and, hence, inferior to himself in a field that he (the former candidate) had mastered. Evidently, a sensitivity to the narcissistic needs of his analyst had joined with his resistance to find a successful hiding place for his oedipal ambivalence in his idealizing transference and his identification with his analyst. It is equally evident that the training analyst failed to analyze and resolve the candidate's idealizing transference to, and his identification with, the analyst—something that should be a continuous part of the analysis and find its resolution in the termination process.

It is the failure to work through the idealizing transference and the identifications with the analyst, that leaves behind a predisposition to ideologize psychoanalysis in the new generation of analysts. One needs to be able to see analytically with one's own eyes, to think analytically with one's own head, and to feel analytically with one's own heart. Instead, the ideas and practices of the analyst acquire a specious veracity, even if they happen to be correct, for they remain untested by the novice analyst. Theoretical ideas and technical rules that require continuous testing and evaluation are treated as canonical. Analysts become enthusiasts, zealots, and ciphers instead of being adventurous observers and empirical thinkers. Training analysts begin to rest their authority, not on a knowledge of the analytic process that works and which they are able to impart, but on their position, power, and authorization by an older generation that they have themselves similarly venerated and feared. The "correct" psychoanalytic texts become quasi-sacred texts that are assigned the authority that only the phenomena should have.

No theoretical position in psychoanalysis can protect its adherents from this idolatry of ideas. Freud's epistemic legacy of a body of knowledge, considered by him to be made up of empirical ideas built up from and tested by clinical observation, cannot deter an adherent from treating it as an infallible system of absolute truth or a critic from seeing in it only the imaginings of an eccentric, ingenious mind. Indeed, because hostility underlies idealization, the zealous adherent easily collapses into the repudiating critic, if the reaction formation that sustains the idealization should succumb to disappointment.

Of course, we like to think, in this period of competing theories, that the adherents of other schools of thought in psychoanalysis are invested in an ideology. How otherwise could they give credence to ideas that are so clearly and self-evidently wrong in the veridical light shed by our own? Such an attitude is the expression of an ideologically motivated reluctance to bring our own ideas down from Olympus to be tested in the sweat and toil of the free market of ideas. The crucial test of the analyst's relation to psychoanalysis is his willingness to put his ideas to the test of reason and experience, because the only real strength of ideas is to be found in their usefulness in knowing and, when possible, in changing life and the world for the better.

There are a variety of indicators that psychoanalysis is being treated as an ideology. The analyst who conceives of a second analysis as a means of "refreshing" his identification with his analyst has acknowledged that he survives as an analyst only by means of a dependent identificatory tie to his analyst. His convictions concerning what is workable and what is not, what is true and what is false in psychoanalysis are fundamentally governed by his ideas concerning the convictions of another—his training analyst.

Has not such an analyst made his analyst into an idol, himself into a proselyte, and analysis into magic? The answer to this question can be decided by the quality of the analyst's attitude to psychoanalytic knowledge. One suspects the worst, if mingled with the necessary and appropriate respect for privacy and confidentiality about patients there is a hermetic secrecy, or if a legitimate insistence upon high standards of training, practice, and research masks a guild possessiveness about psychoanalytic knowledge. The training analyst who sees no difficulty in undertaking the supervision of a candidate, who has recently terminated a training analysis with him, is a promising psychoanalytic ideologue. So is the analyst who claims that the theoretical innovation he has espoused can only be understood and observationally confirmed by those who are convinced of its truth.

The Thomistic "credo ut intelligas" is fitting for religious philosophy based on infallible faith, but it is not tenable for psychoanalysis, which is based on hard-won fallible observation. The analyst, who defends a theoretical innovation against falsifying clinical evidence by claiming that the falsifying observations are artifacts of his critic's theory, is himself manifesting the ideological attitude toward psychoanalytic knowledge of which he accuses his critic. These are a few manifestations of an ideological attitude toward psychoanalysis.

This argument is linked to a concept developed by Rangell (1982) of transference to theory. I have focused on the part played by unanalyzed idealizing transferences and identifications with training analysts. Rangell presents a more general account of the influence of the training institute as an "analytic family" with its oedipal vicissitudes. He describes, for example, the way object relations within the "analytic family" of the institute can become symptomatic and offer a field for displacements that are hard to detect and analyze. But the central issue elucidated by Rangell (1982) is the transference to theory of which he states that the "unresolved elements can establish roots for a blind acceptance of present theory, whatever it may be, as much as for an urge to overthrow and displace it, no matter with what others" (pp. 48–49). This is the same process as the one I have referred to as the transformation of psychoanalysis into an ideology. It is also to Rangell (1980) that we owe the psychoanalysis of the compromise of integrity, a topic that has deep links to the subjects discussed here.

If psychoanalysis is not an ideology, does it provide a basis for a critique of ideology? Is it compatible with some ideologies and incompatible with others? If it does not entail an ideology, does it entail a way of life? Does it have implications for the conduct of social, political, and economic life beyond the sphere of intimate personal relations? Freud's few remarks on communism indicate a sympathetic interest in communism as a social experiment aimed at trying to find a more equitable distribution of goods and services. His comments are tempered by a critique of Marx's failure to take into account the role of sexuality in the motivation of conflict among men and women which resulted in Marx's dangerously naive utopianism. Many of the communist governments of Eastern Europe prohibited psychoanalysis because they believed that it fostered an egoistical individualism incompatible with communist fraternity. Some of the democratic governments that have replaced them wish to foster psychoanalysis apparently because they believe that it fosters the kind of individual initiative and responsibility for oneself that are needed by democratic institutions and a market economy. If these perceptions are correct, it would appear that psychoanalysis does have social, political, and economic implications in so far as different social, political, and economic organizations require different attitudes, expectations, and motives at work in the people whose lives they organize.

But are these perceptions correct? Is not psychoanalysis a body of knowledge and a method of psychological investigation that seeks to examine the unconscious psychological roots of ideological beliefs and investments in the absence of any ideological commitments or investments of its own? If conflicts due to ambivalence are at work in the political life of a patient, the analysis must seek to resolve this ambivalence but without trying to make the patient into a conservative, liberal, or socialist. If a female patient's dedication to feminism is rooted in a denial and repression of some sexual aspects of her femininity, the analysis must help her work through these conflicts without needing to abate her advocacy of rights and opportunities for women. Yet, if we press too far in trying to make psychoanalysis into a value-free, value-neutral science and therapy we soon lose touch with reality in that direction. There follow some clinical and theoretical reflections aimed a redressing the balance.

Without trying to, our analytic work does alter the values of our patients. A severely hysterical woman patient held extraordinarily redneck views about the punishment of offenders. She was a staunch advocate of capital punishment. Reports of crimes aroused in her phantasies of the cruel public punishments that were owed the miscreants. Among the unconscious factors contributing to this attitude to criminals were feelings of revenge toward her father and men generally, castration wishes, sadistic voyeuristic impulses, and envious hatred of disordered, unruly boy cousins whose misdemeanors had been indulged by her mother in contrast to the reliably swift punishment she had received. In the course of the analysis, her memories of these cousins did not change, but she was able to experience waves of pity for them along with remorse for having wished them so much ill. She recounted how one had died intoxicated behind the wheel of his car while another was serving a prison sentence for fraud. Her analysis had altered her conscious social attitude to crime and punishment from one of retribution to one of prevention, with all the modifications in political, social, and economic ideas that such a change involves. Psychoanalysis alters affective attitudes and values en route to the resolution of conflicts.

A male professorial patient, who was being treated for a debilitating depression, was a convinced socialist (in the Swedish or British sense). His sense of social justice made him an advocate of the welfare state. The state with its seemingly limitless powers of taxation should protect all citizens so far as possible from the helplessness of unemployment, illness, accident, and injury. Motivating his political beliefs there was an oedipal rebellion. His father was a rather prominent local conservative. His wish, if not to slay, then to imprison the dragons of free enterprise and corporate profits in the chains of taxation for income redistribution and social services, owed something to an unconscious, unresolved oedipal rivalry. But a more significant determinant was a severe oral trauma subsequently exacerbated by inadequate parenting during the birth of a sibling. His depressive anxiety about abandonment, about being unloved and helpless, caused by unsatisfied need, made itself felt in a dependent, oral transference. He developed an intense need to have his analyst protect him from the ordinary hazards of life. If he missed a session because his bus was delayed, he felt rejected and mortified by being required to pay for the missed session, at once frightened and unbelieving that his analyst could neither protect him from such occurrences nor avoid charging him on account of his own need. He believed the analyst to have unlimited resources of wealth and power. As the transference and the traumas that gave rise to it were worked through, the patient did not abandon his concerns about social justice, but he became realistic about his adult responsibility for his own welfare and about the capacity of governments to provide social services. He had become able to consider political, social, and economic alternatives. Thus social and political beliefs and values are sometimes altered by indirection, as religious beliefs often are, in the course of an analysis that does not seek these results but occupies itself only with the resolution of neurotic conflicts.

Theoretically, in the explanation it provides of the psychogenesis of this suppression, the psychoanalytic explanation of group formation and its account of group dynamics runs counter to the suppression of individuality by social collectivities that is espoused by many ideologies. So completely did Plato in *The Republic* seek the destruction of individuality in his ideal republic that he destroyed family life, making it impossible for men and women to form permanent ties, for mothers and fathers to own their children, and for children to know their mothers and fathers. Children were to know only collective parents—all the women and men of the older generation—so as to become in themselves collective beings who would rejoice and grieve for the same things, in the same way, at the same time. The two major forms of modern ideological totalitarianism, national socialism and communism, sought to invade family life, weaken family ties, and terrorize family members with the threat of betrayal. They achieved this by exploiting the inevitable ambivalences toward each other of parents and children, and by forging such powerful identificatory ties, especially in the children, with the state, its leaders, and their doctrines that, for many children, betrayal in thought and affect became a reality. Political betrayal of parents became a permanent possibility and its socially rewarded enactment became a more frequent occurrence than one would like to think. The problem of practicing analysis in such a society, even if it were not forbidden by the state, is not difficult to imagine. One of the first tasks of the analysis would have to be the resolution of the defensive libidinal tie to the state, should one exist, and this work would inevitably be experienced by the analysand as a treasonous attempt to subvert and degrade him. Psychoanalysis cannot thrive in such social and political environments, although courageous analysts manage to keep psychoanalysis alive even in such adverse circumstances.

The Platonic, Nazi, and Marxist ideologies conceive of the political and social collectivities as superordinate to the individuals who make them up. These ideologies include the assumption that the state has an existence and a life of its own that transcends the individual. One finds the same assumption underlying Hegel's philosophy of history and his political philosophy. The psychoanalytic understanding of the origin and dynamics of groups suggests that this view of the state is an illusion, one that political ideologues need in order to realize their visions for the transformation of the human condition, an illusion that under particular historical circumstances can be made to appear all too real with the help of the secret police and other instruments of suppression—but an illusion, nevertheless.

Freud hypothesized that a group is formed out of two identifications: an idealizing identification with a leader and an identification based upon similarity with others who have made the same leader into their ego ideal. An ideologue invites just such an identification with himself and his ideology, his doctrine of salvation. These identifications give the leader the authority that enables him to exercise power over his followers and, under the right historical conditions, the means to take over government, impose his ideology on everyone, and thus make it into a social reality. Of course, political, judicial, and social institutions have an existence of their own and they yield power to those who control them. But they do not have a life of their own. Who gives life to them, who controls them, by what means, and to what ends is ultimately determined by the dominant mass of idealizing identifications formed by individuals. The road to power of the few, of ideologies and their prophets, is paved with the need of the many to submit to idealized objects.

Ideologists do not like this understanding of the origins of power. They need individuals to deny that they have sacrificed a measure of individual freedom with the belief that autonomy for the individual can only be realized through the group. At the level of explicit statement and doctrine, ideologies are at odds with psychoanalysis concerning the primacy of individuals and groups. At the level of action, ideologues reveal their uncanny knowledge of the dynamics of the idealizing identifications and how to exploit them. In totalitarian regimes, the instruments of suppression are aimed at dissident minorities and rely upon the need of majorities to form idealizing identifications in an escape from individual responsibility.

Psychoanalysis does have an affinity with and a dependency upon the basic principles of liberal democracy, for its ability, if not to exist, then to flourish. For example, liberal democracy includes freedom of thought and speech; the freedom to pursue one's own welfare so long as this pursuit is not damaging to the welfare of others; the right to contribute directly or by representation to the making of the laws that define the general good of the community; the right and the ability to elect to office and remove from office those who govern. These relations to the principles of liberal democracy are shared by psychoanalysis with other natural sciences, literature, the arts, scholarship, and critical thought generally. Psychoanalysts as citizens have a responsibility to support these principles just as psychoanalysts as members of an organized profession have the same responsibility to establish and maintain these principles in the conduct of their societal and institute affairs. It is for this reason that the International Psychoanalytical Association (IPA) insists that the constitutions of member societies embody these principles and that their members respect them in both spirit and letter.

But psychoanalysis has a special affinity to these principles. Free association is a radical form of freedom of thought: the freedom to think and put into words the thoughts that one's own ideals and anxieties forbid, let alone the prohibitions of others. A mathematician, a physicist, a neuroanatomist, an organic psychiatrist can pursue his enquiries, make original discoveries, and publish them in a totalitarian state so long as the dictatorship is sensible enough, for example, not to force scientists to employ the dialectical logic of Hegel and Marx.

In such a society, life is not so easy for creative writers, musicians, and artists, although restricted fields of creative activity may remain. For psychoanalysis life is next to impossible. Psychoanalysis can survive these conditions, while remaining true to itself, only in secrecy as an underground movement as it did in some Eastern European countries during the postwar period, or by means of self-falsifying and self-destructive dissimulation of the sort that befell what little was left of psychoanalysis in Germany during the Nazi regime.

At the heart of psychoanalysis there is the ideal of an unconstrained, open search for the truth of the individual life that is incompatible with ideological thinking with its commitment to self-evident verities that cannot be questioned. One ideal of psychoanalysis is to allow reality testing the freest possible range no less over a person's ideals, morals, religious beliefs, and political convictions than over his drive life, his objects, and his world. Psychoanalysis finds itself at odds with ideologies because they demand that observation and thought be governed by visionary ideas and values that are exempted from critical investigation. It is this ideal that demands candidate analysands and training analysts bring the idealized transference into the analysis and work it through before termination. No matter how genuinely distinguished, how justifiably venerable, how worthy of idealization the training analyst may be, the unresolved idealized transference leads to the cult of personality which is no more desirable in psychoanalysis, including the cult of the personality of Freud, than is the cult of personality in politics or anywhere else in human affairs.

In psychoanalysis there is also the ideal of the primacy of the individual life and the individual's responsibility for it. Freud (1900) concluded the *Interpretation of Dreams* with the assertion that "there seems to be no justification for people's reluctance in accepting responsibility for the immorality of their dreams" (p. 620). Where else could responsibility lie, no matter how thoroughly involuntary dreaming may be? The individual is thus responsible for his drive life and its derivatives just as he is responsible for his own well-being. But these are hard responsibilities to bear; individual responsibility is, at best, only a partially attainable ideal. The libidinal identificatory bonds that form groups and give to ideologies their power over individual thought, feeling, judgment, and action offer paths of escape which all of us to some extent follow. The ubiquity and tenacity of these identifications is well illustrated in the life of Charles Colson, a former Nixon aide who had declared, prior to his imprisonment for criminal activities on behalf of the President, that for Richard Nixon he would kill his own grandmother. Having "seen the light" of Christianity while in prison, he has recently been the recipient of a handsome fundamentalist award for charitable activities on behalf of prisoners. No doubt Mr. Colson's grandmother is now safer than she was before, but we can be equally sure that, "saved" as he may be, Mr. Colson's hostility will now be available for targets selected by his new fundamentalist Christian ideals. One need not think that there is necessarily anything cynical or manipulative in Mr. Colson's transformation or that it is less than genuine, in order to doubt its efficacy. The substitution of one ideology for another is not the same as reducing one's dependency on ideology and gaining a measure of freedom. From the argument above, it is clear that shifting allegiance from one school of thought to another in psychoanalysis is nothing more than abandoning one ideology for another unless it is primarily based on the critical and reasoned consideration of unmistakable clinical evidence.

Wise people who have cared about individual freedom have long been aware of this vulnerability in men and women to alienate their own freedom. The citizens of the ancient Athenian democracy sought, in part, to protect themselves from this predisposition by banishing those they found to be too powerful and too charismatic. The American Constitution, following Montesquieu, separated the three powers of government, and when, after the 1930s, it appeared that a popular President, such as F.D.R., could become too powerful even despite the separation of powers, the citizenry voted to limit the number of terms that a President might remain in office. The British parliamentary system provides for the removal of a government by a majority vote of the House of Commons made up of the elected representatives of the people. Thus it is that the IPA requires component societies to have constitutions that provide for limited, fixed terms for their offices to which members are democratically elected by members. However, it must never be forgotten that Hitler's Nazi party won 43.9 percent of the votes in the 1933 German election. Democratic institutions can no more protect citizens from extremes of political folly than psychoanalysis as a body of knowledge can protect itself from analysts who would make it, in whole or in part, into an ideology.

Accordingly, it is important, in conclusion, to emphasize that throughout we have been talking about ideals to which human beings, including psychoanalysts, only approximate. Idealizing identifications with Freud, Klein, or with lesser figures such as Kohut, Winnicott, Fairbairn, Lacan or their representatives in the shape of our training analysts can cause any of us to become more zealous in the defense of the ideas of the master than in the testing of these ideas, which is the only means of their valid defense and which always risks their falsification. Sometimes the best that an idea can achieve is to have been the stimulus for its replacement with a better idea. Similarly, while we may be more or less united in our identification with psychoanalysis we are also differentiated by national, political, linguistic, and cultural identifications and investments. What differentiates us in these ways can easily divide us.

Freud wrote of how he was swept by patriotic excitement during the early part of the First World War, even though the army with whose valor, strength, and victory he was identified pitted him against his British, French, and Russian colleagues. In the end, his patriotism was no match for the strength of his attachment to these "enemies," and his disillusionment with the war and its senseless suffering. Freud's self-analysis also contributed to his return to reality about the war. He gives eloquent testimony to his struggle with his own nationalist feelings in his letter (Freud, 1926) to members of the B'Nai B'Rith lodge:

> Whenever I have experienced feelings of national exaltation, I have tried to suppress them as disastrous and unfair, frightened by the warning example of those nations among which we Jews live. But there remained enough to make the attraction of Judaism and the Jews irresistible, many dark emotional powers all the stronger the less they could be expressed in words, as well as the clear consciousness of an inner identity, the familiarity of the same psychological structure [p. 368].

The primitive power of nationalist ideology has demonstrated its strength with the fall of communist ideology in Eastern Europe. Communism, with its ideal of a fraternal utopia, had seven decades in the Soviet Union and four decades elsewhere in Eastern Europe to establish its ascendency over national identities, with no success whatsoever. The current centripetal forces of Western Europe are matched by the centrifugal forces of Eastern Europe. One reading of this situation is that communism, despite its internationalist utopianism, actually inhibited the development of a stable basis for cooperation among nationalist, ethnic, and cultural groups in the search for solutions to common economic, social, and political problems. Nationalist, ethnic, and cultural goals, for the time being at least, seem to have acquired, in some regions, a greater importance than economic, social, and political well-being.

Nationalism everywhere poses a problem for psychoanalysis. No science can be confined to national boundaries. And psychoanalysis, unlike other sciences has been from early in its history primarily an international organization as a profession. Yet psychoanalysts are also citizens, which means that they are identified in themselves with their national communities. How is an analyst to solve a conflict between an obligation that he feels to his country and one that he feels to psychoanalysis, especially under conditions of political violence or war? How is organized psychoanalysis, the European Psychoanalytic Federation (EPF) or IPA, to best act when its members or prospective members are divided on account of nationalist conflicts? These problems do not have solutions in the way in which problems in Euclidean geometry have solutions. For solutions are often in the nature of compromises; they require tolerance for disagreement; they need the participation of persons with differing views and commitments because often, however sympathetic to other viewpoints we may be, we may not have all the relevant information, and we may not be able to accurately grasp in imagination the predicaments in which others find themselves.

We ought not to expect of psychoanalysis more than it can offer us.

REFERENCES

Freud, S. (1900), The Interpretation of Dreams. *Standard Edition*, 5. London: Hogarth Press, 1953.

——— (1921), Group psychology and the analysis of the ego. *Standard Edition*, 18:69–143. London: Hogarth Press, 1955.

——— (1926), To members of the B'Nai B'Rith lodge. In: *Letters of Sigmund Freud*, ed. E. L. Freud. London: Hogarth Press, 1970.

——— (1933), New introductory lectures on psychoanalysis. *Standard Edition*, 22:1–182. London: Hogarth Press, 1964.
Golding, W. (1959), *The Lord of the Flies*. New York: Capricorn Books.
Plato, *Republic*, tr. B. Jowett. New York: The Liberal Arts Press, 1948.
Rangell, L. (1980), *The Mind of Watergate: An Exploration of the Compromsie of Integrity*. New York: W. W. Norton.
——— (1982), Transference to theory: The relationship of psychoanalytic education to the analyst's relationship to psychoanalysis. In: *The Annual of Psychoanalysis*, 10:29–56. New York: International Universities Press.

12.

REMAINING IN THE BUNKER LONG AFTER THE WAR IS OVER: DEPLOYMENT IN THE INDIVIDUAL, THE GROUP, AND THE NATION

RENA MOSES-HRUSHOVSKI, Ph.D.

WHO ARE THE "DEPLOYED PERSONS"?

We all tend to utilize deployment[1] in certain situations. For example, when under pressure at times we act like soldiers carrying out duties assigned to us, even if they are contrary to what our conscience tells us; we do so without looking to see what we or others feel. At times a trifling issue takes on the proportions of a life-or-death matter when we feel it puts our honor in question. Similarly, we all may rigidly enter into roles or positions when we experience our self to be threatened.

In pathological deployment, however, the loss of self is more conspicuous and more ongoing; it becomes almost chronic to a point where growth and development are blocked. These patients are deployed into grievances and into presenting themselves belligerently with continuous complaints of suffering. They are constantly switched on to see others' faults and wrongs, real or fancied, which serve as a basis for their complaints (Feldman, 1993; Moses-Hrushovski, 1994). They resemble the unconsolable patients described by Weinshel (1989).

[1]By deployment I mean a rigid "self-programming" into a system of attitudes, roles, positions, and behavior aimed at protecting the person's self-esteem and dignity, consoling them for what they had experienced as humiliating; and correcting, as it were, the injustices done to them. Deployment involves the narrowing of the experiential focus to the point where one aspect of current experience draws off an excessive amount of cathexis.

They are tense individuals who find it hard to relax. They seem to be constantly on their guard not to be suddenly discovered and caught in their weakness. Many of them seem to lead a double life: Professionally they function well, but concurrently they seem to be immersed in blindly "correcting" past injuries to the self through repeatedly enacting corrections in the present. It is as if they had inserted a deep structure into their perceptual and behavioral apparatuses that automatically sets them to deploy a battery of functions against their unbearable feelings—especially those of shame, humiliation, and guilt. They seem driven to use their muscles to immunize themselves from painful feelings, torturing thoughts, and inner contradictions that would paralyze them were they to allow themselves emotional contact with such affects.

In the professional literature these patients are described as difficult (Cooper, 1984), or "stuck patients" (Steiner, 1993). Most of them have been in dynamic treatment before, but claim that they were not "touched" emotionally or helped. One of the difficulties in their treatment relates to the nature of their motivation. They do not want to seek relief through expressing their feelings and their psychic pain or through mourning what had been hurting, lacking, or lost. Rather, they come with a strong need to erase and to actively forget whatever they had experienced in the past as painful, shameful, and offensive to them; to disconnect self injuries from the specific concrete situations in which they had occurred, and to express their grievances so that the *other* would listen with empathy and see how right they are. They are motivated not so much by a wish to try and understand the nature of their suffering, their problems, and conflicts in a way that could lead them to be ready to invest in inner work and change. Instead, they show a powerful tendency to compulsively repeat their past behavior, to justify it, and to explain themselves so that the *other* would understand but also change him- or herself.

It is as if they are remaining in their bunker after a life-long battle to fight against their political enemies who oppressed and humiliated them, so that they could obtain the rights due them. They wrestle unwittingly in the struggles of their past through persons in the present, refusing at the same time to go back to relive the stressful situations of the past which is where they are in fact stuck. To let go of their deployment would mean for them to reexperience the unbearable pain they had experienced in the past. They would then still be the children of their onetime quarrel situation without adequate resources to assert themselves. It would mean also to expose themselves to the danger of being misjudged and humiliated by the other who would see all this as solely their problem (e.g., being jealous and envious). The other would not see the reality to which they had also been exposed.

A different kind of unconscious motivation of deployed patients who were "angry persons" relates to a mixture of despair and a sense of mission. After years of suffering and of having been humiliated victims, all that is left for them now is to demonstrate how they had been wronged and to protest against it. At least the next generation might profit from it, they feel; they themselves are beyond despair. In their deployment they are not only using retaliation and erasure to deal with jealousy and unconscious guilt. An important ingredient in their motivation is their sense of a "political" mission to fight for the rights of the exploited and the abused! They do not want to understand because understanding means to forgive. They do not want to be immune vis-à-vis the suffering of humanity they see. Humanity is much too forgiving to rapists and to murderers, they feel.

Thus many of them show a stubborn and resolute determination to hold onto their misery until the other will acknowledge the injustice and the unfair treatment they had been subjected to, until the other will take responsibility for their part. In that way, the heavy burden of responsibility that they unconsciously feel to be on their shoulders would be more fairly divided. Only once this has happened do the deployed patients feel that they can deal with their own parts; only then could their tranquility, that had been disrupted, be restored; only then would they be able to reconcile themselves with their important others and reach intrapsychic harmony and interpersonal agreements. Their life-long battles have the quality of a sacred mission, like that of a holy war.

Once I came to gain a better understanding of the unconscious motivations of deployed patients and of their power dynamics, as well as more insight into my countertransference reactions evoked thereby, a significant change occurred in my therapeutic approach (Moses-Hrushovski, 1994).

As noted, shame, humiliation, embarrassment, and guilt had been unbearable feelings for them. Just as anxiety is the central motive behind the defense mechanisms of the ego, so is shame the major force behind the deployments: Shame for their awkward behavior, shame for their appearance, shame about their parents, and shame for feeling ashamed of them; shame for having had fantasies, feelings, thoughts, and wishes that had to remain hidden from others, all of which restrict these persons consciously or unconsciously. These, then, are feeling states which often mean that their lives are determined in major ways not by their self, not by what they wished, thought, and felt capable of, but by their shame! (Levin, 1971; Wurmser, 1981; Morrison, 1986; Lewis, 1987).

Grunberger (1971) talks about the relationship between shame and narcissism. He describes a feeling which seems relevant to both individuals and groups:

> Each time the child is confronted by an instinctual impulse that has not been narcissistically enhanced and integrated, this want of narcissistic confirmation will renew the pain of his narcissistic wound. He is reminded of his paradise lost and in contrast to his earlier narcissistic omnipotence he has a searing sense of inadequacy and insignificance that can be compared with shame. Shame that the ego falls before its ego ideal [p. 224].

A state of shame and humiliation typical for these persons relates to what they perceive as an imbalance of power, whether it is the constant feeling of not being treated like equals or the feeling of being looked down on or made fun of. For the deployed patients the world is divided into two kinds of people: those who coerce or rape others and those who are coerced or raped themselves. Rape becomes for them a symbol that includes a variety of states of oppression and of pressures, from invasions into their privacy, to actual sexual abuse. It is a symbol vis-à-vis which they are constantly deployed—cognitively, emotionally, and conatively.

They utilize a host of countershame strategies to protect them from the paralyzing threats of shame and defeat. Thus they tend to offend others in various contemptuous ways to get even and to try not to feel offended. They humiliate others when they expect to be humiliated; they "castrate" others in order not to feel castrated; they turn the tables on the shamer in order not to be blamed and shamed themselves.

Though these are strategies used to counteract shame in specific situations, they often are conceived of as unchangeable character traits, as givens both by themselves and by their important others. It is difficult to identify the deployments when they are activated as well as to tease out the specific mixture of shame and guilt (Adler, 1989) that is behind the deployments since they are enacted in such a speedy, powerful, and automatic way that the patients, as well as the analyst, hardly notice what they actually feel, do, and think or why they do it.

"Being prepared" is a feature of deployment. This means to be constantly in control so that their weakness, their failures, or mistakes or whatever may be interpreted as such, will not be exposed. Once they are prepared ahead of time to watch for the catastrophe to come in order to avoid sudden defeat, this often turns into a self-fulfilling prophecy.

Another variant of this mechanism used to avoid situations of being suddenly shocked and shamed, is to be prepared for the worst, while somewhere they know that their worries are exaggerated; such knowledge supposedly calms them. But in fact the state of tension is thus actively preserved.

A different kind of strategy enacted unconsciously to counteract feelings of shame is to enter or even to produce a state of panic in which they freeze. As terrifying as one feels in panic, it seems somehow safer than experiencing worse states of distress. When one becomes lost in panic and freezes, unable to move or find a way out, one can avoid the anticipated fright of being exposed to shame in public, for example, where, so one feels, one's honor would be lost at once and forever.

A frequent device used to protect oneself from the shame related to confusion and weakness is to turn feelings into facts. Feelings then become objective; now they are reality! Thus, one does not have to deal with shaming and other complicated conflicts within oneself, and also one gets the strong other off one's back.

A further frequent refuge from the feelings of humiliation, shame, and guilt derives from the activation of certain inner rules which are piously observed and seem to provide security vis-à-vis the chaotic states that threaten from within. These rules are actively cut off from the stressful situations in which they had been adopted as well as from the functions they exert; power is applied to sever these connections in order to sustain the pseudosecurity the person feels he or she has achieved by maintaining the status quo. When the deployed patients are invited in analysis to explore the nature of these rules in the context of the situations and circumstances in which they were established, a door is often opened to reach painful states they had previously tried to avoid through these rules.

I am reminded of Mr. K whose rule it was to provide any family member or friend with money, invariably much more than requested, as soon as they hinted that they were in need. Mr. K did this without considering their real needs, his relationship with them, or his own financial state. It was a law for him, he said, to help those who were in need of money. It turned out that this compulsive deployment into helping financially was overdetermined. It "corrected retroactively" the stressful state from the past when he had felt devastated at not having been helped at a time when he needed it most. By actively doing to others what in the past he had felt deprived of or frustrated with by an important person, he corrected, as it were, the self-injury from the past. Also, by being a better person than the other, he gained points of moral superiority which helped him to feel worthy vis-à-vis both his disavowed guilt feelings and his important others.

Toward the end of the treatment we discovered another function behind this rule. Once he had gained more tolerance for his shame and guilt and once he became more ready to own his role in interpersonal relationships, the analysand could talk about his guilt and shame when he had exerted pressure on a girl friend to undergo an abortion and did not "even" pay for it. Until that time he had done all he could to erase this event, to put it aside, to cut off the link between the torturing feelings he had had then and the event. What had remained was the rule to pay forthwith whenever somebody asked for help—a correction in the present of denied experiences from the past.

Here, thus, was insight we had obtained into the functions of his behavior. But of no less importance, and perhaps even more so, was his constant attention to his self organization in the following ways: (1) to see the rules he blindly followed that determined his behavior and feelings; (2) to locate his deployments that were like character traits expressive of his identity that was not to be questioned to see how his self image caused him to rely on rules that dictated his life patterns rather than on himself and on what he felt, wished, thought, openly and flexibly, in the present in accordance with the changing needs of his nature and his situation.

The deployment into rules which were major vectors for the patient's behavior can be seen also in the following examples:

The rule of never being late when enacted rigidly, irrespective of the circumstances, is often based on painful emotional experiences that have been erased. What thus unconsciously is corrected through following the rule are catastrophes: such as having had accidents of wetting or soiling when the person was not on time; primal scene experiences one was suddenly exposed to; or miscarriages when in fantasy one was too late to save the mother. Thus the person's self organization is affected by catastrophes to be that they prepare for rather than by their feeling, thinking, wishing selves. The rules become their master and not they the master of the rules.

A rule of never waiting in line that unconsciously protected a particular patient from being in touch with specific events of humiliation and abuse that he had experienced in the past, is yet another illustration; or a decision unconsciously taken in times of rejection, never to ask for what one wants or needs, waiting instead until the other will notice and initiate action; or taking what they felt they were entitled to, at times feeling then like thieves, rather than risk asking for whatever it was and being refused; that would be too humiliating.

It turned out to be a long process of working through until they were ready to look clearly at what had been driving them in life, to help them disidentify with their laws, which led to self-defeating behavior and to a noncreative life. Gradually it became more feasible for them to own their disavowed parts and to mourn what had been painful, humiliating, and lacking in their personal history.

The following case may illustrate the formation of deployments as they came up in the therapeutic process. Ilana was referred to me by the police after having smashed a shop window in the main street of her town. From what she brought up in her therapy, it gradually became clear that this act was an expression of the fury she felt about the arrogance of her older brothers as well as her teachers who she felt frequently dominated and humiliated her. She was 16 years old when she began treatment with me. She had just left high school, after having felt that the effort of doing her homework and keeping up with the high standards expected of her were beyond her capacity.

In her treatment she talked about the fears and difficulties she had had in school. This had begun in the first grade when she was diagnosed as dyslectic and sent for special remedial sessions and for psychotherapy. To be singled out and to need special care humiliated her (as if she were retarded), but so did the one-up position of the therapist. She stopped going to treatment after several weeks. What added to her difficulty in learning was the family's move to Spain for two years. She had no knowledge of the language, and being different in dress and behavior added to her feeling of being shamed and ashamed. Ilana continued to share her feelings about school. In math and in the art courses she achieved high grades, but in all subjects based on reading she was weak. After she received a negative grade in one exam along with a hurtful remark from the teacher, she decided that she absolutely must leave school. Though she suffered particularly from one teacher, all the teachers, she said, turned out to be enemies for her. She saw them as nonhumans, as if they were a different species. She knew that it was an unfair generalization, but this was how she felt. She talked about her feelings toward the species of teachers, and how she moved gradually from hating one particular teacher to hating them all. She became a punk in appearance, demonstrating thus that she is not just a piece of furniture, or a grain of dust that has no degree of uniqueness and is trampled upon. She made friends with some Basque terrorists and used drugs for a while. When she talked about these phenomena I felt that this was one root of dehumanization as it occurs in individuals, in groups, and in nations.

Ilana continued to talk about her powerful experience of leaving school. In her daydreams she frequently returned to that moment when she got up and proudly said "Goodbye" and left. She felt that this was perhaps the first time that she cared for herself, after all those years when she had felt she didn't really exist in all these humiliating environments. At last she could mobilize her power and take a space for herself; now she could breathe freely. From the moment that she decided to leave school and stop caring so much about what the others thought of her, she felt she was a person who could start her life anew.

I have presented the details of this experience because I have found that humiliation in school situations in addition to the family background and its effects is a frequent and major factor behind the formation of deployments. This effect of school situations is, I believe, not given enough attention in the formation of personality disorders in general.

Another central theme in Ilana's treatment was her deep sense of injustice in relation to her older brothers. While she, the girl, was expected to do house chores, the boys were easily exempted. Her father took them to football games; she, who was interested in sports, was not invited to go along. She could never rely on her parents' help when her brothers teased and abused her, since the parents thought that children should manage on their own.

One of the ways Ilana tried to deal with her humiliation, her resentments, and her envy was to adopt a masculine deployment: she recalled how she would march along with a Walkman, listening to music while she embroidered dreams of glory in which she was famous like actors she admired, and strong in body and soul. She tried to be hard and resolute, talking like a man she appreciated. It was partly an identification with her successful father and a disindentification with her mother whom she perceived as weak and miserable. Yet it was also a way of not feeling envious, helpless, and inferior; and it was intended to correct the injustice involved in her upbringing.

While bringing up other fears, insults, and shame from different phases of her life, realizing how she gradually deployed herself into a position of war, she recalled a terrifying and humiliating experience from the first grade that she had never related to anybody. Boys had run after her during recess, taken off her underpants by force, and had made fun of her. She remembered that her decision was never again to wear a skirt, a rule she followed to this day.

Working through several stressful events in which she had experienced being pressured and pushed helped her bring up various emotional states. One related to her father having on many occasions made decisions for her without considering what she felt and thought. When going along with his decisions, she felt that doing so without expressing her fears and doubts erased her inner world. She was paralyzed and felt canceled out. Once she had given in, whatever psychic energy remained at her disposal was mobilized toward restraining her murderous rage for the sake of survival. She also remembered games of rape she had played with girl friends at age five and six in which her feelings of fear, worry, and excitement were revived and mastered as were her masturbatory fantasies around rape which both excited her and were humiliating. Working through her various deployments against shame, guilt, and humiliation enabled her to accept her feminine role with pride, complete her studies in art, and establish a stable and loving relationship with her boyfriend.

THE FAMILY BACKGROUND

When I reviewed the background of deployed patients, I found several common etiological factors which threw light on the particular dynamics of these patients and are relevant to the forms of therapy. All these persons suffered from failure of empathy in early caregiving. At least one of the parents would have a narcissistic personality. All patients felt exploited, were expected to gratify their parents' needs, and felt they were not related to as separate and autonomous persons.

Another etiologic factor was the experience of excessive shaming on the part of the parents which made those who were shy even more ashamed. There was also a tendency in one or both parents to admire the child because of special talents that many of these deployed persons had, as well as a quality of and drive for power perceived in them from early childhood which increased both their feelings of grandiosity and their tendency to tyranny, as well as the shame when they could not meet the parents' expectations.

All the deployed patients had suffered from a traumatic event in their preoedipal or postoedipal phases, such as a death in the family, serious illness of a family member or of the person himself, or moving from one country to another (Herman, 1992). The parents were so absorbed in their tragedy that they were not open to signs of stress in their children, who felt even more lonely and deserted because of the parents' reaction. Furthermore, since it was impossible to "reach" the parent who was disconnected emotionally, they felt that whatever they tried to do was not good enough. Therefore they tended to remain in a position of despair even after both the circumstances and their resources changed. What many of them transmitted was the feeling that they had had to grow up too fast and too abruptly; they needed this to be corrected by a more gradual and flexible weaning now. Until then, they were perceiving themselves either as children who have no adult inside them to soothe them in times of stress; or as adults who were erasing their child parts, and unable to create a dialogue with them.

A different kind of trauma that most of the deployed patients had experienced in their childhood was physical or sexual abuse by a member of their family, a relative, or a neighbor. They have a strong feeling that they must hide something, whatever it was that now came to stand for the terrible secret, be it because of guilt for not having objected to the abuse, because of a fear of betraying the adult or because of the stain of shame they seem to carry with them secretly (Arvanitaki et al., 1993). Much of their psychic energy is then invested in deployment in order to prevent being humiliated once again.

FORMS OF DEPLOYMENT

There are many forms of deployment and in all of us we can find deploymental aspects. I shall briefly delineate some of these forms.

1. One major form of deployment takes is: to assume *roles* and to fulfill them in reality or in fantasy. This may be the role of the consoler: or of a "Living Statue" (Volkan, 1990) when the person is expected to be a symbol to compensate for a loss the parent had suffered, to play the role of the parent to the parent, to be the savior, or to be a part of the parent that had been disavowed. The invitation to enter a role arises from the parent's thwarted needs. The response of choosing to play the role to please the parent is not of less significance than to compete with a sibling or to expiate guilt feelings. Deployment into the role of the "good guy" who tends automatically to give up what he or she feels, thinks, and wants to appease the other is frequent. This may lead to a state of self-effacement so that the person ceases to know what he or she feels and wants.

A typical role of deployed patients is that of the "black sheep." Through assuming this role they unconsciously protest against what they had perceived as arrogance and hypocrisy on the part of their parents or siblings. They express their hurt and resentments through demonstrating to the world what had been hidden out of guilt and shame, and to make those whom they accuse feel that in fact they are by no means as successful as they appear to be. Thus, the deployed patients who failed, are the evidence for their parents' failure. This is their "sweet revenge," and this is at the same time their attempt to provide more space for their hurt feelings that had not been recognized.

While a role provides calmness and a sense of self-esteem, especially after times of stress when the tranquility of continuity and routine has been lost, there is a risk that one may lose oneself in the role. It is easier to become the role than to adopt it flexibly, shifting from one role to the other according to different, changing needs and circumstances.

The transformation of the roles in the treatment process back into the "erased" feeling states and the capsulated situations in which they were formed, was one of the channels in search of the lost self and of the person's real and complex identity.

2. Another frequent kind of deployment is the assumption of attitudes and positions that are automatically, rigidly, and often unwittingly activated. They then determine one's functioning and feeling to a great extent. These are a variety of positions in which much power is unconsciously invested; for example, the position of the victim of the rapist or that of the abuser; positions of the "Sleeping Beauty" or "Peter Pan"; positions of those who keep postponing whatever they have to do, or of passing their pressures on to the other, or of sitting on the fence without committing themselves to either side, unwilling to give up either option—unable to resolve the conflict.

The contemptuous position is frequently taken both as a weapon and a defense. The contempt continues to be enacted long after the passive experience of humiliation and psychic pain has been forgotten. It often becomes unwittingly expressed through positions and gestures. Not to give importance to thoughts, feelings, and experiences is another variant of the contemptuous position. The contempt often becomes like the water in the story of the sorcerer's apprentice. The contempt has been enacted in order not to feel certain insults and maintains its existence despite the changed circumstances. Created as a defense of the self, it now defeats the self.

The last position I will mention is the familiar position of the offended person who remains unreconcilable no matter how much understanding has been achieved in analysis. As well known as this position is, to us analysts it is nevertheless often enacted in such a subtle way that it remains unnoticed. To identify this position in the context of the present, both in the analytic situation and in life, to stop acting on it automatically, and attend to one's ways of dealing with distress, becomes an important goal of analysis. These positions are identified as a lever for reaching painful and disruptive areas from which the patients attempted with all their power to escape.

One major obstacle for change lies in adherence to the deployments which in the past had been means for survival. Identification of the emotional elements that cause the deployed patient to remain in the bunker long after the war is over is a therapeutic aim that continues from the beginning of the treatment to its end. One of the major factors of "being stuck" is the tendency to libidinize the affects. These persons are locked in their roles and positions as if these were the enactment of soothing masturbation fantasies to which they are addicted. Most of them remembered having masturbated since early childhood, had tried to stop it, but found it particularly difficult to give up. The working through of their deployments also enables them to become more tolerant of their guilt feelings. This reduces the intensity of the regressive pull.

In thinking of the power of being drawn into one's fantasy life or into an ideological world in which one's personality is totally wrapped up, I am reminded of a Jewish joke (Weinreich, personal communication). A group of vacationers were traveling on a ship when a terrible storm broke out; soon the boat began to sink. While all hurried to the lifeboats, two of the passengers were totally absorbed in a Talmudic debate. Another passenger passed by and shouted at them that the ship was sinking—they must hurry to the lifeboats. They stopped the debate for a moment, looked at him, surprised, and asked, "How is this relevant?" and continued their scholarly argument.

Let me bring another illustration of deployment, through the presentation of the last session of a small group of which I was therapist in the framework of a training program for group analysts. From the first meeting I was struck by the high quality of their work as well as by the atmosphere created by the members of the group, the therapist, cotherapist, and observers that seemed to have contributed greatly to the process of growth we all experienced. It is hard to convey the unique climate that prevailed. There was a feeling of unconscious active responsibility (Rangell, 1981, 1992) on the part of the members as they were struggling away from compulsive doing (by being inactive) toward the mode of being; from being cautiously on guard while as yet concealing their real feelings, thoughts, selves, toward opening themselves to self-expression and spotting the deployments that interfered with their development and change.

One of the members commented that he would never have imagined the amount of shame he had had to overcome when at last he dared to tell the group about his origins from a broken family and the feelings of humiliation that he had tried to counteract all his life through many strategies, always feeling himself to be false and inferior. Another member followed by saying that now, after many years of silence, she had written a letter to her parents opening the door for a renewed attempt to communicate.

Mr. M shared with the group his most significant experience from this eight-day workshop. What had always been distressing as long as he could remember was the fear of a catastrophe. He always felt that he had to be prepared for it and was unable to ever relax. He was surprised and greatly relieved when he dared to reveal to the group a traumatic experience of sexual abuse he had never mentioned before out of shame and guilt. Not only did the world not collapse, they did not reject him, and he remained alive. On the contrary, he felt much more accepted by the group that had showed him empathic understanding and care. Until then, he was consistently on guard against being caught; torturing himself with thoughts of the worst that could happen, partly out of his fear of being punished and partly in order to rid himself of his tension. His deployment into concealing his secrets had prevented him from being free to communicate, from being creative, and from being able to love another person.

Mr. Z, another member of the group, had behaved quite aggressively toward anyone who took the floor during the fourteen intensive meetings over eight days. When the group tried to link his domineering position in the present to the constant fights he had had with his dominating brother, about which he had talked, he became extremely defensive. He insisted that there was no connection whatsoever. It was his mission to save groups from monopolizers, he said. After that he withdrew sulkily into the position of the offended person who has been wronged and was now misunderstood. There was a different more vibrant quality to his voice as he started to talk next time and the group listened intently.

He said that he could not fall asleep now, that he was troubled by doubts. He had become confused and did not know anymore when he was false and when genuine. Then he dreamed that he was hovering over the streets or maybe sliding on the snow. The police came after him to arrest him. He now invented stories and lies to get them off his back. When he woke up, he suddenly realized that for so long now he had behaved as though the police were after him; that much of his verbal behavior everywhere had been to fight against unknown enemies; that he had acted out the role of an innocent victim, abused and oppressed. What moved him in this workshop particularly was that the group had not retaliated, nor given up on him. They did not let him get away with his obnoxious behavior, but this was because they actually cared about him. Thus he could soften his deployment and come nearer to his inner truth. Perhaps he could now rely on himself to know when he was genuine and when false. The group was moved by how he turned from his deployment in the direction of development; they felt they too could now trust him more.

Mrs. L commented that she was upset. She wondered whose company she would be able to enjoy when the group had ended. She was not sure she would find anybody. A group member asked her whether she felt that she had been hurt by the group. She responded that she had felt abandoned the night before. It turned out that several group members had gone to a show. Since she had a big car they were happy to go with her. One after the other, they now started to talk about the dreadful experience they had had when she was driving quite dangerously. But nobody had dared say this openly, feeling how anxious and defensive she was and worrying that anything they might say would only make her driving even more frightening to them. The loud laughter which soon filled the room, while each of the cotravelers described their fantasies and their fears, was accompanied by the utter surprise of the driver who thought she had driven more carefully than usual. It soon became evident, as she began to explore her behavior, that she had been deployed into a position of dangerous driving, unconsciously enacting thereby various feeling states and buried feelings from the past. For instance, her deep resentment about her parents' worrying about her driving was reflected in various ways. It often seemed to her that they unconsciously lived their own insecurity through her. For many years she had held a driving license but did not drive her car, as their attitude in addition to her own fears made her feel quite impotent. In her individual therapy she had worked on her fears and begun to drive again. But her resentment was still active, she now realized, as if she were saying through her behavior: "If you do not trust me, I will make this a self-fulfilling prophecy." She sensed that there were other feelings and meanings that needed to be worked on in her therapy.

A final example will be the deployment of Mrs. W who was head of a department in a hospital. She took the role of the leader in the small group, aiming consciously to be helpful and constructive in her interventions. But, in fact, she filled the space with endless attempts to find quick solutions to problems that were brought up. An interpretation pointing out her rivalry with the group therapist, and her need to act in order not to become aware of what she was feeling, did not stop her from continuing to explain away her own feelings and those of others, though she became quieter and began to listen. In the last meeting it came as a great surprise when she, for the first time, spoke gently in an authentic voice and sobbed. She was no longer resolute and well organized as she had been before. She smiled with one eye and wept with the other, she said. She had felt so overburdened all her life and never stopped to unpack all the luggage she carried with her, to make the weight on her shoulders lighter by putting away what was not relevant to her present. She realized that she had acted here as well as in other places in the rigid role of trying to help others almost without listening to what the other felt and thought. She had a really heavy load as a physician, but this was a different kind of load. Some of it related to her role in the family with a sick father and a depressive mother, when all expectations were turned onto her. She felt that she could never be the child who played, as some of the other group members dared to be. She realized that she, too, must not remain the know-it-all adult who is expected to help and wants to impress everybody.

She hoped that when she went home from the workshop, she would not automatically reenter her old position. Another kind of deployment she had mentioned was to do everything possible to win, as if she were in the courtroom—a position she had adopted vis-à-vis her self-righteous sister. She now felt that she could also be the child who cried. Until then what mattered most to her was how she looked to others; thus she would not expose her weakness or allow tears to smudge her makeup. Now she felt that what was more meaningful was what was inside herself, not the mask of shame that strangles (Wurmser, 1981). Tears filled the eyes of many group members, the therapists, and the observers.

It was extremely moving to participate in this unusual process of the melting of the deployments of a person who had been so powerful in her position that most others had given up trying to reach her.

The last kind of deployment that I shall mention here, and which will connect us to the political aspect, is what I call the "terroristic deployment." Such patients were caught in a sadomasochistic relationship in treatment as well as in life (Novick and Novick, 1991). Persons with this type of deployment would immediately attack fiercely whenever they felt offended by what they saw as disregard, insult, or abuse, while they immediately disconnected themselves emotionally. Their violence was at times verbal: loud, abusive, harassing, and cursing, or expressed in fantasy ruminations of revenge such as killing the enemy. Their transference was often extremely intense, resembling a psychotic transference. Whenever they experienced being forced into doing something against their will (e.g., to free associate or to weaken their control) they would attack fiercely. At such a point everything that had been slowly, painfully built up over long analytic work, collapsed. At such moments it was extremely difficult to rebuild the bridge between the patient and myself. Often they identified with terrorists ideologically. They were convinced that only through power can change be brought about in the world. Working with a patient with such a deployment was extremely difficult and frustrating, and much work on my countertransference reactions was needed (Moses-Hrushovski, 1992).

When I succeeded in reestablishing the emotional connection with them and survived the many tests they required me to pass, it was a great relief to realize that what was taken to be psychopathic or psychotic behavior was in fact a deploymental device in the life-long battle they were enacting. The person who seemed to be totally closed to feeling was actually sensitive and soft. It was after having fought a long uphill battle while the unique configuration of injustice was being jointly discovered as it had been experienced in the context of their developmental and social matrix, that they became willing to relinquish their grievances and take fuller responsibility for their feelings, actions, and their life.

It was especially while working with these patients and building contact with the psychic reality which they had found unbearable, that I began to pay more attention to the political aspects interwoven in clinical work. I was helped by the use of deployments as signs to reach the bunker in which these persons had helplessly and stubbornly entrenched themselves.

ASPECTS OF DEPLOYMENT IN THE POLITICAL ARENA

Just as there are political factors in the clinical field, so there are many emotional factors that have their impact on political behavior. I shall start with Vamik Volkan's description (1990) of how a tough politician who was deployed in his refusal to sign any peace agreement was affected by emotional factors.

> In his memoirs, President Jimmy Carter tells a moving story about how a *tough politician's* decision to sign a peace agreement was prompted by his regard for children:
>
> During the last day of the peace talks hosted by President Carter at Camp David in 1978 with President Anwar el Sadat of Egypt and Prime Minister Menachem Begin of Israel, the tough politician—Begin—remained adamant in his refusal to sign any agreement. Carter was frustrated by Begin's attitude and by the fact that the morale of the participants was getting very low. At one point a group photograph was taken of Carter, Sadat and Begin and the Israeli leader

> asked to have three copies signed by colleagues, so that he could present them to his grandchildren. Sadat autographed the pictures and Carter, after obtaining the names of Begin's grandchildren, wrote personalized inscriptions. Afterwards, Carter took the signed photographs to Begin's cabin. In Carter's own words the following took place: "I handed him the photographs. He took them and thanked me. Then he happened to look down and saw that his granddaughter's name was on the top one. He spoke it aloud and then looked at each photograph individually, repeating the name of the grandchild I had written on it. His lips trembled and tears welled up in his eyes. He told me a little about each child and especially about one who seemed to be his favorite. We were both emotional as we talked quietly for a few moments about grandchildren and about war." This superficially insignificant incident apparently caused Begin to have a change of heart about the peace agreement. Soon after the Carter / Begin interchange the Camp David Accords were signed [p. 46].

A phenomenon of group deployment can be seen in the Israeli settlers' political organization. David Grossman (1988) described the use of what I call deployments to ward off feelings of uncertainty and confusion, which are analogous to the power ploys that individuals use with their important others when they are involved in a struggle. Many of the settlers were convinced that Israel would be overrun by treacherous Arabs from all sides if it gave up its strength, its territory, for a peace that could not be trusted. They are deployed as a means of survival to keep in mind the scenario of another Holocaust, but also as an obstacle to prevent opening negotiations that could advance peace. David Grossman studied the attitudes of members of Gush Emunim (the main Israeli settlers' organization) toward their Arab neighbors.

In one of his meetings with members of a settlement in the West Bank, Grossman explored their thoughts on how the neighboring Arabs perceived and experienced the influence of the Israeli occupation. He described how a settler responded immediately that they, Gush Emunim, are not to blame for the situation and others murmured agreement. Grossman continued to ask, "Let's assume that you are right. Let us assume that history will confirm this in time. Now I ask only for a little flexibility of thought, and ask again: 'what in your opinions, does an Arab in Silwad or Ain

Yagrud, in his everyday life, in his most private mediations in his relations with his children, in what does he most feel the influence of your presence here, in a place he sees as his land?' " The immediate response "we haven't taken one meter of land from Arabs" (p. 36) came from one woman. Grossman describes that the people in the room were not able, even for a little while, to shift their point of view; they did not allow themselves even a split second of empathy and uncommitted participation in the lives of those whose fates are intertwined and interwoven so much with theirs. "Like fossils, they did not succeed in freeing themselves from those very bonds which they are unwilling to admit exist" (p. 39). "Then Yehuda said," Grossman continues to tell, that the answer is simple: "that he does not want to think even for a minute about the situation of the Arabs around him, because he is caught up in a struggle with them, at war, he said, and were he to allow himself to pity, to identify, he would weaken and endanger himself. The people in the room nodded. There was a hum of agreement" (pp. 39–40). In the vivid description of the closing off of one's empathy to others, and even more so to victims of one's own actions I found much similarity to the "deployment." It is stubbornly preserved as a self-survival-strategy.

In the same vein we can see the words of Ms. D. Sheleg, the editor of the Journal *Otiot* (Letters) that appeals to the religious members of the settlements particularly: Yotam Benziman when a journalist, asked her why she does not publish the positive experiences with Arabs who come and drink coffee and are friends. She replied that it may be true that they do not educate for tolerance but the population they belong to feels threatened by the published articles that "justify" Arabs.

I was struck by the deploymental aspect in a small extremist group whose members closed off themselves and their empathy to others out of the fear to feel shame and guilt that would weaken, break, or disintegrate them. In a meeting of Palestinian and Israeli-Jewish teachers I worked with a group that combined rightist Israeli-Jewish and more moderate Israeli-Palestinian teachers. When in one session the Israeli Jews ruthlessly accused the Arabs of ingratitude for the benefits that the Israeli State had provided for them, and especially attacked them for violent acts by Arabs throughout the country, I felt that their aggressive assaults served also to defend them against their own guilt and shame; and I said so (cf. Moses, 1983). It was amazing to realize that for quite some time nobody from the Jewish group had any notion about what they as representatives of Israeli Jews could possibly feel guilty about. It became clear that the guilt and shame relating to the humiliation and atrocities that tragically are carried out in the service of the Israeli occupation could not be owned at that moment.

In many other meetings the deployment of returning time and again to the wrongs of the past instead of working for the potential of the present and future has been experienced and spotted as a major obstacle to reaching a real peace agreement. Horowitz (1993), an Israeli journalist, told us how a Palestinian journalist said in a meeting held in Spain that one could not expect that everything would fall into place just by putting the two peoples, or their representatives, together. What the Palestinians need more than anything, the Palestinian journalist said, is freedom and the development of their independence, while the Israelis need recognition and psychological acknowledgement to overcome their fears." He explained that they do not understand how Israel, strong as it is, with a strong army and so many resources, could be afraid of Arabs, but he realizes that they are afraid and that they need help in overcoming these fears. I thought that Horowitz had sensed and phrased the dynamics of the group deployments on both sides.

Becoming aware of the deploymental aspects which we find on both sides could be one of the steps on the way to reconciliation and peace and might perhaps actually diminish terrorist acts. Gideon Levi (1993), an Israeli journalist, was writing about a group of Jews and Arabs who met with a Rabbi and an Imam in Israel and tried to unite against fundamentalism on either side. This small group attempted to deal with fanaticism and the individual correlates of fundamentalism. These similarly function to ward off all signs of weakness in the deployed individual and group; the group of the Imam and the Rabbi tried to break stereotypes by learning to meet each other in a friendly atmosphere. The fact that both groups regret the present state of affairs and want to improve what can be improved, and are able to mourn, rather than leave unfinished business that interferes with both inner and interpersonal peace, is another component in this process.

Despite the difficulties that deployed individuals (Moses-Hrushovski, 1993) as well as deployed groups have in giving up what they owned and dreamed about for so many years, which served as a consolation and strengthening device, it seems that there is perhaps some readiness to stop automatic functioning and open oneself to the present and future needs and possibilities. How to combine not forgetting the tragedies of the past and doing whatever is possible to prevent them from happening again, and yet at the same time not to let the events of the past close us off, individuals, groups, and nations, from being human and reach peace is a constant concern of us all, here in Israel and elsewhere.

Various programs for change have recently been planned in Israel. For instance, the Ministry of Education has crystallized a program for preparing elementary and high school children for the problems that will arise in the process of peace with those who were perceived as enemies. The new direction invites an emotional and cognitive adaptation of the world of concepts involved in the need to attend to the changes that will ensure, we hope, the historical event of signing the peace agreements between Israel and the Palestinians. To the extent that the unrealistic dreams on both sides (Barron, 1993) will be given up and mourned, the deployments that interfere heavily with reconciliation and dialogues worked through, and the commitment to recurrently find ways to revive the hope that threatens to die will motivate us—the chances to actualize the dream of peace that just has been born will improve.

REFERENCES

Adler, G. (1989), Transitional phenomena, projective identification and the essential ambiguity of the psychoanalytic situation. *Psychoanal. Quart.*, 58:81–105.

Arlow, J. A. (1992), Altered ego states. *Israel J. Psychiatry & Rel. Sci.*, 29:65–77.

Arvanitaki, K., Jodoin, R. M., Lester, E. P., Lussier, A., & Robertson, B. M. (1993), Early sexual abuse and nightmares in the analysis of adults. *Psychoanal. Quart.*, 62:572–587.

Barron, A. (1993), Easing the mental strains of peace. *Jerusalem Post*, December 27:4.

Benziman, Y. (1994), Kol Hair. *Ha'aretz*, Hebrew, June 24.

Coen, S. S. (1989), Intolerance of responsibility for internal conflict. *J. Amer. Psychoanal. Assn.*, 37:943–964.
Cooper, A. M. (1984), The unusually painful analysis: A group of narcissistic characters. In: *Psychoanalysis: The Vital Issues*. New York: International Universities Press.
Feldman, M. (1993), Grievance. Paper presented at the Israel Psychotherapy Association Conference on Psychotherapy and Aggression in Tel Aviv, April 23.
Grossman, D. (1988), Don't pity them too much. In: *The Yellow Wind*. New York: Bantam Doubleday Dell Publishing Group, pp. 34–53.
Grunberger, B. (1971), *Narcissism*. New York: International Universities Press.
Herman, J. L. (1992), *Trauma and Recovery*. New York: Basic Books.
Horowitz, N. (1993), And the poet said you cannot force love on anybody. *Ha'aretz*, Hebrew, December 14:6.
Levi, G. (1993), The twilight zone. *Ha'aretz Supplement*, Hebrew, December 31:5.
Levin, S. (1971), The psychoanalysis of shame. *Internat. J. Psycho-Anal.*, 52:355–362.
Lewis, H. B. (1987), *The Role of Shame in Symptom Formation*. Hillsdale, NJ: Lawrence Erlbaum.
McDougall, J. (1989), *Theatres of the Body*. London: Free Association Books.
Morrison, N. K. (1986), The role of shame in schizophrenia. In: *Essential Papers on Narcissism*, ed. A. R. Morrison. New York: New York University Press, pp. 51–87.
Moses, R. (1983), Guilt feelings of the Israeli side of the Arab-Israeli peace process. *Bull. Freud House*, 7:2–14.
Moses-Hrushovski, R. (1986), Interpretation of the past and present. *Bull. Europ. Psychoanal. Fed.*, 25:15–25.
——— (1992), Transference and countertransference: From deployment against feelings of loss through psychotic regressions to a better capacity to feel and mourn. *Internat. J. Psycho-Anal.*, 73:561–576.
——— (1993), Discussion of Dr. Michael Feldman's paper on "Grievance." Presented in Tel Aviv, April 23.
——— (1994), *Deployment—Hiding Behind Power Struggles as a Character Defense*. Northvale, NJ: Jason Aronson.
Novick, J., & Novick, K. K. (1991), Some comments on masochism and the delusion of omnipotence from a developmental perspective. *J. Amer. Psychoanal. Assn.*, 39:307–333.
Rangell, L. (1981), From insight to change. *J. Amer. Psychoanal. Assn.*, 29:119–125.
——— (1992), The psychoanalytic theory of change. *Internat. J. Psycho-Anal.*, 73:415–429.

Steiner, J. (1993), *Pathological Organizations in Psychotic, Neurotic and Borderline Patients*, ed. E. B. Spillius. New York: New Library of Psychoanalysis.

Stone, A. M. (1992), The role of shame in post traumatic stress disorders. *Amer. J. Orthopsychiatry*, 62:131–137.

Volkan, V. D. (1990), Living statues and political decision making. *Mind & Hum. Interact.*, 2:46–49.

——— Rodgers, T. (1988), *Attitudes of Entitlement*. Charlottesville: University Press of Virginia.

Weinshel, E. M. (1989), On inconsolability. In: *The Psychoanalytic Core: Essays in Honor of Leo Rangell, M.D.*, ed. H. P. Blum, E. M. Weinshel, & F. R. Rodman. Madison, CT: International Universities Press, pp. 45–71.

Wurmser, L. (1981), *The Mask of Shame*. Baltimore: Johns Hopkins University Press.

13.

CAN YOU NOT, FATHER, SEE THE ERLKING? PSYCHOANALYTIC OBSERVATIONS ON GOETHE'S BALLAD, "THE ERLKING"

Hermann Beland

THE COURAGE OF THE ENLIGHTENER

Goethe's ballad, "The Erlking," deals with those unconscious powers of schism and paranoid conflict of the individual and of groups that lead to social subjugations and revolutions. The poem is thus political in the true sense. It uses the invention of a mythical figure, the Erlking, as we can say two centuries later, to give a precise description of the internal psychic relations that can deprive individuals or groups of their ability to discern reality. They then equate subconscious scenes with those of the outside world in a paranoid way, leading to delusional behavior.

The poem was written in 1782, a few years before the excesses of the French revolution shattered the Enlightenment's faith in the reign of reason and the principle of harmony that accompanied it. In 1781 Kant had published the first of his great critiques, *The Critique of Pure Reason,* which can be regarded as the climax and culmination of the Enlightenment's thought. It too shattered all hope in the power of knowledge. Two years after the Erlking, Kant published an article on man's autonomy and the liberation of thinking from heteronomy and fear, the Enlightenment's major concern. He called the subjection of previous centuries to heteronomy and fear a "self-inflicted not-coming-of-age." "Staying little was self-inflicted if it was caused not by an absence of understanding, but by a lack of resolution and courage to make use of one's own mind without being led by others. *Sapere aude!* Have the courage to make use of your own mind! is thus the catchword of the Enlightenment" (Kant, 1783). The "Enlightenment" into which Goethe symbolically ventured in the ballad of "The Erlking" and which had to wait for scientific discovery, was, as we could say today, about the necessity of recognizing the vast problem of unconscious thought processes, even though this concept did not yet exist. It was also about the necessity of recognizing childhood fears, including those of all adults. It concerned the necessity of recognizing the extraordinary significance of paranoid–homosexual delusional behavior for individuals and for society. Goethe's comprehension of the phenomena that called for the courage to make use of one's own understanding thus went much further than Hume or Kant with their critical philosophies of consciousness. Goethe created poems of the unconscious with what German philologists called "magical nature ballads."[1] His poems, which typically express processes of individuals or large groups, thus presage twentieth-century psychoanalysis, Gestalt psychology, and the philosophy of symbolic forms. We will see clearly that Goethe, with his ballad of "The Erlking" in particular, proceeded with a self-knowledge that could only have been artistically shaped and made public with "resolution and courage." This process of acknowledgment and publication bears similarity to Freud's display of courage in interpreting and publishing his own dreams in his dream interpretation. The poem was a work of art, in the form of a nightmare, an unbelievable condensation of paranoid fear, guilt, and acknowledgment of the unconscious. What do we know about the relationship of courage, self-knowledge, creative processes, and the production of a poem as a nightmare? And what do we know about the relationship of courage, dream interpretation, and dream work in nightmares?

---

[1]In his commentary on Goethe's ballads, Erich Trunz (1946) wrote: "The 'Sturm und Drang' ballads were almost all ballads of love; in the Weimar years magical nature ballads appeared by their side. They are genuinely Goethe's own creative achievement. Eighteenth century poetry had, in its sensitivity, developed a feeling for nature, but only as far as aesthetics went, and to a certain extent, religion. Yet in these ballads nature treats man in a completely new way, luring him, robbing him, making him happy and killing him. . . . In these poems, the human unconscious and the depth of the soul's feelings, disdained by the Enlightenment, found expression in words here and thus gained new spiritual recognition" (p. 482).

Not dreams, but their *interpretation,* writes Freud, is the "royal road to the unconscious." The work invested by analyst and patient must be equal to or greater than the dream work for the transference meaning of unconscious dream thoughts to be retrieved from the distortion of the dream work; it must be understood and transformed into an interpretation (Segal, 1991). If this does not occur, the meaning of the related dream remains an unanswered question.

What enabled Freud to work on the interpretation of his own dreams, to reveal the distortion of dreams and their motives, this "deepest and most difficult problem of dream life" (1923b) that had previously, so far as we know, remained a mystery for humanity, and thus to pave an accessible path to the unconscious? The remarkable information he provides answers an open question in the history of science and the history of thought as a whole. It can be found in a brief publication, written in 1923, just $2^1/_2$ pages in length, "Josef Popper-Lynkeus and the Theory of Dreams," and reads as follows: "I think what enabled me to reveal the cause of the distortion of dreams was my moral courage" (1923b, p. 263).

The expression "courage" or "moral courage," as we know, has not become a psychoanalytic concept, and despite its prominence in the history of science, cannot be found in the index of the Gesammelte Werke. Yet it designates a central psychoanalytic category and is part of every human being's "psychoanalytic function of personality," of the function of self-knowledge indicating tolerance of the perception of unconscious content, including the ability to think of this content (Grinberg, Sor, and Bianchedi, 1993). Tolerance of fear and of guilt, as elements of the depressive position, replace what Freud meant by moral courage in psychoanalytic terminology. Both concepts, however, lack the highly relevant element of active initiative so essential in the concept of courage. By tolerance of fear we mean the tolerance of those frightening upheavals in the psychic structure initiated by the revelations of dream interpretation, and by tolerance of guilt the assumption of responsibility for the narcissistically relentless and destructive sides of one's being, revealed by dreams.

In his ballad "The Erlking," Goethe expresses emotional and social connections due, in my opinion, to his moral courage, as Freud claimed of himself, to his tolerance of the perception of unconscious and socially denied content that he acquired on the path to self-knowledge (self-analysis). I will elucidate some of these connections below.

Several elements of nightmares included by Goethe in this ballad tie it even closer to the interpretation of dreams and moral courage than is the case in a painting or sculpture or music which use a medium other than language. Indeed, the function of distortion which, as we shall see, is evident throughout the poem, generally tends to be opposed to the distortion of the dream work. Its purpose in the poem is to bring the social resistance to empathy with the dying child's fantasized agony *closer* to consciousness. In addition, the poet's tolerance of fear and his courage of self-acceptance with tolerance of guilt must have developed *before* the poem was created. Without them it could not have been written (Segal, 1991, p. 85), whereas with dreams, tolerance of fear and guilt occur *subsequently*, thus undoing the distortion through an interpretation. Accordingly, this ballad uses the same means as dreams but has the opposite effect, making conscious what dreams conceal for sleep to remain uninterrupted. If the dream work fails, a nightmare ensues and the state of fear is rejected by waking, whereas successful poetic work leads to a poem about a nightmare and to an acceptance of fear and grief. A comparison of the main functions thus shows they correspond exactly to the *interpretation* of dreams and to the poem, both made possible by the tolerance of fear and guilt.

If we compare how they are formed, we see that the poem owes much of what we admire about it to those elements of dream function that we recognize as describable and as peculiarities such as body rhythm (e.g., riding in fear or lustful excitement, reflected by the different rhythms of different lines), consonance, ideograms, language condensation, symbolization, and the play of metaphors. Splitting characters and dramatizing the action are also taken directly from the dream function.

Many of the questions asked in Goethe's ballad are related to the riddle of the sphinx. The question form plays a significant role in the poem and will occupy us further. Could poems not be understood as reverse dreams spoken by the poet for society, expressing individual emotional experiences and conflicts of his times in symbolic form when they have been worked through and elevated to the level of generality? Are ballads, a particular, dramatic form of poetry, not particularly dreamlike creations? Or better, as in the case of Goethe's Erlking, are they not nightmarelike creations, even though, in sharp contrast to nightmares, they heighten wakefulness and awareness? Should their interpretation, like the interpretation of dreams, not consider the countertransference of the social reader, just as it must understand the meaning of the specific form used? Should it not consider the poet's fate, which gave rise to the theme, and try simultaneously to understand the ballad as the myths of the past; *as history recorded in symbolic, exemplary fashion and as a conflict faced by the poet and by society that has not been worked through*? (This formulation leans on Klaus Heinrich's definition of myth [1993, p. 225].) These are many questions that serve as a transition to the phenomenon of questions.

Johann Wolfgang Goethe 1782
Erlkönig

Wer reitet so spät durch Nacht und Wind?
Es ist der Vater mit seinem Kind;
Er hat den Knaben wohl in dem Arm,
Er faßt ihn sicher, er hält ihn warm.

"Mein Sohn, was birgst du so bang dein Gesicht?"—
"Siehst, Vater, du den Erlkönig nicht?
Den Erlenkönig mit Kron und Schweif?—
"Mein Sohn, es ist ein Nebelstreif."—

>Du liebes Kind, komm, geh mit mir!
Gar schöne Spiele spiel ich mit dir;
Manch bunte Blumen sind an dem Strand,
Meine Mutter hat manch gülden Gewand.<

"Mein Vater, mein Vater, und hörest du nicht,
Was Erlenkönig mir leise verspricht?"—
"Sei ruhig, bleibe ruhig, mein Kind:
In dürren Blättern säuselt der Wind."—

>Willst, feiner Knabe, du mit mir gehn?
Meine Töchter sollen dich warten schön;
Meine Töchter führen den nächtlichen Reihn
Und wiegen und tanzen und singen dich ein.<

"Mein Vater, mein Vater, und siehst du nicht dort
Erlkönigs Töchter am düstern Ort?"—
"Mein Sohn, mein Sohn, ich seh es genau:
Es scheinen die alten Weiden so grau."—

>Ich liebe dich, mich reizt deine schöne Gestalt;
Und bist du nicht willig, so brauch' ich Gewalt.<
"Mein Vater, mein Vater, jetzt faßt er mich an!
Erlkönig hat mir ein Leids getan!"—

Dem Vater grauset's, er reitet geschwind,
Er hält in Armen das ächzende Kind,
Erreicht den Hof mit Müh und Not:
In seinen Armen das Kind war tot.

Translation of J. W. v. Goethe: Erlkönig

Who's riding so late through dark and wind?
It is the father with his child.
He holds the boy snug in his arm,
He grips him safely, he keeps him warm.

"My son, why hide you so anxious your face?"
"Can, father, you not see Erlenking,
The Erlenking with crown and robe?"
"My son, it is a wisp of mist!"

"You darling child, come, go with me,
So lovely games I will play with you.
Pretty flowers you find there by the shore,
My mother has many of golden gowns."

"My father, my father, and can you not hear
The promises Erlking is whispering to me?"
"Be calm now, stay calm now, my son,
In the dry leaves is rustling the wind."

"You pretty boy, will you come with me?
My daughters shall look there after you well.
My daughters will lead the nightly round
And lull and dance and sing you to sleep."

"My father, my father, and can you not see
Erlking's daughters in that dark place?"
"My son, my son, I can see it plain:
It is the old willows that gleam all grey."

"I love you! Your beautiful shape excites
and are you not willing, I will use brute force!"
"My father, my father, he takes hold of me!
Erlking has hurt me, the Erlking has."

The father shudders, he rides fast,
He holds in his arms the groaning child,
arrives his home in toil and travail:
The son in his arms, the child was dead.

(Translation by Renate Beland, 1994)

THE QUESTION

What is the significance of asking? Goethe's "Erlking" ballad opens with a question and its form is marked by its large number of questions. There are seven in all, characterized by the external and internal situation of those asking them as being as conflictual as life itself. Yet they are all questions. So we see that the form of the question is an important element of the poem, calling for clarification. The poem contains a riddle, or rather several riddles, that emerge as we learn of the circumstances leading to a son's death. What is it that kills this boy? Does he die from his fears? Who is the Erlking? What is the meaning of the child having two fathers, a good one who represses what he should know and a bad one, gruesomely real and aware of everything the "good" father no longer wishes to know?

Let us anticipate what comes later: This poem deals with the universal human riddle that asks why parents must put their children through traumatic developments and experiences without being able to prevent the development, thereby, of a grave formation of psychic structures, repetitive in innumerable individual destinies. Traumatic experiences then lead individuals to work through the schism between good and evil, and the fear of persecution in a way we know as perverse. This often leads to an actual delusional act or, throughout history, millions of them: to terror, torture, war, the slaying of a son by his (murderous) father or the death of a son in his (good) father's arms. As with the sphinx, the poem's riddle of who the Erlking is, and who the father and his son are, could be solved thus: Man, I, Oedipus—we may ask why the poem moves us so.

Let us approach the poem first with respect to the question form. *Questions are requests for knowledge.* The question that opens the poem, simply or with precipitous symbolism, turns the listener into both an enquirer and a riddle-solver: "Who's riding so late through night and wind?" Schubert interpreted the poem's reply as something radiantly righteous, ultimately good, meriting grateful recognition: "It is the father with his child." This is, or could be, one of the best, primordial facts of life. The composition of "*It is the father with his child*" no doubt defines "father" in the happiest possible way. What we go on to learn about this father–son relationship seems to confirm Schubert's musical interpretation. The father gives his child pleasure and basic security; he holds him snugly, caring for his physical and emotional well-being. This is what good-enough fathers do. Or perhaps this is how fathers used to be seen? Two centuries ago? Or at two years of age? "*He holds the boy snug in his arms, He grasps him securely, he keeps him warm.*"

Alternatively, could this be an idealization based on a split?[2] I will examine this question more closely below; it includes the issue of the boy's mother. Suffice it to say here that the actions attributed to the father sound perfectly appropriate for a mother as well: she holds the boy snug in her arms, she grasps him securely, she keeps him warm. The overall interpretation will determine if this is so. In any case, if answers like those given in the first verse define the good side of a father's life with his child, they are extremely gratifying. This means that questions, or requests for knowledge, also express the desire of adults to share their children's anxiety and sense of danger, to help them deal with their fantasized fears through understanding and reassure them through their knowledge: "*My son, why hide you so fearfully your face?*"

[2]The theme of fear in Schubert's bass line is a repeated phrase of six rising triplets and two falling quarter notes. There are interruptions, but it is maintained throughout the distinctly positive description of father and child (Konrad Hössler, personal communication).

Up to this point, the father's empathy has been helpful. Parents are good enough, as Winnicott and Bion phrased it, if they accept and calm their children's fear of being destroyed. From here on, however, the father struggles uneasily with the Erlking's imaginary yet real, seductive yet somehow sinister promises genuinely experienced by his child, through which the father discovers the Erlking. The father struggles somewhat helplessly with the boy's fears through his own grasp of the external world of fog, rustling leaves, and old gray willows.

The child then responds with an alarming question. *Questions in the negative* (such as those at the beginning) *serve as reminders of knowledge*. The questions asked by the son who (and this would be a meaningful and feasible interpretation), in his feverish delirium, experiences his agony as a homosexual seduction, rape, and murder are all of this grammatical structure. The father is asked more and more unbelieving questions, incredulous at such a good father's inability to share the reality of such a threatening reality. In the end they are desperate reminders of knowledge that should exist, and would now be the only chance of help, since it would show understanding and an acknowledgment of physical danger, hallucinatory horror, and psychotic fear. Can you not see? Can you not hear? Can you not see there? Can you not, father, see the Erlking?

No, the father sees and hears nothing but the external world. Is his refusal to be drawn into the boy's imaginary world due to his own fear of homosexual seductions? Does the boy's fear continue to grow because his projective identification boomerangs back at him, twice as terrifying, when his father refuses to accept it?

Perhaps the father understands his child's dangerous emotional state after all, and his inability to distinguish between perception and wish (delusion)? And perhaps he does understand which desires his completely split and hallucinating son is trying to "satisfy" with the help of projections? However, if he is aware of all the boy's fantasies, and fears for the sanity of his child, we must conclude that the only way he can think of to reassure him is to name (define) the harmless reality of the visible world, thus calming the child by banishing the freed processes of his inner world back behind the walls of repression. This is sometimes a perfectly valid way of dealing with delusional convictions, but experience has shown it to be ineffective unless the fear is first accepted and the import and purpose of the delusion, the symbolic equation between internal and external reality, are understood. Here this is not the case.[3]

Paradoxically enough in the light of his enlightened rationality, the father's responses now translate the symbols of night and wind of the opening question: Who's riding so late through night and wind? Wind is the soft promise of libidinous and narcissistic satisfactions (*"My father, my father, can you not hear / What the Erlking softly promises me?" "Be calm now, stay calm now, my dear child, / In the dry leaves the wind is rustling."*). Night stands for the sinister elves and the oppressive Erlking with his crown and robe and for the dark place (*"My father, my father, can you not see / The Erlking's daughters in that dark place?" "My son, my son, I see it clearly: / It is the gray gleam of the old willow-trees."*). This ride, this physical experience thus admits us into the "reality" of the son's inner world that his father wishes to reduce to perceptions of the outside world. Moreover, the sensuality of the rhythmic motion too may signify nothing other than "riding."

In the father's answers, Goethe alludes to the split, so central to the Enlightenment and relevant to this day, between technical reason and emotionality, that rules out any contact between reason and the unconscious: the split of the preconscious. The simplistic and reductive elimination of religion and superstitious faith in devils and witches made the world uneasy and dangerous in a new way. The rationality of the Enlightenment was accompanied by the emotionality of the split-off Sturm und Drang and the tearful sensitivity that tend to be connected with irrationality and spill over into the next period's fascination with the devil's elixirs and the scientific–technical and marketing–economic complex.

---

[3]Herzog examined the nocturnal panic states of twelve children of divorced parents (18- to 28-month-old boys), who reacted to the loss of their father with night terror. This could be stopped only by the father. He refers to "father hunger" and the "Erlking syndrome": "A boy needs his father for the formation of the sense of self, the completion of separation-individuation, the consolidation of core gender identity, and the beginning modulation of libidinal and especially aggressive drives. I call the affective state which exists when these needs are not being met father hunger" (p. 230). He refers to the production of phobic symptoms as "precocious creativity," an expression of hostility against the father who has abandoned him, the projection of which returns as a nightmare (Erlking). Herzog is cautious about predicting personality disturbances (Herzog, 1980).

The next question, asked by the Erlking, was in fact a late product of faith in the devil.[4] It is the question of seduction: "*You beautiful boy, will you come with me?*" According to its form and words, this question is also an enquiry after the boy's free intentions, again a completely open request for knowledge. However, according to its content and expressed words, it is intended to prevent prior knowledge (of the deadly consequences of destructive narcissism), to prevent knowledge (the conscious and unconscious motives of the seducer and of the seduced) and to prevent free choice (through the presumed pressure of the drives and through the perversity seeking a combination of satisfaction and self-destruction).

What have we learned so far from our examination of the poem's questions? Its questions and answers could be said to have brought closer to us a few central historical and psychological dimensions of modern times. These dimensions are characterized by unconscious paranoid structures, in which split father images become internal and deadly external reality. We must, however, admit that we have not as yet come much closer to the problem of the question itself and the meaning concealed behind its specific form.

THE SPLIT MOTHER IMAGE, DUALITY AND (ONCE AGAIN) THE QUESTION

Not only questions, but duality are central to the poem's form. The symmetry is strict: Each two of the middle verses of the poem describe the dialogue between father and son and the Erlking's seduction with "games" and "dances," while the opening and closing verses deal with the benevolence of the father to his son and the second and penultimate ones with the Erlking's evil-doing and the strange, three-way contact between both fathers and the son. Most of the poem's thirty-two lines have nine syllables in the

[4]In 1764 Wieland translated the charming wood spirits in Shakespeare's "Midsummer-Night's Dream" by the German word "Elfen" (elves). Over the last three centuries, elves have appeared as powerful nocturnal beings, and taken the form of vampires, werewolves, witches, incubi, and succubi, representing the fear that (male) sexuality would be totally destroyed. The word *Erlking* comes from the Danish word for "elf king," or *Albking*, and a word meaning "*elf*" also appears in the German word for "nightmare," *Albtraum*. The Erlking's "robe" can be understood, and has always been translated as, a train, but it could definitely also be the Devil's tail. Together with the crown, it is a last relic of his reign over souls in the period of frenzied Christianity and witch hunts (see E. Jones, 1912).

original German text, often with two rhythmic sections, the division usually falling after the fifth syllable. Particularly pungent are the repetitions "*My father, my father—My son, my son,*" which occur four times, with a possible fifth repetition: "*Be calm now, stay calm now.*" This repetition both intensifies the failure of the attempts to calm the boy and expresses his growing unrest, which eventually becomes a fear of death. Both these accentuations point to the mother's absence, and already we can sense that she may be represented by the duality, or may be "canceled" by it.

The duality is continued in the contrasts of the content and in the false dualisms. There is a good and an evil father, each with masculine and feminine characteristics. The paranoid split between good and evil initially seems relevant only to the paternal images of external and internal reality, whereas the maternal characteristics seem to be divided only according to the pleasure principle (the Erlking's excitement) / reality principle (father's holding), but not according to the schism between good and evil.

We have already seen that the description of the good father's behavior ("*. . . holds the boy snug in his arms, . . . grasps him securely, . . . keeps him warm*") would also be linguistically valid for a mother. Women go on to play a central role in the Erlking's parapraxes. The Erlking's mother "*has plenty of golden gowns,*" a parapraxis of tremendous narcissistic enhancement belonging in the feminine (and homosexual) realms. A child is also more likely to pick flowers on the seashore for his mother rather than his father. The Erlking's daughters shall "*take such good care of you . . . / And lull and dance and sing you to sleep.*" This is all exquisitely motherly, but there is only a grandmother and her granddaughters, for the Erlking has no wife. She would be a heterosexual intruder, superfluous also in the homosexual world because the Erlking, just like the father, has a feminine half. *The child's mother is psychologically removed.* Her attributes, split and divided between the halves of the five split pairs mentioned above, are subject to the mixed perverse split between good and evil.[5]

The gratifications used by the Erlking to tempt the boy are perfectly suitable for children, typically innocent and good.[6] Yet we

[5]Two fathers, male-female, good-evil, conscious (external)-unconscious (internal), pleasure principle (excitement)-reality principle (holding).

[6]The simplest of temptations, that of candy, is missing, but there are cultural and historical reasons for this; sugar cane was planted and the sugar industry established only in the early nineteenth century!

know that here everything has a perverse and destructive intention. What Horkheimer and Adorno (1944) wrote about propaganda in the "Dialectic of the Enlightenment" applies literally: It "manipulates people; when calling out freedom, it contradicts itself. It goes hand in hand with mendacity. It is the community of lying, which binds leaders and those led by them through propaganda, even if its contents, as such, are correct" (p. 272).

The false unities found in the poem are also relevant to the problem of duality, serving as a contrast and an appendix to the tearing of the context into two false halves. This is so with the equation of internal and external, inner reality and outer reality, wishes and perceptions, past and present, all evident in the child's hallucinations. Other unities like the absorption of the feminine in the masculine, the maternal in the paternal can be seen both with the good and the persecutory fathers. The concurrence of impotence and omnipotence, lack of knowledge and omniscience fan the child's delusional fear of murder, which accompanies his dying.

Could a unified interpretation be valid for the various levels of the poem's duality—the symmetries, the polarities, pairs, contrasts, splits, equations of contradictions and hybridizations, all determined by the number two? I believe we may be permitted to draw on the significance of duality in dream symbolism and assume it to represent the child's mother, who has been removed. We can assume that her presence, split between excitement and nonexcitement, has its place in the similarly split paternal aspects. Here we find the psychological structure of an open paranoid homosexual triangle, made up of a persecutory father, a loving father, and a son. The suggested interpretation of duality as one of the poem's structural patterns corresponds in terms of content to the psychological removal and division of the woman (mother) and child and the division of their attributes, as occurs in a paranoid homosexual setting.

OEDIPUS, LAIUS, THE SPHINX, AND THE ERLKING

An interesting analogous structure in the Oedipus myth occurs after Oedipus kills his father, when the sphinx tests him for life and death with the question of her riddle. The sphinx is an exact analogue of the Erlking's masculinity-femininity, with a female head and torso and a male, animal lower half with a snake's tail (the sphinx was itself engendered by mother-son incest). This is the first analogous duality. The sphinx can also be interpreted as the persecutory half of the loving Jocasta (van der Sterren, 1974, chapter 6). This is the second split corresponding to the father–Erlking split in the poem. Oedipus is a knowing criminal, who does not learn by asking, but rather forces his knowledge through murder and incest, kills the sphinx and drives Jocasta to suicide.[7] In the Erlking, the son dies long after his mother has been psychologically removed.

In the Oedipus myth, it is the sphinx who asks the question.[8] This suggests that the questions and the duality that structure the Erlking should be taken as a function and a syntactic reflection of the mother. Her image, split and displaced to the fathers, nevertheless provides the psychological backdrop for the whole poem.

Mythologically, the Erlking corresponds perfectly to the myth of Laius, Oedipus' father. When he was living in exile in Pisa with Pelops, son of Tantalos, Laius seduced the latter's son Chrysippos. Laius was considered the first man in the Greek world to indulge his love for boys. He wanted Chrysippos, kidnapped him, raped him, and drove him to suicide. Laius was therefore cursed by Pelops and persecuted by Hera, who also sent the sphinx to Thebes. According to the curse, Laius would be killed by his son. The

[7]There is one place in Sophocles' King Oedipus that different philologists translate in different ways: Oedipus should kill "tous tekontas," his parents. It seems that the plural can always be understood as the singular as well, but most translators choose the plural. It is found in the all-revealing conversation between Oedipus and the herdsman, who had saved him:

Oedipus: Did she give it to you herself?
Herdsman: Aye.
Oedipus: To do what with it?
Herdsman: I was to kill it.
Oedipus: She was so hard—its own mother?
Herdsman: Aye, through fear of evil oracles.
Oedipus: Which?
Herdsman: They said that he should kill his parents (tous tekontas) (King Oedipus, 1173–1176).

[8]The famous riddle that the sphinx is said to have acquired from the muses is simple in comparison with the answer, which also includes Oedipus' fate. The answer is: Man. The question concealed in the riddle should thus actually be: "Who are you?" "What sort of person are you?" "Who are your true parents?" "What have you done with your parents?" "What have your parents done with you?" If the riddle of the sphinx is taken in this sense, the questions need not be greatly altered to be adapted to the questions in the Erlking.

oracle added that this son would sexually possess his mother, the wife of Laius (see Nebel, 1964, pp. 121–122).

The negative Oedipus complex is thus older from a mythological standpoint and induces the positive one as vengeance. This ties in with Freud's hypothesis about man's prehistoric trauma, which he views as recurring ontogenetically in developmental dispositions to psychoses and neuroses. In the beginning was the distress of the ice age, which explains the developmental riddle of sexual latency; this distress was, however, perpetuated socially as well through the cruel but shrewd despotism of the archaic leader of the primal horde. He claimed sole ownership of power and of women through castrating or banishing his sons, until they put an end to his tyranny by murdering him and possessing their mothers. Freud saw their remorse over this as the beginning of the feeling of guilt, the prohibition against patricide, the prohibition against incest, the beginning of exogamy, of religion, law, and political organization—the beginning of civilization. While despotism and castration reigned, man is said to have acquired paranoid cruelty and homosexual–masochistic talents. This was a congenital disposition for fundamental psychic defensive stances, a combination of the split between good and evil and the gender split with an intolerance for guilt, that so strongly resists a modification through therapy.

Freud's hypotheses on man's prehistoric development would no doubt have gained wider acceptance had he detached them from his obstinate psycho-Lamarckism. Yet this connection is easily undone, and the questions taken up by Freud must be dealt with scientifically. The lack of acceptance for his hypotheses lies more probably in the fact that they paint a catastrophic picture of humanity. "Since history, as a correlate of a unitary theory that can be structured, represents evil rather than good, thought is in truth a negative element" (Horkheimer and Adorno, 1944, p. 236, n. 10). The myth of Laius, the Erlking, and Freud's prehistoric psychology all fit together.

"AND ARE YOU NOT WILLING, I SHALL USE FORCE!"

Let us leave mythology and return to the Erlking and to a psychoanalysis of the clinical relations between paranoia and homosexuality. Freud's analysis of *Memoirs of a Neurotic,* published in 1903 by Daniel Paul Schreber, president of the Saxonian senate court, concluded that the author's paranoia stemmed from a defense against his own feminine attitudes and his unconscious castration wish that he had projected onto God. Aged about 50, Schreber became firmly convinced that God (clearly endowed with attributes of his father) had resolved to emasculate him and take him as His wife to engender new persons of Schreber's spirit. The heaviest paranoid symptoms left the president of the senate, according to Freud, "when he decided to stop resisting castration and submit to the feminine role God had intended for him" (1911, p. 63). Freud continues that Schreber was then able to lead a normal life "except for one area: that he would devote a few hours each day to fostering his femininity, convinced that it would gradually progress until the goal set by God would be reached" (1923a, p. 93). Freud's famous formula on paranoia was: " 'I (a man) love him (a man).' This is reversed into: 'I do not love him—I hate him.' 'I hate him' is transformed through projection into: 'He hates (persecutes) me, which will then justify my hate for him' " (1911, p. 63).

Today we can hardly conceive of the vast progress this represented in the understanding of psychoses. Analytic research continued on the role of idealization. In the after-treatment of the Wolf Man who had developed a severe paranoia, Ruth Mack Brunswick found an unresolved idealizing transference to Freud. She analyzed the hate and the death wishes effective behind the idealization, not as a defense but as the patient's disappointment at the frustration of his passive homosexual wishes. He had felt better after a dream in which his mother had smashed all the icons in his room. Rosenfeld (1949) commented "that the dream represents the patient's recognition of his analyst's successful work, particularly the throwing out of the idealized saint image of Freud that he had made for himself" (p. 46; see also Brunswick, 1928).

In Rosenfeld's own examination of the question whether paranoia prevents homosexuality or vice versa, he concluded that paranoid fears are genetically older and systematically primary. The homosexual idealization of a good male figure denies the existence of a male persecutor. Experience shows that the even older split mother image lies behind the male persecutor, with the projection of the child contained in the persecutory part of the mother (Rosenfeld, 1949, n. 22). Melanie Klein's more precise understanding of projection as projective identification later allowed the understanding of the delusional destruction of reality by symbolic equation (Segal, 1957), as is so inevitably done in the poem. Yet how does this lead to compulsive delusional behavior? I quote Hanna Segal (1994):

> Phantasy always contains a wish to act; we all want to fulfill our dreams. But in the case of acting on delusion the wish becomes a compulsion, sometimes a compulsion which goes counter to all conscious wishes and intentions. Why this compulsion? It is, I think, due to the fact that those misperceptions arise in relation to projective identification, and that there is an unbreakable tie between the self and the object of such projections [p. 399].

The examples given by Segal to elucidate the psychotic bond through projective identification are appropriate to the concrete level of the poem: murder or death from the delusion of being murdered. She writes: "Often the wish to murder is an attempt at expelling and getting rid of the wish to kill or to die. The murderer of the 'Babes in the Wood' tried to kill himself at the age of three. Killing those other children was an attempt to externalise a part of himself that had to be annihilated, and thereby get rid of the suicidal impulse" (1994, p. 399). Correspondingly, the child in the Erlking delusionally experiences the return of his projected wishes as reality. This always happens whenever wishes come up against a No, frustration cannot be tolerated and an omnipotent faith then takes hold of a phantasized wish: the wish character disappears and the phantasized image has become delusional reality.

We can now list the various meanings of "*And are you not willing, I shall use force!*".

1. On the concrete level, this is a paranoid, delusional crime: the child must be killed since he is the victim of a projective identification, the content of which is to be destroyed. This is the psychological aspect of ideological crimes controlled by a collective delusion.
2. On the same level, because of a murder motivated by delusional love, the "beloved child" must die since he is guilty of (all) frustrations.

3. On the symbolic level, and from the point of view of fear, this is the projection of a castration wish. After the collapse of a positive homosexual attitude, the content of the projection returns with great force.
4. A realistic explanation: A mortally ill child experiences the fear of death during a nocturnal ride in his father's arms and experiences his death as mutilation by a man and as sexual penetration.

"I LOVE YOU! YOUR BEAUTIFUL SHAPE INVITES ME"

Having become aware of the condensed levels of emotional behavior expressed in the poem, we can turn our attention to the concluding question of the overall effect the poem has on us as readers and listeners. The climax undoubtedly lies in the realism of the cry *"The Erlking has hurt me,"* rendered definitive by the final statement *"In his arms, the child was dead."* Psychologically this is, as we have seen, the end of the split between good and evil and the taking back of the projective identification. The extraordinary impact of the poem is due, in my opinion, to the fact that we as listeners are made to identify with all three characters of the poem at the height of the tragedy and thus experience the realization of depressive anxiety. We have been feeling with the child all along, but empathize with him especially at this moment of the irreversible lethal act that originated from a wish. We feel the horror of the father, whose denial of internal reality has broken down so that he has become a helpless witness of his child's destruction. Yet he feels incomprehensibly guilty, if only for having refused to accept and understand the child's perceptions of fear. When we identify with the father, we know that consciously we do not want to know anything of homosexual desire and of paranoid madness. The crucial effect, however, comes from our identification with the Erlking—the least conscious, perhaps, but the most important psychologically. The consummation of this identification comes, at the latest, with *"I love you! Your beautiful shape invites me,"* since this is one of the first conscious experiences remembered by every person. And everyone has also experienced the ensuing violence and terrible consequences of the frustration of love.

During the removal of the split, the object of love-hate is attacked. Death's success inevitably leads to the shocking realization that one's own power has irrevocably destroyed the object of love. The poem reveals the accuracy of this depressive despair and presents it as the crucial task. This work of art reveals the centrality of man's depressive situation and, most astoundingly, allows an absorbing listener to purposely relive one of his or her own painful experiences by identifying with all three characters. "It is when the world within us is destroyed, when it is dead and loveless, when our loved ones are in fragments, and we ourselves in helpless despair—it is then that we must re-create our world anew, reassemble the pieces, infuse life into dead fragments, recreate life" (Segal, 1947, p. 190). The creation of the poem is evidence that this exact process had taken place in the poet's mind,[9] and its influence over two centuries proves that it is evoked over and over again in the listener's mind. The combined effect of the two works of art, Goethe's poem and Schubert's equally immortal arrangement for voice and piano, intensifies and alleviates the listener's receptive identification and his working through of the poem's ending.

If we review the analysis presented and return to the beginning of our study, the comparison drawn between Goethe's ballads of the unconscious, especially "The *Erlking*," and Kant's broader critique of cognitive ability may now seem more legitimate. Unconscious paranoid thinking based on splits and projections is a dominant power in humanity; the present and the future depend on their being acknowledged and overcome. This small poem, containing a courageous confession, is perhaps a watershed in the struggle to overcome paranoid thinking, and an astonishing aid in accepting one's own paranoid thoughts (and homosexual defenses). Such thoughts can be surmounted only by the painful acknowledging sorrow to which the poem invites us, with its astonishing power of identification.

[9]Eissler describes Goethe's life situation that formed the poem as he worked it through. Three factors seem to have concurred: the death of his father, the climax of his transference of love to Charlotte v. Stein in the sixth year of Goethe's "protoanalysis"; and his intense attachment to Charlotte's youngest son, 8-year-old Fritz, whom Goethe took into his house for several months to help him. The poem represents the overcoming of homosexual seduction through acknowledging the catastrophe in the work. It is part of his work of mourning over the loss of his father and overcoming the (incestual) transference love, nourished at this time by all three sources of infantile attachment to the father, the love for his mother and that for Cornelia, the sister he had loved so much (Eissler, 1963, p. 780f.). All this knowledge does not explain the poem. On the contrary: The poem "explains" the poet.

REFERENCES

Brunswick, R. M. (1928), Supplement to Freud's History of an infantile neurosis. *Internat. J. Psycho-Anal.*, 9.

Eissler, K. R. (1963), *Goethe. A Psychoanalytic Study*. Detroit: Wayne State University Press.

Freud, S. (1911), Psychoanalytic notes on an autobiographical account of a case of paranoia (Dementia paranoides). *Standard Edition*, 12:1–82. London: Hogarth Press, 1953.

——— (1923a), A seventeenth century demonological neurosis. *Standard Edition*, 19:67–105. London: Hogarth Press, 1953.

——— (1923b), Josef Popper-Lynkeus and the theory of dreams. *Standard Edition*, 19:261–263. London: Hogarth Press, 1953.

——— (1932), My contact with Josef Popper-Lynkeus. *Standard Edition*, 22:219–225. London: Hogarth Press, 1953.

Grinberg, L., Sor, D., & Bianchedi, E. T. de (1993), *New Introduction to the Work of Bion*. Northvale, NJ / London: Jason Aronson.

Goethe, J. W. von (1782), Erlkönig. In: *Goethes Werke*, Vols. 1–14. Hamburg: Christian Wegner V., 1952, Vol. 1, pp. 154–155.

Heinrich, K. (1993), *Arbeiten mit Ödipus: Begriff der Verdrängung in der Religionswissenschaft*. Dahlemer Vorlesungen Bd. 3. Basel; Frankfurt am Main: Stroemfeld / Roter Stern.

Herzog, J. M. (1980), Sleep disturbance and father hunger in 18- to 28-month-old boys. *The Psychoanalytic Study of the Child*, 35:219–232. New Haven: Yale University Press.

Horkheimer, M., & Adorno, Th. W. (1944), *Dialektik der Aufklärung*. Frankfurt am Main: S. Fischer, 1969.

Jones, E. (1912), *On the Nightmare* (Der Alptraum). tr. H. Sachs. Leipzig and Vienna: Franz Deuticke.

Kant, I. (1781), *The Critique of Pure Reason*, tr. N. Smith. New York: St. Martin, 1969.

——— (1783), Beantwortung der Frage: Was ist Aufklärung? In: *I. Kant, Werke in zehn Bänden*, ed. W. Weischedel, Vol. 10, pp. 53–65. Darmstadt: Wissenschaftl. Buchgesellschaft, 1968.

Nebel, G. (1964), *Sophokles, König Ödipus. Dichtung und Wirklichkeit*. Frankfurt am Main / Berlin: Ullstein.

Rosenfeld, H. A. (1949), Remarks on the relation of male homosexuality to paranoia, paranoid anxiety, and narcissism. In: *Psychotic States, A Psychoanalytical Approach*. New York: International Universities Press, 1966.

Segal, H. (1947), A psychoanalytic approach to aesthetics. In: *Delusion and Artistic Creativity. The Work of Hanna Segal*. London: Free Association Books and Maresfield Library, 1986, pp. 185–206.

——— (1957), Notes on symbol formation. *Internat. J. Psycho-Anal.*, 38:391–397.

——— (1991), *Dream, Phantasy and Art.* London-New York: Tavistock/Routledge.

——— (1994), Phantasy and reality. *Internat. J. Psycho-Anal.*, 75:395–401.

Sterren, D. van der (1974), *Ödipus.* München: Kindler.

Trunz, E. (1946), Anmerkungen des Herausgebers (Comments of the Editor of Goethe's Poems). In: *J. W. v. Goethe, Gesammelte Werke.* Hamburg: Winkler, 1952, Vol. 1, pp. 411–596.

Part IV

At the Psychopolitical Border

14.

MORAL CONFLICTS, PUBLIC OPINION, AND THE POLITICAL PROCESS

LEO RANGELL, M.D.

I will begin in the middle, so to speak, and work both ways. Living in Los Angeles, the entertainment-news center of the world, and having been a psychoanalyst for over half a century, I have followed a succession of news events and broadcasts which have captured and entranced larger public audiences than any fictional programs, through the eyes and thoughts of a psychoanalyst. Bisecting this half-century, in the 1970s, as an example, I (1980) took it upon myself, as part of my daily task to study in depth the unfolding of the public drama of President Richard Nixon (a fellow-Californian), which led eventually to his resignation. The object of the analysis was the relationship between the leader and the led, and the role of public opinion in the process.

As an entry to the subject of the irrationalities of large-group processes, I will begin with a memory and historical–political datum of almost sixty years ago I called to mind in a lecture in June, 1992. Asked to speak at the eightieth birthday of a medical school colleague, at an alumni reunion 55 years after we had both left the University of Chicago (at the Centennial celebration of the University, which happened to also be the Centennial of psychoanalysis), I recalled that after our graduation, my classmate called me as he came from Chicago through New York, where I was interning. It was 1937. He was on his way to Spain to join the Abraham Lincoln Brigade, to fight against Franco. Years later, and probably forever since then, he was not rewarded but forced on the defensive for this. He had been right too soon. Richard Nixon, and the U.S.

government before and after his Presidency, registered and kept tabs on people who were "premature antifascists." To be right too soon was wrong. George Romney, who, in 1967, as a strong Presidential candidate, came back from abroad critical of the Vietnam war, immediately lost his standing, and his political career, never to be revived. In each case, at each time, the public is the jury. Political correctness (PC), which was to play a part in each era, is nothing more than the center of public opinion at a particular time.

While psychoanalysis focuses on conflictful states in individuals, the type of irrationality I have just described is ego syntonic and culture syntonic enough to slip by uncontested. Such global rationalization—I can call it pseudoimbecility, a syndrome described by Mahler (1942) as utilized defensively to hide behind by children—is widely operative, and imperceptible in large-group life. It is this largest-group life, and in particular its handling of moral conflicts, which is the central subject of this presentation.

At the time of the celebration in 1992, the campaign was in progress for the national Presidential elections in the United States, between President George Bush and Bill Clinton. Businessman Ross Perot had also entered the contest. The country had in the recent past been subjected to a series of conflictful emotional crises, starting with the Anita Hill–Clarence Thomas confrontation over alleged sexual harassment, followed by a number of other gripping legal trials which galvanized public interest. By serendipity, the immediate thought I had when I received the invitation to speak on my friend's behalf, was synchronous with the subject which was occupying my thoughts and writing at that moment: I was involved in moral issues.

Forty million viewers were glued to their television sets during a week in October 1991, watching the Hill–Thomas hearings, without commercial breaks, from Friday night through the Senate vote on Tuesday. To understand the deep meanings of the total phenomenon, what transpired on the screen, and the numb depression which settled over the country after the verdict, would be to apply analytic insights, in a quantitative sense, more than in individual analyses throughout the world for many years.

To those watching, there were repeated references to fantasy, delusions, unconscious motives, transference, split personality. One reporter (Moran, 1991) wrote:

> It would appear to have been a situation ripe for the wisdom of a psychiatrist. . . . The subject matter that was aired on national television in October— . . . that appalled Americans but held them in thrall—was the stuff of psychological motivation, matters that Freud and his heirs have claimed as their dominion of expertise–love, sex, desire, aggression, competition, and ambition.

Yet almost no psychiatric or psychoanalytic opinion was in evidence. Official psychiatry, which had indeed been turned to by several Senators, to see if they had any opinion or could "shed any light on the confusion," expressed an almost exclusive concern for protecting the field of psychiatry from misuse, stressing their strong opposition to "armchair diagnoses" of public figures. This proper and necessary caution stemmed from the protests that arose both inside and outside psychiatry during the 1964 national elections, against unprofessional opinions rendered by psychiatrists about the mental health of the then-Presidential candidate Barry Goldwater. The ethics code of the American Psychiatric Association was cited against clinical assessments without having conducted psychiatric examinations and having obtained authorization for such reports.

Psychoanalytic knowledge, to me, has always been applicable to man in all his pursuits. Psychoanalysts readily study and interpret films, novels, works of art, historical figures, but demur from applying psychoanalytic understanding to, and conversely extracting psychoanalytic knowledge from, the type of human dramas to which our country has been repetitively exposed. With the new technology being continually expanded, we now watch Congressional Committees in session, and are present in the courtroom in the midst of high drama. As a more immediate participant, the citizen in this democracy, his or her conflicts and responsibilities, become increasingly an issue to understand and address.

The riveting few days to which this country was exposed that October 1992 was not without precedent or a solitary event, but fell into line in what I regard as a connected series of historical times. In the fifties, there were the McCarthy years, with the moral pall over the country; in the 1960s the divisive Vietnam War, when the credibility of our Government reached a new low; in the 1970s, the famous, and infamous Watergate; in the 1980s came Iran-Contra, with again an equal degree of injury to the trust engendered in the top levels of our Government; in the 1990s, the Hill–Thomas "affair" (I say "affair" advisedly), with its own specific challenge and trauma.

In all of these experiences, the audience comprised no less than the nation. The type of political process introduced in each instance presents, if one would study the total phenomenon, a three- or four-tiered structure. There is an issue, the behavior in question, the main protagonist(s), their supporting casts, equally under scrutiny and public concern, and in the invisible background the people as the ultimate judge. To be acknowledged as at least potentially involved, in the preconscious of the proceedings, to be brought into public awareness to different degrees in the different incidents, is to be no less than the President of the United States.

In each of the experiences cited, the character of the leader at the tip of the pyramid was by no means for me the main subject of psychological interest. My study of Watergate was not a psychobiography of Nixon. When asked by reporters whether I had interviewed Nixon, I replied that if I had, I could not write about it, since the material would have been confidential. The data for my conclusions were all in the public domain. A main thrust was why and how the available leads and evidence were selectively denied, screened, or suppressed (i.e., covered up) by the general public, and the necessary conclusions not drawn. The center of gravity in each historical instance, which gave each pyramid its weight and stability, was not at the top but lower down toward the base. The psychoanalytic issues of most significant interest to me were the relations between leaders and led, the characteristics at the top levels of power, and the links between them as a composite and the broad base of the people.

In each of these national trials, which shattered the nation within the remembered lifetimes of many alive today, the public was subjected to an experience of similar affective quality, uncertainty of data, mounting negative "evidence," high moral stakes, and the mental state of the nation in the balance. In each case, the external resultant was an aggregate of anxiety, depression, guilt, and shame, with disgust not far behind. Clinically, all such composite affective states have unconscious as well as conscious roots. This can be a lead as to what is operative here too. Conspicuously absent, or at least felt to be powerless, was outrage; perhaps largely "in-rage" as well. For the most part, anger, rage, the inner process toward spontaneous reactions, were widely repressed, or suppressed.

To briefly comment on these events individually: My main analytic immersion in this aspect of psychopathology was in "The Watergate," which I studied as my extra patient for eight years. If this is surprising, since Nixon's official troubles covered only two years, *The Mind of Watergate* (1980) was not limited to Richard Nixon, or to the break-in into the Democratic National headquarters. The subject preceded the office crime and continued after Nixon's resignation. The analysis continued through Gerald Ford's term as President, his pardon of Nixon, and the election of Jimmy Carter, which was also a sequel and derivative of "the Watergate." Gerald Ford was the first and only President in our history appointed by one individual, a privilege reserved for the only President who was about to leave the office in disgrace.

To cite a few sample findings and conclusions from this study, from which we may have hunches or gains to extrapolate to the others. A datum: Of the forty "men under Nixon," thirty-nine went along with what they knew was wrong. The one who desisted and resigned from the group left because his wife told him she would divorce him if he stayed on! (His name is the most forgotten among the roster of participants; it is Hugh Sloan Jr.) I postulated that under similar circumstances the same ratio might well apply in general human enterprises, in business and corporate life, in academia, in science, and in psychoanalytic group life as well. In conflicts between expediency and moral principles, it is only a question of how high the stakes are before the latter are overcome.

For twenty-five years before Nixon's first election as President, his nickname in public life had been "Tricky Dick." Nixon was elected for his second term by the second largest landslide in American history five months after the Watergate break-in, three months after this was reported in the *Washington Post* as having been traced to the White House. From a close examination of the evolving investigation, during the two years from the triggering incident of the Watergate break-in to the resignation of the President, the responding public consistently lagged far behind the evidence available. I formulated a mechanism of "identification with the corrupt," to be added to Anna Freud's (1936) "identification with the aggressor," and postulated an unconscious bond of the people to Nixon based on the universal wish to join in the ability to overcome the superego without guilt. From a multitude of observations and complex findings, I concluded that the people were in collusion with Nixon in covering up the facts, and preventing their recognition and absorption as long as possible. Open acknowledgment and opposition came reluctantly only after the "smoking gun." Without it, which Nixon himself, with almost Dostoevskian overtones, provided, he would never have been in serious trouble.

Among a number of theoretical formulations which derived from this study, "the syndrome of the compromise of integrity" is on a par with neuroses in human affairs. While conflicts between the id and the ego result in neuroses, from compromises of the id, conflicts between the ego and superego result as routinely in compromises of integrity, at the expense of the superego. Ego–superego conflicts are as ubiquitous as id–ego conflicts, as decisive in determining character and external behavior. Ambition, power, and opportunism, which I designated as "the three horsemen of the syndrome of the compromise of integrity," are sought and encouraged in normal child development and are desired in the course of life, but any of these can become hypertrophied to the point of becoming malignant. John Dean (1976) wrote confessionally of his *Blind Ambition*. "Narcissism is the enemy of integrity" (Rangell, 1976, 1980). There are borderline states between neuroses and compromises of integrity, clinically and in life, as much as there are between neurosis and psychosis. There are people who are sick, and those who are bad, and some who are on the border between the two. Struck by the same phenomena, Karl Menninger (1978) wrote on "Whatever Became of Sin?"

Looking back at earlier history, the McCarthy era was our last national shame before the Watergate. The two were connected by Nixon, who paired with Senator Joseph McCarthy, and did for the House Un-American Activities Committee what McCarthy did with his Senate Investigatory Committee. I was already a psychoanalyst during the McCarthy hearings in the 1950s, and listened as such. I recognized then that I was seeing psychopathology not less in degree or scope or importance than in my clinical work. The oppressive McCarthy period held sway as long and tenaciously as it did only because it was held up and kept intact from above and below. Although Eisenhower (and Truman before him) as President personally escaped the odium which followed, he never exerted his position to disempower the offensive Senator from Wisconsin, but gave full rein to his appointed Secretary of State, John Foster Dulles, who fanned and augmented the noxious atmosphere. At the same time, from the base below, the people for their part provided enough of the receptive paranoia necessary to keep the malignant fumes alive. The words of Edward R. Murrow still ring out, quoting Cassius, "The fault, dear Brutus, is not in our stars but in ourselves." That the people suffered from an internal conflict, however, and the ambivalence within the average individual and the country as a whole, was evidenced by the relief at the final victory associated with the person of Attorney Joseph Welch. It was only when the people had had enough that they were receptive to his words, which were then able to turn the tide, "Let us not assassinate this lad further, Senator. You have done enough. Have you no sense of decency, Sir, at long last? Have you left no sense of decency? . . . If there is a God in heaven, it will do neither you nor your cause any good" (Matusow, 1970, pp. 95–96).

McCarthy in the 1950s, Vietnam and Watergate in the 1960s and 1970s, in the 1980s the secret arms deal to Iran, accosted the ears and eyes of the again-stunned public. There were the same compelling television dramas, their national leaders again tainted and under the lights. "Did they or didn't they take part . . . how much did Reagan know"? Although the accusation in this case was much more serious than that against Nixon, in the area of treason rather than a break-in and robbery, in the face of testimony and revelations which were generally perceived as incriminating, only staff members were exposed and questioned, and relatively lightly treated. The President in each case was protected. No smoking gun was made available here, nor was one sought. In the case of Nixon, this tumbled into view by the most casual revelation, and was acknowledged only when it could no longer be denied.

Oliver North, who, after stonewalling for a long time, confessed in his own self-aggrandizing way, was lionized. "Ollie for President" placards, not calls for punishment, appeared in profusion on the television screen. Identification was with charisma, power, guts, and derring-do, and a disdain for rules and the superego in life. North had contradicted National Security Advisor John Poindexter, Robert MacFarlane had said that the information was known up to the top, and had made a suicidal attempt to escape from his conflicts. North, in a later book, claimed that Reagan and Bush both knew, contradicting his own previous testimony. Another stream of claims and testimony accused Reagan of an even more evil act, the "October surprise," conspiring with the Iranian captors to hold back the liberation of the hostages until minutes after the Reagan inauguration. This, if true, is more deeply offensive to the American people, a more venal violation of human rights, than the criticisms of Carter by Reagan about attitudes toward the hostages, which cost Carter a second term of the Presidency. But nothing could dislodge Reagan, or come between his heroic image and his admiring public. Impervious to emerging facts and reality, Reagan, according to general opinion, could be elected again. Unconscious identification with the hero, still an idol and idealized paternal image, easily maintained his appeal over unwelcome knowledge.

Analysts derive theory from their observations, which help not only toward understanding but toward making further observations. Man's inner life is a balance of three forces interacting and adjusting to each other. There are instincts at one pole, ethical guidelines at the other, and the rational ego between the two determining the outcomes, inner feelings, and outer actions. In intimate and personal lives, the instincts press and need to be dealt with on a routine basis by the person's ego seeking mastery and solutions. On the wider social scale, the more distant and anonymous and less immediately personal it is, the more the balance is shifted to an active interplay between ego, or self, and conscience. On the sociocultural and political scene which we are examining, the ego–superego dyad has center stage.

When the public is judging Nixon, or forging an attitude toward a paranoid culture one is living in and surrounded by, as during the McCarthy era, or the Cold War in the 1950s, or Vietnam of the 1960s, the inner balance within the depth of each individual, from whom allegiance is requested under some unspoken threat, is a conflict between self-interests and moral conscience. The same holds in less oppressive times, when the conflict engendered by outer events touches on the same inner duality, although with a less immediate feeling of external pressure. Confronted by a troublesome revelation against a trusted leader, a moral judgment to be made about the actions or motivations of an admired paternal figure, the same inner forces are stirred and stimulated, and the same necessity to choose between the self and what is right. Was Reagan convincingly incriminated by the Contra stain, or could we in good conscience let things lie and continue our trust? The same conflict between expediency and morality, which exerted the inner pressure on "the men under Nixon," and in the larger jury throughout the country as well, presses all involved in this series of conflicts, to different leaders at different times, with the same predictable results. Each individual will serve the self and the conscience in different proportions, and differently in the same individual at different times. The determining ingredients on each side of the scales are in a state of delicate balance.

Although at the distant social level, the full force of instincts is sublimated and less in evidence, the basic instincts, of sex and aggression, are not absent or dead but latent and in check. The "sexiness" of a candidate is not without its unconscious effects. As in a dream, or unusual event in life, primitive forces await an opportunity to emerge and be felt. It is no accident that a film with the straight title, *Basic Instinct,* although negatively reviewed, is high at the box office. The opening scene, of a woman thrusting an ice pick into the chest of her lover at the moment of orgasm, assures its success.

The Hill–Thomas television show in the Fall of 1991 was the next public event to command 40 or 50 million viewers. This one had all the ingredients: sex, aggression, gender, power, accusation, denial, and the explosive political issues of abortion and race, all subtle and refined, at a high intellectual level, the Supreme Court, the President, lying and the truth.

Again I saw a pyramid of participants. In this one, just under the tip is Clarence Thomas, above him President Bush, who nominated him, and alongside Thomas, Anita Hill. Some distance down at a broader horizontal is the Senate Judiciary Committee—fourteen Senators. At the base again is the American people. My view is that it is the latter that gives the structure its stability and character. The people are watching the Committee, judging the principals, and the principles, in their behalf. In judging the performance of their elected representatives, the people are indirectly judging themselves. In this case, one of the two principals is to be believed, the other deemed to lie. That both can be truthful, that the male had suggested a sexual closeness and the female declined, which would not disqualify the aspirant for the judgeship, was ruled out by Thomas himself, when he stated that he had made no overtures whatever to Ms. Hill, and that if what she said was true, he would not qualify to be a Supreme Court Justice.

The moral scores of this Judiciary Committee, in the test conducted before the eyes of the electorate, were no more inspiring of confidence or admiration than those of any of the prior public servants under Eisenhower, Nixon, Reagan, and now under Bush. A lie was already built in at the top, when Bush said he had nominated the most qualified person for the job, rather than a minority person, who held the views he wanted, and who was also qualified for the position, for political reasons to his advantage. I said that an analyst might have shed some light on what took place. Extrapolating from the methods and goals of the psychoanalyst, whose efforts and credo are also directed toward exposing hidden and obscured and defended truths, it is not always the demonstrated historical fact upon which conviction rests, but the relentless incorruptibility of the process of the approach. Of highest priority is the analysis of distorting impediments, both in the subject and the investigator. Countertransference in an analyst, or bias in a judge, mild and checked, is compatible with satisfactory performance, but if frequent and severe, and undiagnosed and unchecked, renders the process and the outcome dubious.

Without any of these guidelines being articulated, the viewing audience was witness to a miscarriage of justice in what was technically a judicial process. What disappointed the national courtroom was not the outcome but precisely the process. The same outcome, come to by an honest and credible investigatory process would have been readily accepted, would even have made many people happy. Instead, the audience witnessed a cynical deviation from their task by individual Senators, and by the judicial body as a whole. The country watched with increasing unease as Senators Spector, Hatch, and Simpson in particular abrogated their investigatory roles for prosecutorial ones, became advocates (for Thomas) rather than fact-finders, and as the Committee allowed evidence and questioned witnesses with striking asymmetry (also in Thomas' favor).

The miscarriage was bipartisan; the Democrats, for their part, were pathologically passive, reminiscent of the similar fatal behavior of their national candidate Michael Dukakis three years before. Five out of the seven Democrats on the Committee had themselves been involved as defendants against ethical charges, which many felt played a part in silencing their voices in the present hearings. One of these, Chairman Joseph Biden, seemed to bend over strongly to make it easier for the hostile (to Anita Hill) Senators. He also ruled that a lie by Thomas revealed in this procedure about testimony by Thomas at prior hearings could not serve as evidence in the present phase. Thomas had said in the earlier phase that he had never discussed abortion with anyone; in the present hearing, Hill spoke of discussions with Thomas on the subject. An angry refusal by Thomas to answer questions, declaring, with strong emotion, that "God will be my judge," was met by one friendly Senator telling Thomas how proud he was of him for taking that position. The Committee accepted his refusal with no pursuit of the crucial question. The Committee did not seem to be impartially and objectively directed toward acquiring the necessary data.

An analyst might also have pointed out that the emphasis given to "who leaked (the information about Anita Hill?)" was a displacement, which is a defense mechanism in individual dynamics, to keep something else hidden and repressed. The country as a whole seemed to go along with this deflected interest, to have a respite from the embarrassing and seemingly insoluble spectacle before their eyes. A number of Senators defended themselves, saying it was not they who leaked, instead of objecting to this sidetracking of the issue. Nina Totenberg, a reporter for National Public Radio, had to face a charge, before the issue dissolved and disappeared. The shift was so patent as to be more like a comedy maneuver.

Following the outcome, the affective result was the same depression as in the connected series in the 1950s, 1960s and 1970s. The reasons given for the emotional pall were contradictory, in keeping with the unconscious repression behind them. The public, as individuals, were split. Most people believed Hill, yet were relieved to see Thomas approved. Blacks and women were part of this trend. The people also were glad it was over. There was no protest about another witness, Angela Wright, having been denied a hearing before the Committee, who was to be a second accusor of Thomas corroborating Hill's claims. The vote in the Committee was 7–7. The confirmatory vote in the full Senate the following week was 52–48. With all the doubts, the public leaned toward accepting Thomas. The demoralization of the national viewing audience followed previously established lines. They could not face their composite agreement, and their complicity in the result, even in the face of their shame in the method.

The fifty-fifty division in this and other such issues mirrors the split within each individual psyche between self-interests and moral restraints. As passive observers of the repetitive dramas around them in life, unfolding live on their television screens, people in their inner minds veer from left to right and back, like a needle on an instrument panel, toward serving their self-interests, or leaning toward morals, discipline, and self-denial. The pointer shifts, sometimes abruptly, more often slowly, with each statement, mood, or new revelation in the plot which flits across the screen. But just as the outer split reflects the inner division, the internal balance within the individual also brings about the two major competing groups in the external political world. Most elections, and other political disputes of the populace, veer around the fifty-fifty mark. Most outcomes, of elections or stands on divisive public issues, vary between 60 and 40 percent. It is the middle band, moving this way or that, which spells the difference in each case.

Following Hill-Thomas, other national dramas have come forth in quick succession, riveting the audience, as tests of the public's judgment and the rationality of its reactions. In viewing further live events, the people have been repeatedly immersed in a series of compelling court spectacles more dramatic than any fictional counterparts. These dealt with the raw instincts, sexual and aggressive, not more subtle derivative compromise formations. I am referring to two rape cases, a nationally televised police beating, an urban riot, and before this paper is finished, a brutal murder, with a legendary sports hero the only suspect. The dramatis personae of all of these are not unknowns but celebrities, involving no less than the Kennedy family, the world heavyweight boxing champion, the second city in the United States aflame, and the greatest football player of our times being indicted for a bloody carnage. Entertainment, sports, politics, and crime fuse into one continuous public product.

In two rape cases, the public, as did the courtroom jury, listened and were to judge, two versions, by Senator Edward Kennedy's nephew William Kennedy Smith and boxing champion Mike Tyson, of sexual intercourse claimed to be rape. "Did she, or did she not want to, did she assent, did he force it?" In considerations bordering on voyeurism and vicarious participation, in the case of Smith, "did she move her hips upwards or away, did she lie down on the sand a second time, did she remove her panties in the car?" In judging the case of Tyson and his accusor, "What were her wishes or expectations when she went to his hotel room at 2 A.M., on a first date, arranged that very night? Did the Champ use force?" Smith went free, Tyson to jail. It is questionable whether it was differences in evidence entirely which made for the differences in outcome. I would bring up for consideration the possibility that had the sequence of the two trials been reversed, so might have been the verdicts. Subjective factors intrude, may even be decisive. Political considerations, here the feminist issue, aroused shortly before in the Hill–Thomas period, play a part. A conviction may have been necessary after an acquittal. Public opinion and expectations enter the courtroom. These were different in the second trial after the first. To rule against the female victim twice in succession was not likely, even dangerous.

The Rodney King experience made its points too. The burning of Los Angeles, looking like Armageddon, stemmed from two levels of irrationalities, one by the jury, the other by the mob. With regard to the first, the question needs analysis of the unconscious determinants, of how the six men and six women came to their conclusions in the face of the "evidence," seen first hand by millions of viewers who came to the opposite conclusion. The factors of group psychology will enter, of the hierarchy and layering of leadership, power, influence, charisma, contagion, suggestibility, operative as the group of twelve interacted during their secret deliberations.

After the verdict absolving the police officers in the King case came the outburst, an irrational response to an offensive stimulus. Among the reasons, one was normal outrage to an unjust action. But this was combined with long-latent repressed anger. Here the aggressive impulse, not the sexual, gained direct expression, in the individual and the mass. Many commented that large aspects of the wild orgy had little to do with Rodney King. As a dream taps the latent unconscious, the unbridled escapade, of burning and looting and getting "Whitey," felt to have been given justification by an insult experienced widely in common, was allowed to give expression to long frustrated anger and wishes born of chronic deprivation. An opposite reaction inevitably sets in later, the need for the reestablishment of controls. Shortly afterwards, a Samoan was killed by police in the same city. This time, community group leaders succeeded in keeping the reaction restrained. A call for law and order has been a dominant theme in recent history and remains strong. One hopes a repetition of the cycle will be prevented. At the second King trial, the signals from the public are paid close attention. The more moderate verdict could not have been otherwise. What with a change of Police Chief in between, a further triggering of violence does not occur.

History changes and stays the same, in accordance with the French formula, and from deep psychological trends. The repetition compulsion, in an individual life, and in the larger events I have recounted in our group history, needs no underscoring to know its relentlessly recurring effects. Yet beneficial and adaptive changes also do take place, in the collective as in the individual. Unconscious insights, besides conscious learning, goes on automatically. The Holocaust, perhaps, cannot happen again. Nor a quiet Gulf of Tonkin, and its sequel the Vietnam War. Although there was a Kuwait and the Gulf War in response to the Iraqi invasion, that one had to be short. President Bush said Saddam Hussein, President of Iraq, was Hitler, but he let him go. Bush was for being kind and gentle in his first campaign, and revived that theme in his second run. Lee Atwater apologized on his deathbed for his treatment of Michael Dukakis, the Willie Horton ads during the presidential campaign. Ted Kennedy made a "mea culpa" speech in Boston about his political and personal life. Senator Alan Simpson of Wyoming, two weeks after the Hill–Thomas hearings, at a GOP fund-raiser in Cheyenne, Wyoming, appeasing the women he may have offended, rued what he had said about Hill. "I have been . . . a bit too cocky, arrogant, yeah, too smart. . . ." Later in 1994, Oliver North, confessor of lying and perjury, was to be nominated, though not elected to the Senate from Virginia.

Repetitions and changes alternate repetitiously. As history has two opposite thrusts, people forget, but also remember. If the Hill–Thomas episode looked quiet in its immediate aftermath, one has but to think of a few events since then: Carol Moseley Braun defeated Senator Alan Dixon of Illinois in the 1992 primary (Dixon had voted for Thomas against Anita Hill). In Pennsylvania, Lynn Yeakel, a political unknown, running only on her anger at Senator Arlen Spector, won the Democratic primary to oppose him in the Senate race. Spector, concerned, said one issue does not determine an election. Two women won the primary nominations for the Senate in California, for the first time. One of them, Congresswoman Barbara Boxer, had led a march to the Senate against the Thomas verdict. Her having had some House checks bounce did not stand in her way. A patient, in her eighties, says of one of the best friends of hers and her husband's, that she does not think he can ever look her in the eye, because he "named names" before the House Un-American Activities Committee in the 1950s! She is also going to vote against the son of a close friend, a liberal running for office this time on a law and order platform.

Every November, and especially every four years, the people have their say on Election Day, when they become officially the public jury. The inner balance within each individual, always labile and never fixed, can be influenced toward one side or the other, either to protect one's ego and self-interests, even if straining morals, or to stress ethics and the superego, even if not to one's best interests. The two oscillate, which is what keeps the two-party system in place. It is not that each party represents an opposite pole, of self-interests versus social good, but that each stands for a different combination and ratio of the two ingredients. This proportion varies at different times of history. The Republicans were once the party for change, the Southern Democrats against it. This has changed, and continues to change.

The citizen, and the aggregate of citizens, do the judging and deciding. The candidates play hard to this receiver and decider, and learn from them each time what their fates will be. The mood, traits, and mental state of the people are the decisive base. Does the voter respond to charisma or character? Which is the best asset for the President? Is Clinton as bad a character as he has been painted to be in the 1992 Presidential campaign? How much does an affair count? Did he lie about it? What does not having wanted to be in the Vietnam War mean? How much does some trying of marijuana as a young man in the 1960s reflect on his quest for the Presidency? Did President Bush lie about foreign affairs in his campaign? Are the questions about him, his past buildup of Noriega, or Iraq, of the same or greater quality of concern than those directed against Clinton? Are his promises to be believed? The aim in these questions is judgment by the rational ego.

How much of a role do issues play? Ross Perot entered the fray unknown and was promptly favored by one-third of the voters, for one asset, about $3 billion, self-made. Other things about him are now being looked for, but this is what was known at the beginning and was enough. If he can take care of himself, he can take care of us. Morality, family values, are added later. In an interview on the "Today" show, Perot touched the self-preservation nerve of the people quite well. He does not talk, he executes, he stated. "I ask my people not to talk but to execute, execute, execute, deliver, deliver, deliver." I was interested in and reverberated to this; I have written (1986) of "the executive functions of the ego," stressing the importance of the unconscious moments of decision and action. I have felt, as many have criticized, that psychoanalysis does often fall into the trap of standing still at the thinking and feeling phases, at the brink of, and at the expense of doing, acting, i.e., undoing the effects of the irrational forces uncovered. But I failed to hear Perot say what he would execute. He still veered away from the pointed questions to that effect. The intermediate stages prior to action are indispensible, the judging, discriminating, deciding, planning phases, i.e., having an opinion, preliminary to action. The latter alone, without the former, are unreliable, can be worrisome, even dangerous. Perot also said he deals not with personalities but with issues. Here he grasps a good, strong point, but this is so far what he says, not does. The public is waiting; this is still to come. His declarations on issues, of course, will alter his followership; he will lose some, and gain some. But this is desirable, and necessary, for rational action. Many, however, themselves amorphous or even ambivalent on issues, do in fact prefer to keep these aspects vague or undeclared, and will react positively to the promise of action, without caring too much at this phase which actions will be executed.

The final vote is pressed into the ballot by each individual, as the pointer within comes to rest on the mental scale between his deep self-interests and moral concern for others, how uniquely in each case the two are put together. The middle ground which swings and determines elections is not the middle class, or the "independent" voters between the two parties, but the point in the middle within the mind of each individual. This is measured against what each candidate comes to represent by his image, and how close it comes to what the individual voter regards as his own inner view and value. The test for the candidate is how he combines economic gain with ethics, management with morality. Republican and Democrat, "conservative"and "liberal" do not, after time, capsulize these complex and variable inner stances. A creative combination of self-protection and compassion for others, delivered with a sincerity which is believed and trusted, can be inspiring. This, however, does not in itself insure election.

November 1992, the election, following the build-up described having sensitized the electorate on many provocative psychological fronts: Bush was denied a second term. Clinton, whose package is deemed to have had a better combination of ego interests and social good, was given the big opportunity. Boxer and Feinstein both won in California (1992 was deemed "the year of the woman"). Braun was elected in Illinois, a woman, a black, a first on two counts! But Spector, from whom an apology of sorts was exacted during the campaign, defeated Yeakel, and was returned to the Senate. It is certain that at least his manner will change. Public events have reached the jury and affected this election.

While psychoanalysis has been called "the impossible profession," I have added (1974, 1980) to its already impossible task of curing neuroses a goal, or at least an interest, in moral conflicts, not making its task any easier. Related are such character traits as integrity, sincerity, cynicism, hypocrisy. The image of sincerity may be sought and attained, without the substance; one of Nixon's strengths was to look sincere, which is practiced by many who seek office. In the study of values, I would include the analysis of the ego trait of courage, the capacity to proceed to action in the face of anxiety and the anticipation of lack of approval. The Kennedy Foundation now bestows a medal, after "Profiles in Courage," to a political figure who takes a position which is right but unpopular. The 1992 award went to Governor Lowell Weiker, of Connecticut, who raised taxes, to the accompaniment of protests and boos! Those who do this, by definition, have tough going. Paul Tsongas, whom *The New Yorker* wrote could not be insincere, did not last long in the 1992 presidential race. He was much praised, by both parties, after he left the race. The great Chicagoan, Adlai Stevenson, who epitomized the straight and sincere, as well as eloquent, ran for the presidency twice, and was defeated each time.

At the time of the lecture I referred to at the beginning of the chapter, psychoanalysis was one hundred years old, as was the University of Chicago. This Centennial celebration coincides with "the Century of Freud." It was not far from the University, in Hyde Park, in 1924 (not very long before I first came there; I did not realize then that I would come to have such a direct interest in what took place), that the famous Leopold and Loeb case, in which Clarence Darrow introduced unconscious motives into a murder trial, established a precedent in human understanding and the legal system which strongly influenced the rest of this century. As a bit of history, Freud received two invitations, from Col. McCormick and William Randolph Hearst, to come to Chicago at any sum he named to "psychoanalyze" both murderers and testify in their behalf. When Freud declined for reasons of health and that he could not offer an opinion without a personal examination, according to Freud's biographer, Ernest Jones (1953–1957), Hearst offered to charter a special liner to transport him to the United States.

I believe today that the advance made in that historic legal argument was incomplete and subject to misuse. The demonstration of unconscious motives, which underlie every act, elucidates the nature and composition of responsibility but does not remove it. This subsequently gray and divisive area of morality, guilt and jurisprudence led to an inconsistency over the years which has increasingly made a mockery of justice. My own researches and writings over decades have led in the opposite direction, toward understanding and fostering an increase rather than decrease of individual responsibility. Not only passive but active mental processes originate in the unconscious. In 1991, this country celebrated the two hundredth anniversary of the Bill of Rights. With the freedom of the individual which this guaranteed came increased responsibility. Increased freedom gained socially and politically, and internal autonomy won psychologically, by analysis or in life, bring with them a commensurate increase in responsibility and accountability.

No less than justice and democracy are at stake in these considerations, the jury system in one, and government by the people in the other. In the types of group processes I have been describing, the challenge to the individual at all levels of responsibility is the ability to retain individual judgment within the surround of the group. This applies to small or large groups, the push of the media, the force of authority, the atmosphere of the surrounding culture of the times. This is of course the utopian view of democracy, but is not automatically its attainment. It applies and is tested at every level of activity of the citizen of a democracy, from his expression of opinions in conversation with his peers, to jury duty, to his voting for representatives who will govern in his behalf. But mainly the test is to have one's own opinion in the midst of group thought.

Another and ultimate group is the group of nine who constitute the Supreme judges of what is right and wrong for all of us in this land. That is why the appointments to the Supreme Court command such compelling interest. Each of these, almost by definition and requirements for the position, is an individual who thinks for himself, while open to influence by the others. Are each of them actually chosen and granted this chair for precisely these traits, or for having opinions and subjective predilections (biases) in the direction wished for by those who appoint and / or confirm them? In the end, this ultimate group sits where it is because the people elected the Senators, who confirm the choices of the President, elected by the people. The base is the citizen. It is his or hers to act, and direct. To the extent that this has become only theory, not practical or possible, democracy has become warped. Ideal, even satisfactory, performance of this routine task, or duty, is beset by impediments from within and without. To many, this has led to a feeling of democracy in crisis.

April 22, 1994: Richard Nixon died of a stroke at the age of 81. At the Memorial service at the Nixon Library in Yorba Linda, California, the uniquely history-making former President was eulogized and praised as he had never been in life. The tone was somber, tearful, and respectful. President Clinton and all four living ex-Presidents were in attendance, constituting a photomontage of American history rarely seen. Among those who spoke, Senator Robert Dole broke into tears, while former Secretary of State Henry Kissinger described Nixon's accomplishments to be "as much moral as political." Spiro Agnew, who was forced to resign as Nixon's Vice President, came for the occasion, declared Nixon "the greatest statesman of our time." In what might have been the kindest reconciliation of all, George McGovern, into whose Democratic campaign offices at the Watergate complex the fateful break-in had occurred, came to pay his respects. To a question by a reporter, he stated that he had had differences with Nixon, but that the two had made peace, and he "really had the feeling that an old friend had left the scene."

In a letter to Ernest Jones, during the course of a highly irregular and critical relationship, Freud (Paskauskas, 1993) writes Jones that they should be satisfied with each other in spite of their disagreements, that "only speechmakers at funerals deny such traces of reality" (p. 607).

But the subject never dies, although the facts may never be fully known. Two months later, an op-ed article in the *New York Times* (Emery, 1994) brings evidence, though still circumstantial, from BBC interviews, newly released tapes at the National Archives in Washington, and files and notes of the late H. R. Haldeman (Nixon's chief of staff), that implicate Nixon for the first time in complicity with intelligence operations that led to the Watergate 2½ months before the break-in, and the start of the cover-up immediately after the event.

June, 1994: This paper does not wish to be closed. Having brought it up to date with additions and revisions since the original presentation two years ago, I was about to close when another explosive event has burst into the news which dwarfs all others in public and media attention, the O. J. Simpson murder case. The ex-wife of perhaps the most celebrated athlete of our age, and a male friend, are found brutally murdered, their necks slashed, their bodies multiply stabbed. O. J. Simpson, a public image of heroism, a figure of awe and worship, is at first a mourning ex-husband but quickly becomes the suspect. For three or four days, he appears on television at the funeral and with his children, an object of national sympathy, perhaps comparable to, if not more so than to Jackie Kennedy. It is at the same time naggingly marred by evidence being gathered and reported, blood at his home, in his car, and on his clothes, a quick trip to Chicago that night, and a national wondering amd anxiety about what was to follow.

His celebrity status quickly bears results. After he is named as the only suspect, and while being "taken" by the police, conferences are held, between defense, prosecutors, and detectives, during which O. J. is able to leave the premises and to escape into the city in his car. Could any other suspect have been allowed to escape thus? The new, respected Chief of Police comes on the air to explain and defend the lapse. There follows a "chase," which turns into an escort, by a squad of police cars, through the Friday night traffic of the freeways of Los Angeles (L.A. again! Of course, the center of entertainment), watched by the entire country, some say the world. O. J. is in control of the procession as he holds a gun to his head. No crime, or sports event, or court coverage, has ever equaled this in dramatic interest, one commentator says "in the history of the Republic." No fiction can match it. This is live, and involves a legendary superhero, pursued for murder. Ninety-five million people watched the first day; one out of every four television sets were turned on.

O. J. is now in jail, the decisions are in the balance, the parameters of possibilities span between being freed and the death penalty. The Grand Jury has been dismissed, unable to cope with the criticisms and contradictions at this level. The Preliminary Hearing which replaced it has been watched by a far greater number than any of the previous supertrials before it. While the instruments of justice are in official motion, the court of public opinion is in the background, unspoken, and is the unconscious key. Two years ago, the same defendant was in court when his wife was found badly beaten, hiding in the bushes, afraid he would kill her. He characterized their problems then as family spats, "no big deal."

He was sentenced to probation, community service, and therapy. The latter lasted a few months, became telephone therapy when Simpson moved out of the city to perform his occupation, and he discontinued because he said there was nothing more to talk about. "How long could I say the same thing?" The judge then, who is now under criticism, comes on the air, and states, in self-defense, that he ruled as he did because that is what the prosecution wanted, he "was not star-struck."

The public then was behind the prosecutors; the outcome was dictated by the perceived public wish. The stakes have been raised; the case is now murder. The question is what that wish is now, and what are its directions, or changes. During the freeway chase, crowds of people were excited, motivated, and creative enough to stand on overpasses, and along the freeway, in time to cheer the caravan on; "Go, O. J., go," was the chant. But as the case proceeds and the evidence mounts, the public is divided. The conflict between hero worship and what is right is not a simple one, and will not disappear. It will in fact go both ways. As Simpson's plight becomes worse, he elicits both increased sympathy and the wish for justice. It is a close balance between fame, money, glamour and unconscious identification, versus the progression of objective evidence.

It is not automatic which will be stronger. Psychoanalysis can understand more than it can influence.

REFERENCES

Dean, J. (1976), *Blind Ambition*. New York: Simon & Schuster.

Emery, F. (1994), Watergate—Worse than you thought. *New York Times*, June 19: Section 4, p. 7.

Freud, A. (1936), *The Ego and the Mechanisms of Defense*. New York: International Universities Press, 1946.

Jones, E. (1953–1957), *The Life and Work of Sigmund Freud*, vols. 1 & 2. New York: Basic Books.

Mahler, M. S. (1942), Pseudoimbecility. *Psychoanal. Quart.*, 11:149–164.

Matusow, A. J., Ed. (1970), *Joseph R. McCarthy. Great Lives Observed*. Englewood Cliffs, NJ: Prentice-Hall.

Menninger, K. A. (1978), *Whatever Became of Sin*? New York: Bantam.

Moran, P. (1991), *Psychiatric News*. Washington, DC: American Psychiatric Press.

Paskauskas, R. A., Ed. (1993), *The Complete Correspondence of Sigmund Freud and Ernest Jones, 1908–1939*. Cambridge, MA: Harvard University Press.

Rangell, L. (1974), A psychoanalytic perspective leading currently to the syndrome of the compromise of integrity. *Internat. J. Psycho-Anal.*, 55:3–12.

——— (1976), Lessons from Watergate: A derivative for psychoanalysis. *Psychoanal. Quart.*, 45:37–61.

——— (1980), *The Mind of Watergate. An Exploration of the Compromise of Integrity*. New York: W. W. Norton.

——— (1986), The executive functions of the ego. An extension of the concept of ego autonomy. *The Psychoanalytic Study of the Child*, 41:1–37. New Haven: Yale University Press.

——— (1992), The Inaugural Aaron Hilkevitch Lecture, presented at The University of Chicago Centennial, Chicago, IL, June 11.

15.

THE LEADER AND THE LED—THEIR MUTUAL NEEDS

RONNIE SOLAN, Ph.D.

Professor Moses has amply written about leadership issues related to the psychology of politics. In the present paper I intend to interlace conceptually some of Moses' thoughts with my own, thus creating an encounter (a contexture, as we would say in French) of ideas encompassing both common denominators and divergences. I shall, thereby, present Moses' views and my own perspective on them and on the issues they relate to in four sections. I shall focus (section I) on Moses' claim concerning "the extent to which irrationality pervades the life of groups, of leadership, of decision making" (Moses, 1990c, p. 215); (section II) Moses' formulation of the object-relations in terms of mutual needs of the leader and led; (section III) Moses' elaboration on the phenomena of denial, shame and of dehumanization; and (section IV) Moses' classification of various types of leadership.

THE ROLE OF REPRESENTATIONS IN CHOOSING A LEADER

The choice of a leader raises questions about the processes which motivate it. What is the role of internal representations in the processes of followership? What are internal representations enlisted in the service of adaptation? To what extent do internal representations, reality testing, rational thinking and relation to uncertainty affect the processes of choice? What are the motives for a certain choice? What motivates different people to choose one leader or another, or to break with a particular leadership and exchange it for that of another? What drives people to choose different leadership figures during times of stress from those selected during times of tranquility?

Moses says that "Politicians (leaders) serve, firstly, as the target for the projection of a variety of wishes and affects that cannot be directly expressed or even consciously tolerated by the follower" (1990c, p. 208).

From infancy onward, continual processes of conservation (introjection, internalization, identification, etc.) of constant and new experiences enrich the reservoir of representations. An "organizing activity" (Sandler, 1987) of these internal representations regulates familiar affects and images of the self, of the object and of the interaction between them. These processes can serve to identify an image or affect, an environment or a feeling, and to locate the familiar, the strange, and the threatening.

An image identified by perception (Sandler, 1991) as familiar and friendly may elicit hope and trust in its ability to realize known representations; whereas any strange image may provoke resistance, denial, or rejection, and uncertainty may evoke anxiety. The process of locating and identifying objects or experiences as similar in the outside world to the inner known representations, draws from one's reservoir of perceptions a chain of associations with additional familiar representations. Thus, we feel attracted to or repelled by persons who remind us of those who are similar. These, in turn, spark the endless wish, or perhaps the projection, to reconstruct and realize known experiences with similar persons.

The extent to which this process of location and investigation of the unknown takes place depends on the richness of our reservoir of inner representations and on the chain of associations that link them and regulate them..

I would like to illustrate my idea by an example: When we see an unknown person with some unknown small persons we may feel ourselves confused and in uncertainty. We try then to locate these strange people in order to feel that we are in a known space and in mastery of the situation. Chains of associations, which link these people to our inner representations of peoples, emerge in such situations. These associations of inner representations allow us to identify the unknown people in the outer world as father and children who remind us of a similar father and similar children from our personal history. From this process further chains of representations and locations may emerge such as the language they use, the authority of the father toward his children, his leadership and the tenderness, admiration or obedience of the children. Now, the unknown changes into the familiar and the uncertainty into mastery of our known representations.

The regulation of representations is accompanied by an economic-narcissistic struggle to achieve a balance between antagonistic perceptual representations that have been aroused: between representations laden with gratification, trust and mastery, on the one hand, and those that are terror-laden, on the other; between representations related to each other through fantasy, symbolization, and sublimation processes, and those which remain forever primal, such as representations of ultimate gratification or of narcissistic injuries (Solan, 1986, 1989a). Balanced regulation demands inner resilience and flexibility to temper the dimensions of threat and trust. It may sublimate the intensity of the wish to meticulously reconstruct known representations or to avoid changes.

The same process occurs when we choose a leader. The leader sparks in each one of us chains of associations linking his image to our inner known representations. Then our needs and hopes that the chosen leader will reconstruct some of these known representations emerge, so that our sense of well-being, security and mastery will be realized through him. If the leader fails to realize our familiar representations, we feel disappointment and strangeness in the unknown spaces of our relation with him or her.

I suggest, therefore, that the mutual needs of the leader and the led are related mainly to processes of locating and identifying what is familiar or what is strange. It is related to regulatory narcissistic processes for coping with threats, and to achieving maximum gratification with minimal injuries, strangeness, rejections and disappointments. This task is meant to regulate the delicate balance between the preservation of the self and the preservation of the object and of one's interaction with it.

The processes here described may lead to a better understanding of "the reluctance and difficulty to accept change linked to the safety in sameness" as Moses and Bene-Moses elaborated it (1980, p. 118). We know well the resistances to giving up known and familiar ways of being, for hopefully better ones may relate to risks involved in alternative choices which are not fully known and therefore may be frightening. It thus may not be surprising that enemies often prefer to stay entrenched in their hatred rather than risk the choice of peace. Leaders may embody at times hatred, at times risk-taking. The recent peace making processes in the Middle East between the Arabs and Israelis and in the U.K. between the British and the Irish attest to this. "The resistance to change, the need to painfully mourn patterns of being as well as territories to be given up, the mourning of past traumas, the overcoming of the repetition compulsion, the abundant use of projection and of denial with their specific defensive meanings—all these are the main highlights of what seems to be a formidable array of psychological obstacles to peace" (Moses and Bene-Moses, 1980, p. 121).

I would say that the choice of a leader in times of war or peace is related to these reluctances and difficulties. It makes us understand how much the representation of war unites the followers around their leader against their known and common enemy, whereas the representation of peace remains unknown and not common. The representation of peace arouses the wish for calmness linked to the primal "all or nothing" principle. It elicits the need and the hope that peace will be without terror or injuries, whereas war remains in the domain of perceptions connected with victims; thus casualties can be accepted.

THE ROLE OF "JOINTNESS" AND "MEDIA" IN LEADER-LED OBJECT-RELATION

In his paper on "The Leader and the Led: A Dyadic Relationship" (1990c), Moses emphasized that "Psychologically, as well as socially and politically, there can be no doubt that the leader and the followers need each other" (1990c, p. 205).

Representations of object, self and "jointness" come into being through the development of object-relations and the moulding of narcissistic integrity (Solan, 1991). The urge for existential security and for reassuring sameness accelerates the need to reconstruct these representations. Gradually, the child discovers the pleasure available from the realization of mastery and power, as well as from the valuable achievements of both the self and the object

(Solan, 1983). Thus, a person will forever strive to realize these representations in ideal symbols in the outside world or within him- or herself. By "jointness," I mean "An encounter between mother and infant or any partners experiencing simultaneously mutual satisfaction of surrendering while concomitantly safeguarding separateness" (Solan, 1991, p. 337).

"Jointness" represents the intimate communication or any intimacy attained through the mutual and the profound satisfaction of separate partners. It is the simultaneous experience (of partners) which perpetually regulates the safeguarding of separateness and of the surrendering to mutual satisfaction. Each encounter (of "jointness") represents a mutual investment of the partners in a joint object, phenomenon or idea, cathected and meaningful to them. It thus creates a shared "psychic space" between partners and elicits the triangulation (two separate psychic spaces and one which is shared) in object relations. "Jointness" "may evoke those privileged *moments* of the sense of being indistinguishable from one's object (especially between mother and infant)" (Solan, 1991, p. 340). During such very few moments of a blurring of the boundaries between partners one may sense, through the shared space, the psychic adjustment (of partners) of merging and separateness. Each "jointness" alters the balance in one way or another (to extend the merging or the separateness), and so the regulation of the intensity of each within the self and between partners is a dynamically active, ongoing process. It is, in my belief, a normal developmental process which may unfold from the beginning of a baby's life.

The child seeks to find in parental authority the ideals of peace, perfection, power and ability. The symbols of these ideals, which he wishes to join and from which he hopes to draw power, can only temporarily assuage his drives and his sense of worthlessness. The object representations, which are retained from these experiences and conserved in his reservoir of perceptions, are associated with an authoritarian image that repeatedly reassures the child that his sense of threat is appeased; it arouses feelings of safety, security and basic trust (Erikson, 1950; Sandler, 1987).

Conservation of various constancies, such as self- and object-constancy (Solnit, 1982; Sandler, 1986), "jointness" constancy, object-containing constancy, constancy of daily routines, etc., produces representations of separateness, "jointness," boundaries and reality testing. These free one from the bondage to the "not-I," to drives, to the environment and to the superego (Meissner, 1986) unto the "taming of solitude" (Quinodoz, 1991).

"In order to develop a separate and cohesive self" stressed Moses, "and to achieve a degree of individuation, the child needs parents who can allow him a separate existence in an ongoing way" (1990a, p. 48). But contrary to Moses' ideas of the dyadic relationship between leader and led, to my mind processes of separateness must begin as a triad from the very beginning of life and not after a dyadic relationship as in symbiosis. Once the child experiences "jointness" which includes separateness, he will expect to perpetuate separateness / jointness in every interaction just as he will choose symbiosis which denies separateness in a dyadic relationship if that is what he had experienced in his infancy.

I mean that the baby can already differentiate himself from the "not-I," from his very early life on. Mother may confirm, respect and develop this expression of separation in joining her offspring's attitudes or she may deny it. Mother may encourage the investment of them both in the individual space of her baby, in her own individual space or in their shared space. Such encounters will develop the self relatedness and the object relatedness in separateness and in jointness experiences and representations. But mother may also deny their separateness and induce her baby to give up the investment in his needs for separate space or for a shared space for the benefit of her own narcissistic space. Such investments will develop the self-object relatedness in symbiotic experiences and representations. For example, a mother holds her baby in her arms during moments of breast-feeding and she wondrously looks at the infant in the eye while he or she looks back at her. Suddenly the baby turns his head away and mother might join him with empathy in regarding the new voice he has turned toward; she may enjoy with him his discovery (separateness and jointness). But mother might also be offended by his abandonment of her and react to it by pulling baby back to her and to their unique pleasure in one another (symbiosis).

The same processes occur with empathy: As "a good mother is empathic with her child." Those who experienced empathy will be able also to reconstruct it.

> And empathy is that faculty which enables us to feel with another human being, to cognitively and affectively put ourselves into his or her place, and therefore to become aware of the other's feelings, needs, and wants. . . . Our empathic faculties will be opened and sharpened vis-à-vis those for whom we have an interest; and blunted or closed off, often hermetically, against those from whom we turn away, or who arouse our ire (Moses, 1985).

Representations of symbiosis, ultimate gratification, perfection or separateness / jointness and empathy are thus accessible both to the leader and to the led, because of gratifications they all experienced with their objects.

The need to reconstruct gratifying situations as representations of "jointness" encourages individuals to invest in partnership, in communal spaces, in a joint object, phenomenon or idea, cathected and meaningful to them. It creates what I call "media" (Solan, 1991). The term "media" represents "those occurrences which, as a result of the mutual investment, have the quality of being cathected by all the partners of 'jointness.' It becomes meaningful for them all to the extent that something of the partners' 'jointness' will be found in it and be enriched by a spectrum of their feelings" (p. 344). "Media" become the symbols of the shared spaces of partners (i.e., the thought of any concrete object, such as a father or a flag, or any abstract object, such as political ideas, leadership, etc.). "The urge for the restoration of the narcissistic injury (linked to separateness) compels the separated partners to encounter each other through their mutual investments in the shared 'media.' It compels them to broaden the transitional 'space' or 'media' in order to find further routes for restorations" (p. 345).

The perpetual regulation of separateness and merging allows different qualities of encounters through "media" to take place; it widens the merging from the intensity of mutual erotization to the smoothing of mutual symbolization, from physical dialogue of the erotic contact of the body to a common language in sublimated dialogue, or in sophisticated moral, social or cultural "media." The "media" unite individuals around them in mutual trust. For example, Churchill's phrase "blood, sweat and tears" (during the Second World War) became a unifying "media" phrase, despite the threat inherent in the words.

TRUST AND DISAPPOINTMENT BETWEEN LEADER AND LED

When a similar chain of representations erupts in many individuals and between them and their leader and his weltanschauung, we can speak of "media" which join people together as a group. Individuals, who commit themselves to "media" and to their symbols, undertake to abide by the rules of a society. In order not to breach these rules for their own personal benefit (Freud, 1930), they are required to restrain their aggression and demandingness (Freud, 1933) and to sublimate them into common symbols. "Joining" around "media" consolidates individuals into a unique affinity group characterized by power and trust. Thus the dimensions of threat are reduced and representations of existential security are realized.

I would like to illustrate these "media" processes with another example, borrowed from a "team task" metaphor. A team task is chosen as "media" by individuals who choose to work together. They place mutual trust in the realization of shared representations of "jointness" associated with the "team task" experience. For all of them, the leaders and the followers, work depends on the ability to realize representations of self-preservation and at the same time on safeguarding the other workers of the team. This can be achieved by regulating simultaneously the work rhythms of each member as well as the representations of the intimacy between them. The shared investment in the work "media" creates the code of a dialogue which may often allow each one of the team members to sense the extent of the other partners' gratification or deception, the quality of closeness or distance, the existing trust or suspicion; each partner senses the other's separate rhythm. Regulating one's investments in "jointness" and separateness temporarily balances and attenuates the dimensions of possible threats, such as failure or injury.

During the stage in which mutual trust is being built in "jointness" between the members of the "task team" (I am thinking, e.g., of a team of soldiers), the workers abandon themselves to the pleasure of the "team task." Each worker feels trust in his or her ability to come close to the other while blurring, temporarily, the boundaries between them; at the same time each one feels a limited trust in the partner's ability not to harm him, and in their ability to protect themselves. Being partners in the "media" team, they experience a pleasurable and sweeping sense of belonging and power. This is similar to that brought about by the function of a unifying leader who is considerate of the separateness of his partners and of the representations of reality.

When one places excessive trust into the leading worker's ability to provide protection from failure (narcissistic merging or omnipotence), this may lead the follower to totally surrender himself to the work. He may be so immersed in the work that he or she denies the threat and the separateness. This leads to an impairment of the functions of reality testing, such as of evaluating the boundaries of the task force and one's own active forces and temporal and spatial orientation. This is akin to the influence of a charismatic, fanatic or dictatorial leader, whose magnetism is rooted in the symbiotic needs of his followers.

On the other hand, a lack of consideration for the rhythm of the team's partners or the neglect of her or his presence may undermine one's ability to surrender to the work "media" and lead to an outburst of rage at the disappointing partner, to a loss of trust in her or him, and to the emergence of a sense of imminent failure.

Moses related to this process by showing that "many groups are idealized and valued first and foremost because of the group leader who symbolizes them sometimes charismatically . . . i.e., more through the idealizing cathexes than through the grandiose self. People take special pride and indeed regard as special not only their job, but the particular small group on the job to which they belong. . . . Adults show (group narcissism) in the various areas of their functioning—vocational, political and geographical" (Moses, 1982, p. 59).

The encounter with images arousing a chain of representations related to separateness and empathy contribute to the choice of leaders that match reality testing to a greater degree. In this case followers place only a limited trust in the leader's capability of realizing ultimate representations of existential security.

The encounter with images arousing a chain of representations related to symbiosis and to perfection may produce unwavering trust or blind trust in the possibility of these images to realize the wish for surrender to, and indulgence in, this rewarding experience.

Thus, for example, an encounter with an image identified as ideal (Solan, 1989b), or as having a containing quality, may arouse representations of omnipotence. It evokes the trust that one is able to surrender to, and indulge in, the familiar representation of power and of ultimate gratification. The unwavering trust in the ability of this image to bring about gratification is so powerful, that the regulation of self-preservation is bound to become unbalanced, giving rise thereby to a denial of the threat and to the ignoring of reality testing.

Moses stressed " . . . that such denial brings about an impediment in the ability to face and therefore to deal with the danger that is being partially denied. By not facing danger, the society, just as the person, is able to deal less efficiently than possible with the approaching threat" (Moses, 1989b, p. 295).

Moses reminded us that when a discrepancy occurs "between the ego ideal and the assessment of the extent to which these goals have or have not been reached, . . . shame is aroused." He stresses that "once the shame has become conscious it relatively quickly becomes mixed with frustration and anger" (Moses, 1989a, p. 411).

"In the normal course of development," Moses tells us, "we would expect the sense of specialness to be gradually transformed. This would parallel the change in the sense of omnipotence and grandiosity, which through repeated frustrations comes to be more in tune with reality. As the sense of omnipotence and grandiosity decreases through confrontations with reality, so, we assume, would the primary sense of entitlement" (Moses and Moses-Hrushovski, 1990, p. 66).

The loss of the ability to realize representations as expected, disappointment with the leader, or misidentification of an image as familiar, will undermine the equilibrium of regulation. Facing the unfamiliar, the "not-I," generates discomfort (Freud, 1933; Chasseguet-Smirgel, 1973): it evokes familiar representations of threat, strangeness or disappointment and induces stress. It undermines the level of equilibrium between trust and threat and thus injures the person's well-being and narcissistic integrity. Thus a sense of terror is produced, great enough to lead to suspicion and to a loss of trust. (These feelings may be one of the sources of racism.) These, in turn, are projected onto the external reality which then becomes all the more threatening—so much so, that the self is overcome with a sense of the horror of annihilation or with a feeling that narcissism and pleasurable existence are seriously injured.

In the face of Saddam Hussein's threats, during the Gulf War, we Israelis tried to regulate these representations of an unknown threatening "not-I" through known representations related to mastery. Thus we tried to create, every day anew, known boundaries and constancies that would better enable us to master the known representations linked to trust in the routines of life. We tried to call upon representations of "rules" for behavior during rocket alerts, and to form constancies in daily schedules. During daylight hours, functioning was almost routine, whereas as of about 5 p.m., levels of alertness rose. However, after having been caught off-guard by a morning Scud attack, we no longer trusted the constancy code we had formed, and once again reacted with horror and confusion linked to representations of the threat of death.

We may think that leadership which is based on idealization and on a split between good and evil can, in some individuals, impair a person's self-control of his aggression. " . . . especially when a hurt or a humiliation has been registered," says Moses, "they easily elicit reactions of narcissistic rage which lead (terrorists) to the commission of acts of violence or to the increase or escalation of such acts" (Moses, 1984, p. 3).

In such circumstances, aggression threatens to explode with demonic rage at any "not-I," stranger and enemy (racism). The group is then led to trust a leader who directs the group's aggression toward any stranger. German neo-Nazis sing: "See the evil in my face; I am the Evil in each one of you; I will empty all your heads of sense" ("The Bad Uncles' Song" [free translation]).

During stressful situations, a recurring search for an object identified as similar to the lost one takes place (lost as a result of its disappearance, through disappointment or loss of trust in it, etc.) (Freud, 1925, 1926): It is a search for a representation of mastery within the self or in an all-powerful external leader. This leader resembles representations of the image-identities of the lost object, or is similar to the identity-representations of the gratifying experience with this object. Simultaneously, all-powerful and authoritative figures often tempt us to place trust in their ability to realize the child's primal wish (representations) that an external authority object be omnipotent.

Moses gave us an example of this process when he speaks of "Begin's sensitivity to injury and insult—both in the name of the Jewish people and in his own name, combined with his sense of grandiosity. Begin's sense of righteous mission, his charismatic certainty in his beliefs and his pronouncements based thereon—created the strong appeal to his followers. . . . By his absolute certitude he reassured their doubts, especially in times of crises or special need. By his charismatic promises he dispels their doubts and fears that they might become victims again. Vicariously, by identifying with him, they can feel sure and strong, unambivalent and protected. In this way they can avoid the reliving of persecutory fantasies in their mind" (1984, p. 9).

The "familiar" image representation of a leader or leadership arouses the hope and trust that danger be eliminated, that narcissistic integrity be restored, that the perfection of the gratifying object be recovered (Freud, 1926, 1933), and that the gratifying situations be realized (Freud, 1914).

When this "familiar" image is common to a group of people ("media") it might unite them arround the "media" in mutual trust. When partners feel that one of them refuses to or avoids investing in the chosen "media," they will experience that partner as a stranger, an outsider, a threatening "not-I," on which their aggression is then projected (see, for instance, the hostility currently directed toward strangers, especially in Germany).

"Members of a nation (may) project their hostile and aggressive wishes and tendencies into or onto an enemy-neighbor," says Moses. "Polarization then takes place: they, the Arabs, are bad and we, the Jews or Israelis, are good. And vice versa, of course" (Moses, 1982, p. 56).

"It is pertinent to take note of two phenomena," adds Moses, "dehumanization and demonization. Individuals in a society become accustomed to focusing their own aggressive wishes, mostly unconscious, on the "bad people" outside. To demonize one's enemy is a further step. . . . The more the enemy is the demon, the more pure we become ourselves. And then, (in) dehumanization . . . the enemy is now seen as someone less than human. . . . This subhuman demon threatens us in such a mortally dangerous way that we must, and may, perforce defend ourselves" (Moses, 1990a, p. 52).

During the Gulf War, because of the investment made in such objects as the gas mask, the Infant Protector and the sealed room and through the processes of getting acquainted with them, they acquired a personalized, friendly dimension and came to be chosen as "media," as a unifying communal symbol that safeguarded our existence (e.g., children decorated the mask containers). People who took their masks with them when visiting others were greeted warmly (at therapy sessions, for example), whereas those who came without a mask, i.e., who had difficulty investing in it or scoffed at its use, became for their hosts that strange "not-I"; aggression surged toward these nonpartners of the "media." Today, with the passage of time, when the "jointness" processes and the shared investment in these protective devices as "media" no longer operate, we once again relate to them with some reservation.

But when the "media" lead to a tough and rigid leadership or to a strong idealistic orientation and a stringent ideology it might trigger a dangerous process. It might lead to a strong moral commitment and under certain circumstances even to two public phenomena elaborated by Moses (1986, 1989a) known as the Watergate syndrome and the Holy Wars.

Moses says: "Ideology is often used to ready a people for war or dehumanization. . . . It changes ordinary human values into values dominated by the needs and demands of a specific group, whether religious or national, or any other group that is united by stringent ideals. . . . Such influence and appeal are fostered through identification with the group and its leader, especially with a charismatic leader, and with the group's 'cause' " (Moses, 1990b, p. 114).

When referring to the leader, Freud made this point (1927), when he said that "It is only through the influence of individuals who can set an example and whom masses recognize as their leaders that they can be induced to perform the work and undergo the renunciation on which the existence of civilization depends" (p. 8).

President Truman defined the good leader as one who can convince the citizens to do what, in their hearts, they know to be right. According to the definition of Israel's General Yisrael Tal (1988), leadership is a function of power not based on authority alone, but rather on the ability to persuade. Tal suggests that without the common denominator of obedience to principles, policies and the dictates of the general program, individuals would act as they please or as they think best and thus it would very soon lead to total anarchy. It is obvious, then, that Freud, Truman and Tal were referring to the importance of "media" in the choice of a leader.

During the Gulf War, in Israel, it indeed seemed that the absence of a leadership figure made it difficult for the individuals to participate in the values common to the nation's fate. Consequently, each individual or family had to fend for itself.

We can realize that the processing of "media" may achieve an equilibrium of regulation under very strict rules. But, when a leader and his or her policies ("media") are disappointing, inappropriate or fail to realize common representations, the balance between trust and threat is likely to be undermined. Daily life routines, boundaries and mastery processes that have been achieved are disrupted, causing changes in social, moral and cultural values, thus leading to economic, political and familial crises (e.g., the events that occurred in the former Soviet Union and in Germany). Unsuccessful or unrequited choice, loss of trust and impotence arouse shame and guilt, demoralization, fear of death, despair can lead to anarchy and desertion. Each individual and each family are then likely to act as they please and to abandon the group responsibility which had unified them.

I share the ideas of Moses that " . . . in times of crises the wish for fulfillment of a variety of needs from a leader increases dramatically. At such times, the critical faculties of the members of the large group weaken, and the expectations for a leader who can be seen to be strong, knowledgeable, and decisive become dominant. . . . we speak of a partial regression to earlier modes of behavior" (Moses, 1990a).

LEADERSHIP WITHIN THE BOUNDS OF NARCISSISM

Weber (1956) differentiates between three types of leadership within "the types of legitimate domination" (p. 215): The rational, the traditional and the charismatic. Moses (1990c), following Zaleznik (1984), differentiates between two types of leaders as extremes on a continuum: the charismatic and the consensus leader. The charismatic leader is needed and turned to more desperately in situations of crises. "The consensus leader, or technocrat, shows the same basic mechanisms, needs, and narcissistic expectations as his followers, but to a lesser degree. The need on both sides here is less strong and less acute; therefore, the relationship or bond is less intense" (p. 208). Moses classifies two more types of leader: the relation between leader and led within the affective dimension of the moderate and the rigid leader. "The moderate and moderating leader is here analogous to the good mothering figure. . . . The (moderate) leader may accept psychic content (projected on him) in its raw and primitive form and contain it. . . . The more flexible, warmer, more moderate leader makes his constituents feel better about themselves because he is a more tolerant and containing person: he thereby encourages a more moderate, more mature, more flexible and permissive social process, and, possibly, social system. The extreme, rigid leader . . . would not only be unable to contain such (primitive) projections and moderate them, but he would also perhaps thrive on them. He would tend to use such projections in order to escalate a conflict situation, to polarize attitudes—perhaps for purposes of demagogic dramatization, i.e., to increase his admiration by the regressive masses. A tough and rigid leader will tend to lead his followers to more extreme positions and more aggressive behavior" (1990c, p. 211).

It seems that both of us agree that the need to reconstruct early experiences—according to the individual perceptual reservoir of representations—appears to be crucial in the relationship between a leader and his followers. We also agree that under stressful circumstances regression is so intense that it strengthens the temptation to surrender to a type of leader that represents charisma.

We both wish to supplement Weber's sociological classification of leadership with psychological theory. In line with the present discussion I suggest to formulate three types of leadership within the narcissistic domain / dimension. And, to conclude, I would like to explore the differences of the three types of leadership from the viewpoint proposed in this essay, that which furthers my understanding of some extreme sociopolitical phenomena prevalent nowadays, i.e., going from freedom of choice, tolerance and democracy on to fanaticism, fundamentalism and totalitarianism.

I believe that the temptation to trust a leader consists of three components:

(1) The need to place blind trust in his ability to realize very primal representations, such as symbiotic, sweeping and addictive representations of union with his or her power and / or its concomitant gratifications. People to whom this appeals yearn to trust a leader who radiates narcissistic merging (Hareven, 1985).

(2) The need to place unwavering trust in the leader's ability to reflect absolute truth and elitism. Such individuals yearn to trust a leader who tempts them with the prospect of realizing childish representations of power and of omnipotence elicited by him (this is a pattern of fanaticism, cf, Haynal, 1980).

(3) The need to place only limited trust in the leader's ability to realize absolute "media" rules. Such individuals long to trust a leader whom they invite and expect to realize mature representations of ability and of reality testing elicited by him (this is a pattern of democracy).

It may well be that a certain degree of charisma is necessary for all types of leadership figures in order to arouse primary emotional representations (albeit of different intensities). But charisma is less necessary for those individuals whose narcissistic integrity (Solan, 1991)—which includes representations of separateness / jointness—allows them to take reality testing into account to respect other's ideas, to safeguard themselves as well as their jointness with the object and their group. In times of stress, these individuals are able to make a flexible transition from a loss of perceptual identity (regression and loss of trust) to an arousal of friendly representations; from a fear of death to mastery, and from aloneness to partnership in "media."

Moses (1990c) named these individuals the "sophisticated work group," who choose their leader mainly for the skills required for the implementation of the group task.

Such shared responsibility, in my opinion, can be assumed only when the representation of separateness / jointness predominates in the reservoir of representations. This is possible only when individuals are willing to share a "media." Then these persons are eager to experience the free flow of communication, of reality testing, of a freedom of choice and criticism. Such individuals need to cooperate with a leadership figure who arouses more mature representations of "media"—which are then the representations of democratic values. This kind of leadership figure invites one to place only limited trust in the leader's power, in his weltanschauung and in realistic truths, as well as in the leader's ability to realize representations of self-preservation and of the partnership of individuals in a unique and powerful group. Such leaders produce in us a sense that they are able to master the separateness and the partnership, thus tempering the dimensions of the threat.

On the other hand, a charismatic leader who transmits and carries both components—narcissistic symbiosis and omnipotence—lures his admirers into an experience of megalomaniac euphoria, with no boundaries or limits, at the expense of a sober view of reality—with all the dangers inherent in this.

And those individuals who have lost their faith in the leader and are unable to converge—not even around the channeled evil—feel themselves to be strangers at home and within the familial / national group. They tend more and more to withdraw into themselves, to gratify their own private needs, to flee from the unknown threat, to flout the rules of society or to sink into depression.

Will those who choose a leader or leadership have enough integrity to stand firm against the sweeping temptation to trust charismatic figures who seduce them to a realization of omnipotence, security and symbiotic representations? Will they have sufficient reserves of representations to preserve their own narcissistic integrity, and that of humanity, against inner demons threatening to burst out? Will those who choose have the wisdom to trust those leaders who arouse in them chains of "media" representations consonant with the freedom of choice and with criticism of the reality in which they live?

REFERENCES

Chasseguet-Smirgel, J. (1973), L'Ideal du moi. *Rev. Franc. Psychanal.*, 37:709–929.

Erikson, E. H. (1950), *Childhood and Society.* New York: W. W. Norton.

Freud, S. (1914), On narcissism. *Standard Edition*, 14:67–102. London: Hogarth Press, 1957.

——— (1925), Negation. *Standard Edition*, 19:233–239. London: Hogarth Press, 1961.

——— (1926), Inhibitions, symptoms and anxiety. *Standard Edition,* 20:77–172. London: Hogarth Press, 1959.

——— (1927), The future of an illusion. *Standard Editon,* 21:3–56. London: Hogarth Press, 1961.

——— (1930), Civilization and its discontents. *Standard Editon,* 21:51–145. London: Hogarth Press, 1961.

——— (1933), New introductory lectures on psycho-analysis. *Standard Edition,* 22:3–182. London: Hogarth Press, 1964.

Hareven, S. (1985), Manhigout (Leadership). In: *Mashiach o Knesset (Messiah or Parliament).* Tel Aviv: Dvir, pp. 62–66, 1987.

Haynal, A. & Molnar, M., & Puymege, G. (1980), Fanatisme et civilisation: La psychanalyse du fanatisme. In: *Le Fanatisme. Histoire et Psychanalyse,* Editions Stock. Paris: Cameron, pp. 57–122.

Meissner, W. W. (1986), The earliest internalizations. In: *Self and Object Constancy,* ed. R. F. Lax, S. Bach, & J. A. Burland. New York: Guilford Press, pp. 29–72.

Moses, R. (1982), The group self and the Arab-Israeli conflict, *Internat. Rev. Psycho-Anal.,* 9:55–65.

——— (1984), Perpetuating the Victim Role. Typescript.

——— (1985), Empathy and dis-empathy in political conflict. *Polit. Psychol.,* 6:135–140.

——— (1986), "Watergate" as a universal phenomenon. In: *Psychoanalyse Heute (Psychoanalysis Today),* ed. H. Lobner. Vienna: Orac Verlag.

——— (1989a), Shame and entitlement: Their relation to political process. In: *The Psychoanalytic Core, Essays in Honor of Leo Rangell M.D.,* ed. H. P. Blum, E. M. Weinshel, & F. R. Rodman. Madison, CT: International Universities Press, pp. 493–498.

——— (1989b), Denial in political process. In: *Denial: A Clarification of Concepts and Research,* ed. E. L. Edelstein, D. L. Nathanson, & A. M. Stone. New York: Plenum Press, pp. 287–298.

——— (1990a), The self, the self-view and identity in the Arab-Israeli conflict. In: *The Psychodynamics of International Relationships,* Vol. 1, ed. V. D. Volkan, D. A. Julius, & J. V. Montville. Lexington, MA: Lexington Books, pp. 47–55.

——— (1990b), On dehumanizing the enemy. In: *The Psychodynamics of International Relationships,* ed. V. D. Volkan, D. A. Julius, & J. V. Montville. Lexington, MA: Lexington Books. pp. 111–118.

——— (1990c), The leader and the led. In: *Psychodynamics of International Relationships: A Dyadic Relationship,* ed. V. D. Volkan, D. A. Julius, & J. V. Montville. Lexington, MA: Lexington Books. pp. 205–217.

——— & Moses-Hrushovski, R. (1990), Reflections on the sense of entitlement. *The Psychoanalytic Study of the Child,* 45:61–78. New Haven, CT: Yale University Press.

——— Bene-Moses, A. (1980), Psychoanalytic perspectives of the Middle East peace process. *Samiksa,* 34:117–129.

Quinodoz, J-M. (1991), *La Solitude Apprivoisee.* Paris: PUF.

Sandler, J. (1986), Comments on the self and object constancy. In: *Self and Object Constancy,* ed. R. F. Lax, S. Bach, & J. A. Burland. New York: Guilford Press, pp. 97–106.

——— (1987), *From Safety to Superego.* London: Karnac Books.

——— (1991), On internal object relations. *J. Amer. Psychoanal. Assn.,* 39:859–880.

Solan, R. (1983), Closeness in the psychoanalytic encounter. *Bull. Psychoanal. Europe,* 20 / 21:65–84.

——— (1986), Refoulement—deni—sublimation. *Rev. Franc. Psychanal.,* 50:533–538.

——— (1989a), Objet transitionnel—symbolisation—sublimation. *Rev. Franc. Psychanal.,* 53:1843–1845.

——— (1989b), Idealization and de-idealization. *Sihot-dialogue, Israel. J. of Psychother.* 4(1):17–24.

——— (1991), "Jointness" as integration of merging and separateness in object relations and narcissism. *The Psychoanalytic Study of the Child,* 46:337–352. New Haven, CT: Yale University Press.

Solnit, A. J. (1982), Developmental perspectives on self and object constancy. *The Psychoanalytic Study of the Child,* 37:201–218. New Haven, CT: Yale University Press.

Tal, I. (1988), Leadership. *Monthly Review I.D.F.,* 35:10.

Weber, M. (1947), *The Theory of Social and Economic Organization,* ed. T. Parsons. New York: Oxford University Press.

——— (1956), The types of legitimate domination. In: *Economic and Society,* ed. G. Roth & C. Wittich. Berkeley, CA: University of California Press, pp. 212–301.

Zaleznik, A. (1984), Charismatic and consensus leaders, A psychological comparison. In: *The Irrational Executive: Psychoanalytic Studies in Management.* New York: International Universities Press, pp. 112–131.

16.

INTERGENERATIONAL TRANSMISSION AND "CHOSEN" TRAUMAS: A LINK BETWEEN THE PSYCHOLOGY OF THE INDIVIDUAL AND THAT OF THE ETHNIC GROUP

VAMIK D. VOLKAN, M.D.

THE FLUIDITY OF PSYCHIC BORDERS

There is a fluidity between the "psychic borders" of a child and those of his mothering person during the child's formative years, and different influences pass from one to the other. We know that a mother's affects are sensed by her children, as evidenced by the findings of Anna Freud and Dorothy Burlingham (1945), who noted that infants under 3 did not become anxious during the German bombing of London unless their mothers were afraid. This has been demonstrated by numerous sources, from the psychoanalytic study of infants reported by Spitz (1965) to the findings of such contemporary researchers as Greenspan (1989) and Emde, Johnson, and Easterbrooks (1988). A mother's unconscious fantasies are also conveyed to her developing child, who will then exhibit their derivatives along with associated defenses and changes of function. The psychoanalytic literature offers many illustrations. When my colleagues and I worked with male and female transsexuals at the University of Virginia we found that a mother's unconscious fantasies about her infant's belonging to the opposite sex from the one biologically indicated was a critical determinant in the establishment of transsexualism (Volkan, 1980; Volkan and Masri, 1989; Volkan and Greer, in press). Apprey (1993a), also at the University of Virginia, elaborated further on the role of intergenerational transmission in true transsexuals.

The type of border-passing most commonly studied, however, pertains to ego and superego identifications and their associated functions. The study of such identifications is one of the cornerstones of psychoanalytic theory concerned with child development. In order to provide a link between clinical and ethnic studies, I focus here on a specific type of identification I call *deposited representation* or *psychological genes* (Volkan, 1981, 1987; Volkan and Ast, 1992, 1994). In this type, an adult deposits an already formed self or object representation into the developing psychic organization of a child as though for safekeeping, and as if to postpone to a future time the resolution of conflicts with which it is involved. The child then unconsciously becomes a "reservoir" of the representation, which brings about an unconscious interference with and influence upon the rest of the child's personality organization. Some "replacement children" (Cain and Cain, 1964; Green and Solnit, 1964; Poznanski, 1972) are indeed reservoirs of the mental representations of dead siblings or other relatives the mother has lost. A mother's inability to mourn and deal with the representation of a dead child or other relative within herself burdens her newborn infant. If a deposited mental representation is not adaptively integrated with the rest of the child's psychic organization, it impedes the full evolution of the child's integrative function or leads to certain troublesome identity formations. Thus we can say that this type of intergenerational transmission or continuity involves more than a child hearing stories about his family's past; it includes the child's identification with the representation deposited within the self—or the struggle against such identification. I emphasize that the concept of deposited representations or psychological genes should not be seen apart from the intergenerational transmission of unconscious fantasies, affective states, and general ideas about identification. I simply focus on it here as a separate entity in order to better illustrate my theoretical exploration.

Not all deposited representations relate directly to such a large-group phenomenon as ethnicity, but when a deposited representation has direct reference to an event in history that affected all members of the large group and especially influenced earlier generations, it does have a crucial bearing on the concept of ethnicity. Children of a large group, in spite of having individual differences, become reservoirs of the mental representations of past generations victimized by some historical trauma. As a result of this process, all the children of the group show certain elements that have been included in their developing psychic organizations.

The mental representations of past generations associated with the shared historical trauma become abstracted and are included in the future generation's ethnic identity, which links all within the large group. Envision us wearing two layers of clothing, one of which is skin-tight and uniquely ours. The outer layer is loose, "like a tent" (Volkan, 1992; Volkan and Harris, 1993a) and covers the larger group (i.e., ethnic, religious, etc.) to which we belong; in this layer is located the representation of past generations and their history. Both are included in the individual's identity and any threat to either one of them causes anxiety. Under certain circumstances the all-encompassing "tent" is the *sine qua non* of identity; its shared fabric may be the primary or sole determinant.

The meaning and function of inherited representations may change as they pass from one generation to the next. For example, Apprey (1993b) illustrates how the representation of people as slaves was modified from generation to generation in the African-American experience. The resulting self representations influence black-on-black crime as well as teenage pregnancies among blacks.

PETER THE HUNTER: CASE EXAMPLE

Peter had been, as a fat little boy, "imprisoned" in the home of two women—his mother and grandmother—when a handsome man named Gregory came into his life. Gregory was a survivor of the Bataan Death March and the Japanese prison camps that had taken the lives and broken the spirits of so many American soldiers in World War II. Upon his return from the war, the soldier must have unconsciously seen a correspondence between the frustrated little boy and his own helpless self representation developed in the South Pacific. Gregory deposited this helpless self representation, as well as the defensive self representation he had developed to deal with extreme helplessness, hopelessness, and fear, in the child's developing sense of self. To Gregory, it was clearly better to hunt than to be hunted—better to be a powerful, armed aggressor than the target of another's aggression. Peter, who idealized

Gregory and identified with his idealized aggressive representation, grew up to become a hunter and an influential participant in the military–industrial complex of his country. He came to know many powerful people, conducted himself with great confidence, and felt that he was the best representative of his company to negotiate million-dollar deals. His omnipotence indicated a malignant narcissistic personality organization, which is that of a person sadistic toward others in the defense and maintenance of a grandiose self. As an adult, Peter had to collect what I call "aggressive triumphs" lest he lose his self-esteem and feel empty or depressed.

An individual with malignant narcissism shares the key characteristics of behavior with the person who has an "ordinary" narcissistic personality. The narcissistic person maintains his grandiose self in his day-to-day activities, and behaves as if he is "number one" in brilliance, power, or beauty, and hence entitled to the best of everything. He expects to be adored by those he considers his inferiors, but he is inwardly fragile in his self-esteem, and envious of others (Kernberg, 1975; Volkan, 1976; Akhtar, 1992; Volkan and Ast, 1994). His covert self representation is that of a hungry self, which, hidden, is split off from the dominant grandiose self. What caused Peter to seek treatment was not a symptom of his exaggerated narcissism, but bulimia, an expression of his hungry self.

By his late forties, Peter had been bulimic for twenty years, vomiting after overeating as often as three times a day. He had developed what he thought of as the most powerful abdominal muscles possible so he could vomit at will. Being narcissistic, he was gratified at having this physical control, and failed to see his bulimia as a problem. His wife, however, had threatened to leave him if he did not seek treatment after he went through his bulimic routine at a dinner party attended by distinguished guests. Anxiety over the possibility of her abandonment brought him to treatment; he was secretly dependent on his wife, although this was not evident in his conduct toward her.

He presented himself at first as one of the most important men in the country. He felt that the manufacture and sale of military hardware, from conventional arms to still top-secret weapon systems, depended on his wisdom. He believed that the American people depended on him for their safety. He had no emotional reaction to the horrors his weaponry could inflict on an enemy people.

Peter had been shot down four times while a helicopter pilot in Vietnam. He had so often defied death that his omnipotence had crystallized. He thought of himself as a national hero; in Vietnam he had shot women and children as well as enemy soldiers from his helicopter, but felt no remorse. Since then he had not killed anyone, but he knew that the weapons he sold had brought death to many. On occasion he hunted animals from a helicopter, sometimes massacring a herd of deer from the air, and traveled to exotic places to kill exotic creatures such as cobras. In a sense, Peter engaged in a private war against animals. The urge to hunt in unconventional ways was especially strong when he faced a threat of separation, as when his wife went to visit her family or his analyst canceled a session, or when his omnipotence was threatened, such as by a legal obstruction to an arms deals he sought to close.

Childhood

Peter's childhood had been traumatic; his father left home when Peter was 2 weeks old, and his parents were subsequently divorced. When his father left, his mother returned with her child to the home of her mother, who cared for Peter while his mother worked. The old woman died when Peter was in late latency, but he slept with her during his developmental years, and, as became evident in treatment, could not integrate her representation; in his dreams she was a witch or an angel seductress with a red bikini, the former image coming from her habit of tweezing hairs from her chin, and the latter from her fondness for bright colors.

Accounts of their life together suggest that both his mother and grandmother were anxious, frustrated, and probably depressed women, who resented the burden of his care, and overfed him until he was fat. They intruded on his autonomy by spoon-feeding him even after he learned to feed himself, and they did his schoolwork for him. When Peter's transference during treatment reflected the environment of his early childhood, he was flooded with paranoid fears and a feeling that he was living as a prisoner in another world under a dome controlled by two women.

At the oedipal age, Peter's mother took him to see his biological father, whom he did not know since there had never been any visits. His mother pointed to a house and told her son to go to the door and ask for his father. When he rang the doorbell, his father, by then remarried, appeared at the door and rejected him, sending him back to his mother who waited on the street corner. The humiliation Peter felt colored all his childhood. It was just before this event, when he was about 3 years old, that Gregory came into Peter's life. He began living with the family, and soon married Peter's mother. Peter called him "Father." For some time he did not work, but stayed home and mothered the little fat boy who idolized him.

In the fourth year of his treatment, Peter captured the meaning of Gregory's arrival in his home in a dream. "Standing with a man who was handsome, as my father [stepfather] used to be, I saw red foxes running along a valley. I pointed out the foxes when he pointed to another animal, a disfigured deer with thick, clumsy legs and no horns." Peter identified the red foxes as his mother and grandmother. Their color recalled the red bikinis associated with his mental representation of his grandmother. He could not remember ever having seen either woman menstruate, but he thought it likely that he had glimpsed their genitals while in bed with them. The handsome man in the dream was obviously his stepfather, who could conquer his mother's "valley," and he himself was the fat, disfigured, hornless (castrated) deer.

Discussion of the dream let Peter understand that he had felt castrated by the two intrusive women, in spite of the oedipal triumph of being the only "man" in the house. When Gregory appeared, Peter hoped he would conquer "his women" so Peter could save himself from their intrusion. He had to idealize Gregory even more after being humiliated by his natural father. Although Gregory was not a sadistic man, Peter's desire for a strong oedipal father led him as a child to perceive Gregory as highly aggressive, and this perception was condensed with the former prisoner's own defensive self representation opposing the helplessness and humiliation he had suffered at war.

What Peter's experience with Gregory meant for the boy can be seen in a series of dreams presented to his analyst in which Peter could walk on water. Such dreams reflected the manifest content of his narcissistic personality organization, but Peter explained after much therapeutic work how he could walk on water. In a new version of his repeating dream he could see a submarine submerged just below the surface of the water, and it was this he walked on. He knew at once that the submarine represented Gregory, who had seen service in submarines; what was supporting Peter was Gregory's representation. Since the submarine belonged to an aggressive military force, the idealized image of Gregory was associated with aggression, weapons, torpedoes, and missiles.

The Bird House and the St. Joseph Statue

A most interesting and direct illustration of Gregory's role in Peter's life appeared in his fifth year of treatment. Gregory and Peter's mother, now in their seventies, decided to sell the house in which they had lived since their marriage, and enter a retirement community. It was in this house that Gregory had assumed the responsibility of rearing Peter, so the prospective move made them anxious. Their anxiety was especially associated with the fate of a birdhouse erected on the lawn during Peter's childhood. It was a multistoried purple martin house on top of a pole set in a firm concrete base. Gregory had made it, taking infinite pains, even to the point of painting numbers on each of the many "apartments" for the bird families to occupy. For decades it had been full of birds that, in due course, had laid and hatched eggs and launched their fledglings. Gregory had banded the legs of all the fledglings, marking each with the number of its family "apartment." If a baby bird had an untimely fall from the martin house, Gregory knew to which "apartment" it belonged, and returned it; a fledgling rescued by a human and returned to the wrong "apartment" would be rejected and die.

In treatment Peter understood that Gregory had built a new version of his Japanese prison camp, where there had been constant horror and death. In the new version (the birdhouse), no occupant could be allowed to die. In an omnipotent way, Gregory had reversed his past reality and developed a new fate for himself and his comrades (the fledglings) by creating a new camp in which all would be safe and happy.

Gregory's self representation in reference to his war experiences had been compatible with that of little Peter, who felt himself imprisoned under a space dome; the child was therefore a suitable repository for Gregory's self representation as a captive. Gregory then attempted to save young Peter, who, like the fledglings, contained his unwanted representation, which was infused with helplessness. I believe that Gregory adjusted to life, and was seemingly without pathology after his Bataan trauma, because of his stable externalization of his helpless, humiliated, and victimized self representation into outside "reservoirs." In making a receptacle for his traumatized self representations, Gregory could solve the conflicts associated with it in the future!

Peter's mother put a statue of St. Joseph beside the martin house as soon as Gregory finished it, thereby offering evidence that both parents unconsciously "knew" that Gregory's unacknowledged objective was reflected in the bird house. Gregory painted the figure's eyes brown like his own. While telling of the birdhouse and the statue, Peter realized he had always thought of Gregory as being saintly, and the Saint Joseph statue symbolically represented his stepfather; Joseph wed Mary and took care of her child, little Jesus. Peter's mother and Gregory had married so Gregory could save and protect little Peter, who represented part of helpless Gregory, by making him omnipotent like Jesus. For Peter to remain omnipotent he must be given the tools with which to express his aggression toward others so he could not himself be made a target of another's aggression. Peter first had to identify with Gregory's externalized helpless and humiliated self representation, and then idealize his defensive aggression and identify with fantasized aggressive Gregory in order to deal with his own humiliated self representation, to which was added Gregory's. The following story illustrates this process.

The Raccoon Experience

Gregory liked conventional hunting, but, in little Peter's mind, as a hunter he was an omnipotent and aggressive representation. Peter was still quite obese as an adolescent, and in the midst of his adolescent passage, he regressed. While he internally reexamined his object relations and psychosexual development, and attempted a second individuation (A. Freud, 1958; Blos, 1979), he experienced a drastic transformation during reidentification with Gregory's helplessness and then his aggressive and omnipotent representations. When Gregory took the young Peter hunting for the first time they came upon a raccoon drinking water from a stream. Peter also drank from the stream, and this probably brought on the illness that caused him to lose fifty-five pounds. He was aware of identifying in fantasy with the raccoon, which represented Gregory suffering on the Bataan Death March and in the Japanese prison undergoing hardships said to have made him lose sixty-five pounds. In the boy's fantasy, pictures he had seen of prisoners of war with their sunken, dark eyes looked like raccoons, though raccoons were not so gaunt.

After recovering from the illness, during which he had physically lost weight and psychologically identified with Gregory's Bataan self representation, Peter took up body building and achieved a well-developed body. Gregory, who seldom spoke of his Bataan experiences, encouraged him, and arranged to have a celebrated military hero call on Peter at school to recruit him for a military academy. This gave the boy great prestige and he enrolled there, keeping up his body building. He crystallized his omnipotent self representation and made the military his career until he went into the armaments business. Meanwhile, the mental representation of himself as a fat boy stayed with him as part of the hungry self that was split off from his grandiose self until psychoanalysis enabled him to integrate his contradictory self representations.

While in the military he married and had children, but was incapable of forming intimate relationships with the members of his family. He distanced himself from his mother also, and ritualistically went hunting with Gregory at least twice a year, thus refueling his grandiose self by being with the older man, adoring him and in turn being adored by him. When stressed, he went on hunting trips that were not simply exercises in sportsmanship, and slaughtered many animals to avoid the recurrence of psychosomatic problems. Besides his hunting trips, his swaggering in the arms industry, and handling his bulimia, he was chiefly preoccupied with a lonely hobby—taxidermy.

Taxidermy

On the walls of his home Peter hung trophies of the hunt he had prepared so skillfully that they looked alive. The different meanings and functions of his work in taxidermy were uncovered in treatment, the first four being connected with his childhood trauma.

1. The stuffed and mounted animals represented Peter himself, who, as a child, had been stuffed (overfed) by his mother and grandmother. He developed cancer phobias; psychological "bad food" had been stuffed into him and might be expected to invade his body.
2. The mounted animals also represented his mother, grandmother, and biological father. His thrill-seeking during the hunt was associated with the excitement of knocking on the door of his natural father's house; when he had done so, he had been rejected and humiliated, and in the symbolic replay of this event he could kill his biological father (usually represented by cobras) and his mother-grandmother (usually represented as red foxes and black bears).
3. His great concern that his mounted trophies look lifelike may have indicated reluctance to do away altogether with his parents since that would do away with any hope of being loved. While his grandiose self used aggression to reassure himself that he needed no one, his hungry self demanded that he keep available a way of gratifying his dependency needs.
4. His obsessive preoccupation with the hides of his kill served the same purpose as the itching phenomenon described by Elbirlik (1980) and myself (Volkan, 1979)—helping to define the borders of the self and gaining control. Obsessive touching of the skin or itching is a means of sensing a physical border of one's psychological being. Other means and functions of Peter's taxidermy hobby relate to his experiences and identification with Gregory's supporting representations, both helpless and aggressive.
5. By surrounding himself with dead animals, Peter identified himself with Gregory's wartime experience of being surrounded by dead comrades.

6. As a "survivor" he had made the trophies a memorial to the deadly environments of his childhood and of Gregory's prison. Now he was not only in control of who would be killed but also who would be stuffed and returned to life (an illusion).
7. Since Peter maintained the illusion of repairing the carcasses he brought home, he could deal with his conscious guilt, although it became clear in treatment that his unconscious guilt remained.

Falling into Water

In Peter's analysis he came to understand his identification with Gregory's self representation, and which of its ego functions defended against helplessness and which supported his belief in his omnipotence. Recalling his dream of walking on the water and walking on a submarine in a way that gave the illusion of walking on the water, he reported a subsequent dream in which, he said, "Once more I was walking on a submarine. It dove and I fell into the water." This was an indication of his attempt to dislocate and dissociate with Gregory's representation. He was no longer its depository, and without it he could work on the surrender of his malignant narcissistic personality organization. Without depending on Gregory's idealized aggressive representation, he had to face the impact of his hungry and helpless self. This dream was followed by exacerbation of his cancer phobia, and he confessed to having always had a fear of flying and being afraid of dangerous game while stalking it. He then began in earnest to integrate his opposing grandiose and hungry selves.

A Mourning Process

Soon after dreaming of falling into the water, in the fifth year of his treatment, Peter went with Gregory, by now a man in his seventies, to shoot rabbits. Peter suddenly realized how weak Gregory had become and how much hunting skill he had lost. This initiated what I consider the process of mourning; he had to mourn the representation of Gregory that supported his own omnipotence and malignant narcissism. His mourning involved a successful effort to gain official recognition of Gregory's bravery on the occasion of the fiftieth anniversary of the Bataan Death March. This award was in effect a mental tombstone with which Peter marked the mental representation of Gregory he had now buried.

The shrinking of his grandiose self came about at this time. His hunting took on a new meaning; he now spoke of the sport of hunting as "communing with nature," and called nature "the good mother." His need for merciless slaughter of wild animals vanished, and his interest in missiles and other weaponry faded. Although he kept his job, he started to be an environmentalist and wanted to convert ICBM silos into storage space for grain.

With Peter's recovery, Gregory lost the depository of his helpless and defensive self representation. When he and his wife moved, dismantling the martin house and the statue of St. Joseph, other "reservoirs" for stable externalization were gone. Gregory became ill almost overnight, and Peter grasped the meaning of this illness, which nearly proved fatal. Peter then faced the dilemma as to whether to continue his psychological improvement or to remain as Gregory's "reservoir." He eventually chose his improvement.

A Different Type of Identification

For Peter, the identifications with Gregory that occurred during his developmental years were problematic, and helped determine the nature of Peter's identity. In the termination phase of his treatment, Peter replaced the maladaptive ones with a new, healthier one that corresponded to his own evolution of new ego functions. Peter spoke of having been seated in his living room when sounds from the chimney indicated that young birds had been caught in it. He was moved to save them, and made elaborate preparations to do so, even trying to climb onto the roof and making a net to catch them lest they come to harm. He finally succeeded in saving them. His associations to his account of this effort made it clear that he had loosened his investment in the idealized aggressive representation of Gregory that had been part of his former grandiose self; Gregory had for years felt responsible for saving fallen birds, and he had also felt responsible for rescuing fat little Peter, who was now, in effect, declaring that he could take care of things himself and had no further need of Gregory (his representation), for whom he had obtained official recognition and to whom he had said goodbye. "He can go on his own way now since I can take care of and depend on myself," he thought.

In separating from Gregory's maladaptive representation, Peter then identified with his saving functions, and made them his own. Here the double aim of a healthy identification is very clear: through identification we keep certain aspects of the other but no longer need the other.

TO THE THIRD GENERATION

Since I know nothing of Gregory's developmental history, I cannot say what kinds of individualized psychological factors were involved in his reaction and adaptation to the Bataan Death March, the Japanese prison, and his eventual liberation, but I believe that the effects of incomprehensible trauma and associated losses, humiliation, and helplessness do not disappear in time, although in the long run the person involved may include stable defenses and creative expression in his repertoire of responses. This certainly has been true of some of the survivors of Nazi concentration camps I studied (Volkan, 1993). In Gregory's case, there was a return of maladaptation decades after the event and after the dismantling of the martin house and Peter's improvement. According to Rangell (1976):

> In spite of the vastness of the unconscious, psychic space is limited. There is room and time in any individual psyche for only a limited amount of cognitive ideation and a finite number of memories, fantasies, and accompanying affects. The product of such space and time comprises the psychic life of an individual, the amount already spent and the amount still left. . . . Traumatic memories of any kind encroach on this time-space and reduce its available quantity; this is why psychic traumata age people [p. 315].

We can imagine—and clinical experience shows—that severely traumatized individuals have a tendency to pass their traumatized mental representation on to the next generation for future resolution since they cannot work through and resolve the conflicts aroused by the unbearable trauma, and since their psychic time-space is crowded. People who, like Peter, come to psychoanalytic treatment may slow down or even stop intergenerational transmission with therapeutic help. In Peter's case, transmission had already taken place before he came into treatment.

What began with Gregory's experiences could be seen in the third generation. One of Peter's children became a veterinarian. There was enough evidence in Peter's treatment to indicate that his child was responding to her father's mental representation as a slayer of animals in choosing for herself a "veterinarian identity."

"CHOSEN" TRAUMA

I use the term *chosen trauma* (Volkan, 1991, 1992; Volkan and Itzkowitz, 1993, 1994) to refer to an event that makes a large group feel helpless and victimized by another large group, and share a humiliating injury. Since a group does not "choose" to be victimized or to lose its pride, some of my colleagues take exception to my speaking of "chosen trauma." I hold that it reflects a group's unconscious choice to add a past generation's mental representation of the event, with its associated change of function, to its own identity. The event in question becomes psychologized, and the way the people share mental representations of it marks their ethnic identity. Once a historical event becomes a "chosen trauma," the historical truth about it is secondary to the power it exercises within the group—the way it continues to be perceived and experienced. Mental representations connected with it are usually condensed with memories of other group injuries and passed on from generation to generation as illustrated by the Gregory–Peter–Peter's child sequence. Findings from the psychoanalytical study of individual patients make us more sophisticated in considering what kinds of "psychological genes" are conveyed, how the process occurs, and its significant influence on group identity. Intergenerational transmission is more than retelling of old history; the simple awareness of past events in one's group does not incite that group to try to massacre their neighbors in circumstances of conflict, but a threat to one's ethnic identity in which "chosen traumas" are intertwined does, whenever it induces intolerable anxiety. The "ethnic tent" (Volkan, 1992; Volkan and Harris, 1993a) may be shaken by a variety of real-world events, from economic collapse, natural or man-made disasters, or threats of conquest, to the megalomanic designs of a leader bent on dominance. It is then that we clearly see how a "chosen trauma" has a role in any attempt to patch or stabilize a group's shared identity.

We have seen how "ethnic tents" were shaken following the disintegration of the Soviet Union: Serbian and Croatian Christians, and Bosnian Muslims were obliged to rethink their identity. Serbs hypercathected their principal "chosen trauma," which took place in 1389 when the Turks conquered them at Kosova. On the six-hundredth anniversary of this event, an ambitious Serbian Communist leader, Sloboden Milosevic, speaking at Kosova, shouted "Never again!" and the coffin of the long-dead Serbian King Lazar was taken on a year-long pilgrimage, passing through every Serbian village in the country. The Serbs have no Serbian identity without their "chosen trauma." It was on an earlier anniversary of Kosova that Archduke Ferdinand was assassinated at Sarajevo, precipitating World War I.

The Inability to Mourn

"Chosen traumas" are linked to a group's inability to mourn, mourning being an obligatory response to change or loss in the normal course of events; both internal and external adaptation to and genuine acceptance of a loss is possible only after a prolonged work of mourning (Freud, 1917). Gregory was unable to mourn the loss of the self representation he had before his experience in the South Pacific, for example, and groups react in much the same way as individuals when attempting to accommodate disastrous happenings.

Disasters such as the explosion of the Challenger 7 Space Shuttle or the great earthquake in Mexico City brought considerable expressions of black humor. Such distasteful jokes had various functions: they reduced the saddening affect on the survivors and helped to displace their guilt over surviving on those who had perished; "protected" from the shock of the tragedy by black humor, the members of the group could initiate mourning in an acceptable and shared way. Different cultures use different ways of coping with a shared tragedy, such as recalling the event in ceremonies, legal processes, and art. The erection of appropriate memorials is part of a shared work of mourning, while Peter's "mental tombstone" used to bury Gregory's representation is an example of an individual case. It is more difficult to mourn loss and humiliation wrought by a human agency than to mourn a natural disaster since the former bring about a loss of self-esteem and group identity. For an event to constitute "chosen trauma" it must be one that cannot be worked through, and losses associated cannot be mourned adaptively, so it is included in the group's self representation and then expelled into subsequent generations. Although succeeding generations experience it as though it were a current happening, the affect it evokes is congruent with issues of shared identity rather than with the historical truth.

Chosen Glories

There are also "chosen glories" (Volkan, 1991)—gratifying historical events that boost the group's self-esteem; these are also passed on as "psychological genes" from generation to generation. Here, however, we focus on the traumas that color group attitudes.

ISTANBUL—NOT CONSTANTINOPLE

Here I give an example based on work done with the historian Norman Itzkowitz (Volkan and Itzkowitz, 1993, 1994). Although Kosova, the Serbians' major "chosen trauma," did not spread into the consciousness of Europe or the West, the fall of Constantinople to the Turks sixty-four years later became a more generalized "chosen trauma" for the Western Christian world, and it remains so on one level or another among many ethnic–national groups.

In 1071 the Turkish Seljuk leader Sultan Alp Arslan defeated the Byzantine Emperor Romanus IV Diogenes near Manzigert, and during the next centuries Asia Minor, the heartland of today's

Turkey, gradually became "Turkified." Soon after the battle of Manzigert, a group of Seljuk Turks captured Jerusalem, which led to the Crusades. By the time the Crusaders entered Jerusalem, the city was no longer under Turkish control; but their perception of the Turks as the enemies of Christianity prevailed. (Later, Jerusalem was taken by the Ottoman Turks.) It was, however, the fall of Constantinople to the Turks, which came three-hundred years after Manzigert, that became a major "chosen trauma" for the Christian world.

Constantinople was conquered by the successors to the Seljuk Turks, the Ottomans, on May 29, 1453. This marked the end of one era in history and the start of a new one as the Byzantine Empire was replaced by the Ottoman Empire. Since Constantinople had been taken on a Tuesday, every Tuesday thereafter was regarded as an unpropitious day by Christians, especially Greeks, who consider themselves the heirs of Byzantium. Reality, fantasy, ritual, and myth have been linked throughout history because the perception of events is colored by shared emotions. In Europe, during medieval and early modern times, those recording historical events tended to disregard real causes and to attribute the unfolding of human history to the hand of God. The seizure of Constantinople by the Turks was seen to reflect God's judgment upon "the sins of Christians everywhere" (Schoebel, 1967, p. 14).

The loss of Constantinople reopened wounds caused by the fall of Jerusalem, and mourning for this loss could not take place to the point of resolution and be set aside. Jerusalem had been regained and lost again, but Constantinople's fall elicited only feelings of helplessness and narcissistic injury, and a storm of emotion. Greeks, heirs to Byzantium, remained to a degree "perennial mourners" of Constantinople's loss. The perennial mourner knows that a loss has occurred, but yearns, consciously or unconsciously, for the return of what is lost, at the same time wishing that he could accept reality fully and be rid once and for all of the burden of trying to turn back time. He seems doomed to struggle continually between "keeping" what is lost, and fully accepting a new reality (Volkan, 1981; Volkan and Zintl, 1993).

After the reality of the Turkish capture of Constantinople became clear, however, the Western world could not escape the blow of this trauma. The desire to undo the loss expressed itself in rumbling about organizing another Crusade. Nothing came of such talk, but the idea persisted. Christians of Constantinople sang together the refrain, "Again, with years, with time, they will be ours," in their attempt to deny the charges and undo their loss; denial appeared also in other ways. If a continuing link between the Turks and the Byzantines could be found, there would be less need for Byzantines and other Christians to feel pain. Many Westerners became preoccupied with the ancient origins of the Turks. For example, Giovanni Maria Filelfo, a humanist, declared that Mehmet II, the Sultan who had seized Constantinople, was a Trojan. Felix Fabri, a German, studied the idea that Turks descended from Turcus, a son of Troyas (Schoebel, 1967).

While these pseudohistorical efforts to find linking continuity between the two sides continued as a way to make loss and change tolerable, a counterattempt tried to unlink them so Byzantines could maintain their identity, and this, in turn, led to stereotyping the Turks. According to Berkes (1964), the Fates played a trick on the Turks because their seizure of Constantinople was condensed with a mental representation of their conquest of Jerusalem. The Turks became the unconsciously chosen targets of stubborn, systematic, and negative stereotyping by the Europeans and historians throughout the West.

Oedipal and Sexual Issues

Besides dealing a narcissistic blow to all the Christian world, the fall of Constantinople led to less apparent symbolism throughout Christendom that linked it with oedipal and sexual issues. Mehmet II, only 21 when he seized Constantinople, is known as Mehmet the Conqueror, or the Grand Turk. He was the fourth son of Murat II; his mother is thought to have been a Serbian or Macedonian slave, although one Turkish scholar recently claimed that she was Greek (Altan, 1992, personal communication). According to the Ottoman custom of the time, he was brought up by a nursemaid, with mentors to oversee his education.

When Mehmet was going through his adolescent passage (Blos, 1979), Murat II, who had arranged a peace treaty with the Serbians and Hungarians, voluntarily stepped down and his 12-year-old son became Sultan, assisted by his two mentors and his father's grand vizier, Halil Pasha. Halil played a major role in returning the older man to the throne within two years, dethroning the young Mehmet, by then 14. The Sultan remained friendly toward his son and took him on various campaigns. Thus it seems likely that the boy displaced the "bad" oedipal father image onto Halil as well as on the Byzantine Emperor. When Mehmet was 19, his father died, and he again became the Sultan. His natural mother died between his first and second enthronements.

Mehmet's preoccupation with Byzantium and his seizure of the city two years after becoming Sultan for the second time should not be attributed solely to his oedipal strivings. Turks already occupied the surrounding Asian and European areas of the Eastern Roman Empire, which basically had been reduced to the city of Constantinople, and it was only a matter of time before they attempted to conquer it. Young Mehmet addressed his task with great youthful zeal, and the Turks made the largest cannons ever seen in order to open a hole in the wall around Constantinople. The cannons were perceived as aggressive and powerful phallic symbols, and they were an object of interest to many Christians for years to come.

The Emperor Constantine was killed as the final Ottoman assault surged through the opening in the city wall. His head was cut off and shown to Mehmet. From a psychological viewpoint it is interesting that, soon after the Emperor's death, the triumphant young Sultan ordered the arrest of Halil Pasha, the other displaced "bad" father, and had him put to death. After Constantine's death, the young Sultan declared that he was the new chief protector of the Christian Church, his mother being a Christian. A son was replacing his father according to oedipal fantasy. It is still alleged that Mehmet the Conqueror slept with Constantine's daughters. Whatever the truth about this, such conjecture echoes an oedipal theme—the father (Constantine) having been killed, the son (young Mehmet) sleeps with his women. According to one story, possibly apocryphal, the young Sultan was told that the corpses of (excommunicated?) Christians did not decay, but remained intact after burial (Adıvar, 1970). Greek priests then opened some

Christian graves in Constantinople by his order and in his presence. Were this story true, it might indicate something more than the conqueror's intellectual curiosity about Christianity; he might have unconsciously needed proof that the enemy—and perhaps the "bad" oedipal father—had indeed rotted away and could not return to haunt him.

The seizure of Constantinople by the youthful and virile Sultan after he opened a hole in the walls of the city was perceived as a rape, and Turks were considered lustful. What was hard to assimilate was the fact that the "rape" was performed not by the father, but the son, who had achieved an oedipal triumph. The city, which was later named Istanbul, became over time the symbol of a fallen or grieving woman. Itzkowitz and I (Volkan and Itzkowitz, 1984, 1993, 1994) describe how this double symbolism attached to the city of Istanbul, celebrated in folksong and poems through many centuries, persists into the present.

Globalization

The expulsion of the Jews from Spain in 1492, and the growing European hostility toward other unwanted elements in their societies, such as heretics, homosexuals, and lepers, were part of the process of nation building that would see multiethnic and multireligious empires replaced by nation-states based on exclusivity of race and religion. Jews, accused of killing Jesus, were a threat to the Christians' identification with the son of God as European groups sought to purify themselves and solidify their identities (Suphi, 1992). Since Iberian Jews found a warm welcome in the Ottoman Empire, Jews and their Turkish protectors were lumped together as the enemy. The Ottomans, however, were not considered deicidal; instead, they posed a threat to the son of God as the conquerors of Jerusalem and Constantinople. Luther considered them God's way of punishing Christians for their sins. Well into the seventeenth century, Catholics viewed not just Islam but "Turcism" as representing the antichrist (Gardiner, 1991). Lacking military power, Jews were persecuted; whereas Turks, with their reputation for ferocity, escaped persecution although they were considered evil. Both anti-Turkish and anti-Semitic sentiment, whether conscious or unconscious, were at the core of the developing European nation-states in the nineteenth century (Suphi, 1992).

Preoccupation with the Turks as conquerors of Jerusalem and Constantinople became globalized as Europeans began "discovering" new parts of the world and colonizing them. For example, in 1539, Mexican Indians took part in a dramatic pageant in Mexico representing the liberation of Jerusalem from the Turks by the armies of the Catholic world joined by those of the New World (Motolinía, 1951). Even today, a variation of this pageant is still performed in Mexico, halfway around the world from Turkey (Harris, 1992). This globalized stereotyping was even incorporated into Webster's Dictionary under the definition of "Turk," which reads "one exhibiting any quality attributed to Turks, such as sensuality and brutality." Few if any nationalities other than the Turks have "qualities" included in their definitions!

The mental representation of the fall of Jerusalem and Constantinople (along with associated meanings) was especially influential during and after the Greek War of Independence in 1821. Before that, for four centuries starting with the fall of Constantinople, Greeks had lived within the Ottoman Empire. In the decades following this war, the Greeks combined Hellenistic and Byzantine elements to develop a new Greek identity (Herzfeld, 1986). Initially the Europeans, especially the British, the French, and the Russians, joined forces in "demanding" and sponsoring the new Hellenic identity for modern Greece. While the Greeks did embrace this new identity, they had to incorporate into it their previous identity as heirs to the Byzantine Empire. The ideologies and identities of classical Greece and Byzantium were not always compatible, so integration of the two sides required massive projections of those Romeic, oriental aspects of identity that threatened cohesion. Turks were "suitable targets" (Volkan, 1988) to receive these projections. They now were perceived as oriental—lazy, primitive, and dirty—as well as lustful and aggressive. This new condensed stereotype appears in Cobb's (1914) *The Real Turk:* "In ordinary life he [the Turk] is affable and dignifiedly curteus [sic]; kind to his children, to animals, and to strangers. He seldom loses his temper; but when he does, beware! He does not encourage street-fighting; yet, if he bears resentment, he may kill you!" (p. 31).

Even Freud (1932) could not avoid stereotyping "Turks." When he wrote to Einstein regarding applying psychoanalytic insights to wars and international diplomacy he was pessimistic, but he could not condemn all kinds of wars and aggression equally. He singled out Mongols and Turks, who were in fact protectors of Jews in the dark ages of Europe, as people who *only* brought disaster.

The Greeks' "Chosen Trauma"

Modern Greeks "reach back" to the fall of Constantinople, and all the mental representations and affects attached to it; this is their most dominant "chosen trauma." Even today, the mental representations of Greek family members of various generations who were "defeated" more recently by the Turks are condensed with the Byzantine's defeat in 1453, constituting a shared element that is by now primarily psychological.

Greek historians, political scientists, and sociologists speak of an ideology known in Greek as *Megali Idea* (The Great Idea), which Markides (1977), a Cypriot-born Greek sociologist, describes as "a dream shared by Greeks that someday the Byzantine Empire would be restored and all the Greek lands would once again be united into a Greater Greece" (p. 10). The Great Idea was first acclaimed at the time of the Greek War of Independence, but Young (1969) points out that its seeds came soon after the fall of Constantinople. Markides holds that it has an "internal logic": we can say that mental representations pertaining to the fall of Constantinople persisted in the minds of many generations, changing function and becoming by today one of the major markers of modern Greek identity. Whenever problems arise between Greece and Turkey, the Greek press, as well as politicians and military men, often refer to the Turks as "rapists" (Volkan and Itzkowitz, 1994). This reflects the symbolic interpretation of the conquest of Mehmet II, and accounts no doubt for incidents such as the receipt by a prominent Turkish political figure of a postcard sent by a Greek woman; in reference to a rape scene pictured on it she wrote, "This is what you want to do to us" (Volkan and Itzkowitz, 1993).

CONCLUSION

Over the years, whenever I have attended a meeting of antagonistic ethnic groups as a neutral moderator, I have been struck by the way in which each group began by competitively citing its "chosen traumas" and glories. I have written elsewhere (Volkan, 1988, 1992) about the meaning of such competition, which indicates the reactivation of ancestors' past injuries and triumphs in the service of repairing each party's ethnic identity, which is being threatened by the encounter. To share the mental representations of the ancestors associated with these significant and shared past events within a group is to validate its ethnic identity.

I compare the way in which shared representations of past generations and events affect the ethnicity of the present generation to the way in which a patient's early unconscious identifications, uncovered only in psychoanalysis, affect his present personality organization. This led me to conclude that intergenerational transmission of ethnic attitudes is a complicated psychological process, and that psychoanalytical concepts can be useful to statesmen faced by the ethnic intransigence now displayed in all corners of the world.

The invisible psychological dynamics of large-group identity are always intertwined with economic, military, and legal "real world" issues. I have not attempted to discuss here how such psychological insights can be applied in practice, having written on this subject elsewhere (Volkan, 1988; Volkan and Harris, 1992, 1993b; Volkan, Julius, and Montville, 1990; Volkan, Montville, and Julius, 1991). I believe that when psychological phenomena are identified and understood in assessing international relations, more adaptive ways may be found to negotiate solutions.

REFERENCES

Adıvar, A. A. (1970), *Osmanlı Türklerinde Ilim (Science Among the Ottoman Turks).* Istanbul: Remzi Kitabevi.

Akhtar, S. (1992), *Broken Structures: Severe Personality Disorders and Their Treatment.* Northvale, NJ: Jason Aronson.

Apprey, M. (1993a), Dreams of urgent / voluntary errands and transgenerational haunting in transsexualism. In: *Intersubjectivity, Projective*

Identification and Otherness, by M. A. Apprey & H. Stein. Pittsburgh: Duquesne University Press, pp. 102–128.
——— (1993b), The African-American experience: Forced immigration and transgenerational trauma. *Mind & Hum. Interact.*, 4:70–75.
Berkes, N. (1964), *Türk Düşününde Batı Sorunu (The Western Question in Turkish Thought)*. Ankara: Bilgi Yayınevi.
Blos, P. (1979), *The Adolescent Passage*. New York: International Universities Press.
Cain, A. C., & Cain, B. S. (1964), On replacing a child. *J. Amer. Acad. Child Psychiatry*, 3:443–456.
Cobb, S. (1914), *The Real Turk*. Boston: Pilgrim Press.
Elbirlik, K. (1980), Organ loss, grieving and itching. *Amer. J. Psychother.*, 84:523–533.
Emde, R. N., Johnson, W. I., & Easterbrooks, M. A. (1988), The do's and don't's of early moral development. In: *The Emergence of Morality*, ed. J. Kagan & S. Lamb. Chicago: University of Chicago Press, pp. 245–277.
Freud, A. (1958), Adolescence. *The Psychoanalytic Study of the Child*, 13:255–278. New York: International Universities Press.
——— Burlingham, D. (1945), *Infants Without Families*. New York: International Universities Press.
Freud, S. (1917), Mourning and melancholia. *Standard Edition*, 14:243–258. London: Hogarth Press, 1957.
——— (1932), Why war? *Standard Edition*, 22:197–215. London: Hogarth Press, 1964.
Gardiner, A. B. (1991), Islam as anti-Christ in the writings of Abraham Woodhead, spokesman for restoration Catholics. *Restoration*, 15:89–98.
Green, N., & Solnit, A. J. (1964), Reactions to the threatened loss of a child: A vulnerable child syndrome. *Pediatrics*, 34:58–66.
Greenspan, S. I. (1989), *The Development of the Ego: Implications for Personality Theory, Psychopathology and the Psychotherapeutic Process*. Madison, CT: International Universities Press.
Harris, M. (1992), Hidden manuscripts in public places. *Mind & Hum. Interact.*, 3:63–69.
Herzfeld, M. (1986), *Ours Once More: Folklore, Ideology and the Making of Modern Greece*. New York: Pella.
Kernberg, O. F. (1975), *Borderline Conditions and Pathological Narcissism*. New York: Jason Aronson.
Markides, K. C. (1977), *The Rise and Fall of the Cyprus Republic*. New Haven: Yale University Press.
Mitscherlich, A. (1971), Psychoanalysis and the aggression of large groups. *Internat. J. Psycho-Anal.*, 52:161–167.

Motolinía, T. de (1951), *History of Indians of New Spain*, tr. F. B. Dteck. Washington, DC: Academy of American Franciscan History.

Poznanski, E. O. (1972), The "replacement child": A saga of unresolved parental grief. *Behav. Pediatrics*, 81:1190–1193.

Rangell, L. (1976), Discussion of the Buffalo Creek disaster: The course of psychic trauma. *Amer. J. Psychiatry*, 133:313–316.

Schoebel, R. (1967), *The Shadow of the Crescent: The Renaissance Image of the Turk (1453–1517)*. New York: St. Martin's Press.

Spitz, R. (1965), *The First Year of Life*. New York: International Universities Press.

Suphi, M. (1992), The expulsion of Safarad Jews: Regression in the development of modern society. *Mind & Hum. Interact.*, 4:40–51.

Volkan, V. D. (1976), *Primitive Internalized Object Relations: A Clinical Study of Schizophrenic, Borderline and Narcissistic Patients*. New York: International Universities Press.

——— (1979), *Cyprus—War and Adaptation: A Psychoanalytic History of Two Ethnic Groups in Conflict*. Charlottesville, VA: University Press of Virginia.

——— (1980), Transsexualism: As examined from the point of view of internalized object relations. In: *On Sexuality: Psychodynamic Observations*, ed. T. B. Karasu & C. W. Socarides. New York: International Universities Press, pp. 189–221.

——— (1981), *Linking Objects and Linking Phenomena: A Study of the Forms, Symptoms, Metapsychology and Therapy of Complicated Mourning*. New York: International Universities Press.

——— (1987), Psychological concepts useful in the building of political foundations between nations (Track II diplomacy). *J. Amer. Psychoanal. Assn.*, 35:903–935.

——— (1988), *The Need to Have Enemies and Allies: From Clinical Practice to International Relationships*. Northvale, NJ: Jason Aronson.

——— (1990), Psychological processes in unofficial diplomacy meetings. In: *The Psychodynamics of International Relationships*, Vol. 2, ed. V. D. Volkan, J. Montville, & D. Julius. Lexington, MA. Lexington Books, pp. 207–222.

——— (1991), On "Chosen Trauma." *Mind & Hum. Interact.*, 3:13.

——— (1992), Ethnonationalistic rituals: An introduction. *Mind & Hum. Interact.*, 4:3–19.

——— (1993), What the Holocaust means to a non-Jewish psychoanalyst. In: *Persistent Shadows of the Holocaust*, ed. R. Moses. Madison, CT: International Universities Press, pp. 81–105.

——— Ast, G. (1992), *Eine Borderline-Therapie*. Göttingen: Vandenhoeck & Ruprecht.

——— ——— (1994), *Specktrum des Narzissmus.* Göttingen: Vandenhoeck & Ruprecht.

——— Greer, W. (in press), True transsexualism. In: *Sexual Perversions,* ed. I. Rosen. Oxford, England: Oxford University Press.

——— Harris, M. (1992), Negotiating a peaceful separation: A psychopolitical analysis of current relationships between Russia and the Baltic republics. *Mind & Hum. Interact.,* 4:20–39.

——— ——— (1993a), *Shaking the Tent: The Psychodynamics of Ethnic Terrorism,* Monograph 1. Charlottesville, VA: Center for the Study of Mind and Human Interaction.

——— ——— (1993b), Vaccinating the political process: A second psychopolitical analysis of relationships between Russia and the Baltic states. *Mind & Hum. Interact.,* 4:169–190.

——— Itzkowitz, N. (1984), *Immortal Atatürk: A Psychobiography.* Chicago: University of Chicago Press.

——— ——— (1993), Istanbul, not Constantinople: The Western World's view of the Turk. *Mind & Hum. Interact.,* 4:129–134.

——— ——— (1994), *Turks and Greeks: Neighbors in Conflict.* Cambridgeshire, U.K.: Eothen press.

——— Julius, D., & Montville, J., Eds. (1990), *The Psychodynamics of International Relationships,* Vol. 1. Lexington, MA: Lexington Books.

——— Masri, A. (1989), The development of female transsexualism. *Amer. J. Psychotherapy,* 43:92–107.

——— Montville, J., & Julius, D., Eds. (1991), *The Psychodynamics of International Relationships,* Vol. 2. Lexington, MA: Lexington Books.

——— Zintl, E. (1993), *Life After Loss: The Lessons of Grief.* New York: Charles Scribner's Sons.

Young, K. (1969), *The Greek Passion: A Study in People and Politics.* London: J. M. Dent.

17.

THE WORKING THROUGH OF THE NAZI EXPERIENCE IN THE GERMAN PSYCHOANALYTIC COMMUNITY

MARTIN WANGH, M.D.

> Alexander Mitscherlich (1947) said: "Only when we recognize and confess what happened and why it happened, and how we were participants in the planning of it, can we, Germans, be healed."

Have we psychoanalysts succeeded in uncovering our own traumatizations and their resulting scotomata which the catastrophe of World War II and that of the Shoah have deposited within us? How far has psychoanalysis itself, especially but not only in Germany, overcome the inability to mourn? Have we already succeeded in erecting spiritual gravestones over the bones and ashes, so that the spirits of the evil deeds, the guilt, the self-punishment, the compulsion to undo, and also the wish to deny it all, which all stand in the way of creativity, can be laid to rest?

Are we already capable of confronting our ambivalences (i.e., to know of both our love and our hate) for both the victims and the evil-doers? Can we recognize our early ties to them and our early identification with them? Can we mourn them completely and keep them afterwards solely as memories? Can we distance ourselves from them as separate human beings, and thereby be free to turn to new objects, lovable as well as hatable ones? Can we find ways to sublimate our losses creatively?

This paper was translated from the German by the author.

A longer version of this paper was presented on November 8, 1991, at the Frankfurt University, upon invitation of the Freud-Stiftung, in Tel Aviv at the Israel Psychoanalytic Institute, as well as elsewhere in Europe, America, and Australia.

The Mitscherlichs' book about the inability to mourn gives us guidelines for these considerations. It is therefore necessary to occupy ourselves in some detail with the course of the mourning process in general. Freud (1915, 1925) defines mourning as "the reaction to the loss of a beloved person or of an abstraction which has moved into its place like fatherland, liberty, an ideal etc." "(Mourning) is a deep, painful mood." It carries with it a "deep lowering of self-esteem" which manifests itself in self-reproaches (as in melancholia). "Distancing oneself from the mourned objects only takes place against intense resistance."

The acerbity of the self-reproaches, Freud speculated, had its origin in the ambivalence which the subject unconciously felt toward the object, during its lifetime. The self-accusations had been accusations against the object. Since the death of the object a part of the ego becomes identified with it, while another part criticizes it. Nowadays we would say the superego accuses the ego. The identification with the criticized object, however, also prevents the giving up of the lost object; the internalization impedes the completion of mourning. This inner accusatory situation is quite akin to the persecutory phase which Melanie Klein postulated to exist in the development of the infant.

I have elaborated on these reflections of Freud, as laid down in "Mourning and Melancholia," because, as we shall see later on, they are relevant for the obstacles to the completion of the mourning process for their Nazi forbears for the present generations of the German psychoanalytic community.

The Mitscherlichs believed that the manic rebuilding of war-destroyed Germany, "das Wirtschaftswunder," supported as it was by the Marshall Plan, together with the denial of reality contained in the formula "the Third Reich was only a dream," prevented the whole German population from falling into a melancholic state.

Already before the war Helene Deutsch (1937) had pointed out that the mourning process as a reaction to a real loss pushes toward completion. When this does not happen other exaggerated reactions take its place. Frequently, these are persistent unexpected depressions and very often psychosomatic afflictions. Other authors (Bowlby, 1960, 1961, 1963; Wolfenstein, 1966; Dietrich, 1989) point out in addition, that a weak ego cannot take on the labor of mourning. This was certainly the case in those who were weakened by starvation, degraded and numbed by being constantly surrounded by death in concentration camps, and those who were children in those camps, or those who as children survived the bombardment of the war that destroyed towns, or even those German soldiers who lived through the years of Russian imprisonment. The survivors of the Shoah, we know, don't have the strength to go through mourning even now, fifty years later. A "conspiracy of silence" arose on both sides, on the side of the victims as well as on the side of the evil-doers. Silence established itself everywhere where shame and guilt, just for being a survivor, pressed upon one's conscience.

Margarete and Alexander Mitscherlich summarized their 1967 work *The Inability to Mourn* as follows:

> The inability to mourn the loss of the Fuehrer is the result of an intense defense against guilt, shame and fear, a defense which was achieved by the [abrupt] withdrawal of previously powerful cathexes. The Nazi past was de-realized. The occasion for mourning was not only the death of Adolph Hitler, as a real person, but above all his disappearance as the representative of a collective ego-ideal . . . [p. 23].
>
> The Germans . . . had received a blow to the very core of their self-esteem, and the most urgent task . . . was to ward off the experience of a melancholic impoverishment of the self [p. 24].

The Mitscherlichs also thought that denial of the past is particularly characteristic of the German personality. In their preface to the English edition of their book (1975) they added that this denial was even stronger after World War I. I can confirm that personally. In my Gymnasium the studies of German history of World War I ended with the victories over the Russians in Tannenberg (August 26–30, 1914) and at the Masurian Lakes (September 6–15, 1914). The desire to overlook reality showed itself in my school also in other ways. For instance, we were handed a copy of the Weimar Constitution only at the time of graduation and without any comment. A few years ago, on the occasion of a meeting in Lindau about the threat of nuclear war I sought to illustrate the masochism of the Nazis through their behavior in regard to the Allied aerial bombardment of Freiburg in Breisgau on November 27, 1944. More than 20,000 people were killed in twenty minutes. I inquired about that at the city archive in Freiburg. The chief archivist told me: First of all, only 3000 people were killed and second, all the documents on that had been consumed in a fire in Karlsruhe, the town to which they had been transported during the French occupation. I did not leave it at that. I consulted the newspaper reports of the time in the nearby Swiss town of Basel. They confirmed the larger figures which a witness, then 12 years old, had given me (Wangh, 1985).

It is of great importance for our theme of the Nazi experience in the German psychoanalytic community to remind ourselves of World War I because what happened then affected the generation of the psychoanalytic leadership in Germany and my own generation most significantly. By the end of World War I Germany had suffered six million casualties; approximately 10 percent of its population (1.8 million dead, 4.2 million wounded, 618,000 prisoners). The Versailles peace pact dictated the loss of land, huge reparation payments, and occupation of the industrial Ruhr as guarantee. The Versailles pact was felt to be a great humiliation. In order to save Germany's pride the "stab in the back" (Dolchstoss-legende) was invented: Had it not been for such traitors as Erzberger (a Catholic) and Rathenau (a Jew)—both were subsequently murdered by ultraright-wing militants—Germany would not have lost the war.

The graver the post-World War I economic crises became, the more people of Hitler's generation and that of my own, educated with so much denial, gravitated toward the National Socialist movement or toward similar groups. A call for revenge filled the beer halls and the ranks of paramilitary organizations; and revenge was the basis on which they were founded in the first place. Revenge is the turning into action of what had been suffered passively. Revenge replaces mourning. As it incites the side that has had the greater loss to start hostilities anew, it eternalizes conflict. It thereby functions as the most noxious form of defense against mourning. It is nursed most profoundly by mythos and fantasy, and is therefore blind toward reality. It is limitless and stirs up the most regressive emotions and forms of aggression. Shakespeare lets the Duke of Exeter exclaim at the funeral of Henry the Fifth: "We mourn in black, why mourn we not in blood" (Henry VI,

Part I, Act I, line 17). "Blood" and death were the key words in the Nazi lexicon.

Everywhere in Germany there were memorials to the fallen soldiers of the 1914–1918 War, but for the fall from the grandiose heights of the Bismarckian, Wilhelminian Reich to the depth of the defeat of 1918 there were no monuments. The knowledge about the degradation of the fathers and the loss of self-esteem was replaced by an ever-growing "resentment" against the "injustice" of the Versailles pact. An increasingly dark, crude, and cruelty-promoting desire for revenge spread. The nearest objects at hand were the Jews, from whom one didn't have to fear immediate retaliation. Had not the historian Treitschke written already in 1880: "The Jews are our misfortune"? And thus, from 1933 on the world became spectator to the evil-doings against the Jews, only to find out soon enough that it was to be swallowed up itself by the unlimited appetite for revenge.

I do not believe that denial and intolerance of what has been suffered passively, and its reversal into active action, and the desire for revenge which springs from it, are attributes which characterize the German people alone. One has to recognize, however, that this mode of warding off pain and loss thoroughly permeated German history of the second quarter of the twentieth century. The difference between the German experience of World War I and that of the Allies, who had lost almost *equally* as many fathers and brothers, lay not in the number of those murdered, but in the defeat. This brought about an enormous depreciation of the fathers and of authority, which could only be mastered by denial and the desire to undo the facts through vengeful action. These two methods were the building blocks of Nazi ideology and practice. Via identification with the uniformed fathers and older brothers, who marched into the war with the Tsching-de-rassa and the flying banners, loss, defeat, shame, and humiliation were to be erased.

I consider these data from World War I as basic in my attempt to sketch from the outside the working through of the Nazi experience by the German psychoanalytic community. The Mitscherlichs postulated in 1967 that such a working through has to occur through a mourning process for the dead of World War II, for the dead aggressors as well as for the uncountable number of their victims. The Mitscherlichs also recognized, however, how great a resistance opposed this process and they therefore spoke of an "inability" to mourn.

In what is to follow, I will try now to explore the way in which the German psychoanalytic community has begun to walk upon this road of mourning. I wish to speak in the main of the operative trends and conflicts. It is as though I want to present the inner conflict of one corpus: only seldom will I make exceptions in this intentional anonymity.

While the "official" death, namely the cancellation of its registration in the bulletin of licensed organizations, of the German Psychoanalytic Society took place only in 1941, the *stepwise liquidation* (Ernest Jones' term as quoted by Thomae [1963]) began in 1933 with the resignation of the Jewish president of the Berlin Psychoanalytic Institute and Society, Max Eitingon. He handed the leadership over to two Aryan members, C. Müller-Braunschweig and F. Boehm. Then came the Gleichschaltung, the exclusion of all Jewish members from the Berlin Psychoanalytic Institute and Society (a process that occurred in all German learned institutions). The two new leaders undertook separate trips to Vienna, in order to seek Freud's blessing, so to say, for this step. His answer seemed to them ambiguous. C. Müller-Braunschweig wrote at the time to Ernest Jones in London, then president of the International Psychoanalytic Association, how heavy at heart he felt: "I hang with body and soul on our science and I love my fatherland" (quoted in Hier geht das Leben auf eine merkwuerdige Weise weiter . . . [p. 131]).

It is to be noted that the letterwriter only speaks of his tie to psychoanalytic science and to his fatherland, no word about his feelings toward his Jewish teachers, colleagues, or his candidates, who were excluded from membership by the Gleichschaltung. ("They went into emigration" was the frequently used euphemistic formula.) Beyond that the letterwriter sent a complaint to Jones that the "Jewish candidates, probably because of their resentment of the political changes taking place in Germany" had not paid their debt to the training fund of the Berlin Psychoanalytic Society.

No doubt, between 1936 and 1939, efforts were still made to teach some sort of psychoanalysis in the now "judenreinen" Berlin Psychoanalytic Institute. Antonovsky (1988) described the spiritual death of basic psychoanalytic thinking in the Germany of that time.

Fourteen Aryan colleagues remained in the Berlin Institute. One of them, Rittmeister, was hanged by the Nazis, when his secret anti-Hitler activity was discovered. Edith Jacobson was incarcerated for two years by the Gestapo, and only while she was temporarily released because of severe illness, could she be secretly evacuated to Czechoslovakia, and from there to the United States. Landau, the then president of the Frankfurt Psychoanalytic Institute, and fourteen other Jewish psychoanalytic colleagues perished in concentration camps.

The question now arises inevitably, what made the two leaders and the rest of the German psychoanalytic Aryan community prone to give in to the pressure of the Nazi regime? Could the German Psychoanalytic Society not have dissolved itself, as the Austrian and Dutch societies subsequently did, in order to evade its forced reorganization? It may not be unimportant to note that the two appointed leaders of the Berlin Society (which was in fact the only significant one in Germany at that time) were born in the same year as Hitler. They thus belonged to a generation which lived in the Zeitgeist of the historical and political events that I described earlier, which fostered German nationalism and its desire for revenge. In this sense they were indistinguishable from my Hamburg host, in whose house I lived as a student, who was of the same age. He was a plumber, and in 1933 still a staunch Social Democrat, but he said to me: "If a new war goes against France, then I go along again." In two papers (Wangh, 1962 [1964], 1968) I spoke of how deeply the soldier generation of the First World War was affected by the disastrous course of that war and by the misery that followed it. As far as I know, one heard hardly any self-questioning from the new leaders of the German psychoanalytic movement about their nationalism and its inner sources. Their ready submissiveness, their ready abandonment of their ties to their Jewish colleagues, their Jewish teachers, and candidates remained unexplored by them. Whatever self-analysis there might have been on this is simply omitted as they participated in the Zeitgeist.

In 1938, the Berlin Psychoanalytic Institute became with their collaboration integrated as "Section A" into the Deutsches Institut für Psychologische Forschung which stood under the leadership of Matthias Göring, a cousin of Hermann Göring, the Nazis' second in command.

After the war the leaders of this Section A fell out with one another. Their brotherly bond broke with the loss of their common love object, Hitler (cf. Adorno, 1970). This became particularly clear when the reconstituted German Psychoanalytic Society sought re-admission to the International Psychoanalytic Association (IPA) at the time of the first postwar congress of the association in 1949 in Zurich. At that time each of these collaborators in Section A sought rationalizations and justification for his actions. One of them was that in their opinion Freud had approved of the Gleichschaltung (Thomae, 1963, p. 77).

The liquidation of psychoanalysis in Germany was passed over mostly in silence. But of course the need to justify contained the unconscious confession of guilt. F. Boehm advised the others that it would be futile to seek readmission in the IPA as "there was too much 'resentment' out there, because of our collaboration at the Göring Institute." The volume: "Hier geht das Leben auf eine sehr merkwuerdige Weise weiter . . . " refers to F. Boehm's opinion on pp. 182–186. At no time did these leaders of the former Section A invite one another to mourn together. They could not confess to each other that they all felt that they had lost something that was dear to them in common: their love for the Führer, Adolf Hitler, their esteem for their leader, Matthias Göring, who died while imprisoned by the Russians. They also could not remind each other of their former common tie to their Jewish models, Freud, Abraham, and Eitingon. They could not reveal to each other the huge degree of dependency which these ties had contained. They could not publicly confess the fear of death under which they lived, at least since their colleague Rittmeister was condemned to death. This fear manifested itself in the gallows humor by which the closet in the Berlin Psychoanalytic Institute in which the writings of Freud were under lock and key, was designated as the "poison closet." How enduring the fear and the compulsion to deny were can be illustrated by an article published *five* years after the end of the war by the leader of Section A, F. Boehm (1951), about the origins of anxiety. He exemplified public anxiety by speaking of the destruction mania of Savonarola and his incitement of the masses, but made no reference to Hitler and the Nazis.

Shame about their spiritual regression and guilt about their actions, and possibly for having survived others, must have played a big role in their motivations to stay silent and their inability to enter into a state of mourning. But guilt, shame, or mourning which cannot be consciously experienced by a parental generation, about which one has to stay silent, is always given over unconsciously to the next generation—this together with the tendency to want to pass over in silence the details of one's past.* This next generation lives then under constant pressure to have to undo something. The German "Suehne-bewegung" (movement of penitence), whose members were in the main the children of participants in the war, has its origins in this sequence. For this reason too, although only with reluctance, the German "Wiedergutmachungsgelder"—restitution payments—were paid out to survivors of Nazi persecution. Yet, one also always finds rebellious feelings against these delegated burdens. In addition, one can observe that what parents stay silent about gets filled in by their children, whose curiosity is not satisfied, with sadomasochistic fantasies about the actual or presumed misdeeds of the parents. I have seen this frequently in the offspring of those parents who escaped the Holocaust and who could never tell their children the terrible details of their barely accomplished escape.

Now I come specifically to the evolution of the working-through experience in the German psychoanalytic community. Here too the delegation of suppressed feelings played a role in the relation of the new generation of psychoanalytic candidates with their teaching analysts. The socotomata of the teaching analysts became scotomata of the analysands. Only slowly, under the impact of the end of the war, with the end of the immediate postwar misery, and under the influence of the development of greater liberty and openness in general, did the strict course of this sequence diminish. Only the second and third generations of postwar analysts were enabled to bring to light the hitherto suppressed facts of the inner ties to the Nazi regime of the colleagues who were participants in Nazi ideology and actions. There had been, of course, some

*In Munich, where I presented this paper, a colleague rightfully pointed out that children, especially small children, are prone to incorporate the unconsciously self-rejecting, depressive feelings of parents, probably in order to diminish the alienation which goes with such self-rejection. They thereby probably try to keep their parents in their own orbit.

exceptions (Draeger, 1971), some few, who already during the war as young physicians, psychologists, or psychiatrists found the courage to question themselves about the degree of their own participation in the Nazi crimes. Yet today still, and that seems to me particularly important, one may observe that many of those who belong to the younger generation of German psychoanalysts feel self-conscious and defensive during encounters with their opposite numbers from other lands.

During the first postwar years psychoanalysts like Mitscherlich, Cremerius, Thomae, and others were very much interested in psychosomatic diseases. They probably responded to the vast need of great numbers of those in the population who could not cope with their many losses. We know that psychosomatic symptomatology is a primary maneuver to keep anxiety and mourning out of consciousness. These colleagues, and other psychiatrists, especially under the leadership of von Baeyer (1964), observed and classified the many pathological manifestations in the survivors of persecution. A new science was born: "Victimology." At the same time sociologists like Horkheimer and Adorno, who after the war, had returned from exile, and had resumed their chairs at Frankfurt University, sought to find answers to the question: how, in the twentieth century, could the traditional German anti-Semitism (not so different from the French or English type) turn into an anti-Semitism for which Auschwitz has become an inerasable word of terror and shame.

From the combined efforts of the aforementioned psychiatrists, psychologists, psychoanalysts, and sociologists grew the symposium, "Die psychologischen und sozialen Voraussetzungen des Antisemitismus" (The Psychological and Social Preconditions of Anti-Semitism) which was held in the framework of the Fourth Congress of "Psychotherapie und Tiefenpsychologie" in Wiesbaden in 1962. I had the honor of being one of the panel participants. The symposium was an attempt to grasp intellectually what had transformed the traditional German anti-Semitism into the demonic possession of Nazi anti-Semitism. Alexander Mitscherlich was the chairman of this panel.

A short time thereafter appeared the first clarification of the history of German psychoanalysis under Hitler. There was the already mentioned extensive research by Helmuth Thomae about the

"Neo-analysis" of Schultz-Henke (1963). The latter served as one of the facilitating theoretical innovations for the deviation of psychoanalysis from its origins. Then followed, as already mentioned, the basic work of Alexander and Margarete Mitscherlich on *Die Unfähigkeit zu Trauern. Grundlagen Kollektiven Verhaltens.* (*The Inability to Mourn. Bases of Collective Behavior*), which searched deeply for both the intellectual and the affective problematic of the Nazi experience.

During this period, and at least for the next decade, the German psychoanalytic community expanded enormously in number. Probably corresponding to the need of the perturbed postwar population, this expansion was fostered and supported by the fact that, at least in West Germany, the health insurance companies were willing to carry the cost of a considerable part of psychoanalytic treatment (they still do). During those years, as Loch (1983) reported, intensive catching up took place with the progress made during the intervening years in psychoanalysis in the world outside Germany.

Thus it came about that on the occasion of the International Psychoanalytical Congress of 1977 in Jerusalem (and that it took place *there* was probably also of special, affective significance) that the German Psychoanalytic Association felt itself motivated and secure enough to propose that the next International Congress be held, for the first time again, in Germany, namely in Berlin.

It was a bitter experience for the German members of the IPA that with much emotion many of the Jewish participants of this congress refused to hold such a meeting in Berlin, the capital of Hitler's Reich, so close to Wannsee, where the Final Solution of the Judenfrage (the Jewish Question) had been decided upon. Forty years had not diminished the pain which these localities reevoked. The German members experienced this refusal approximately as painfully as they had experienced their only conditional acceptance in Zurich, in 1949, almost thirty years before.

Intensive self-questioning followed. Did we really already work through the Nazi catastrophe? A time of great inner turbulence was the consequence. Margarete Mitscherlich-Nielsen (1979), wrote a paper entitled "Die Notwendigkeit zu trauern" ("The Necessity to Mourn"):

> We Germans are viewed in the outside world, whether we want it or not, just as before, from the perspective of the past. These are less prejudgments, than they are postjudgments. . . . Germans cannot withdraw from occupying themselves with their past. In order to develop the capacity to mourn, a special type of memory work is necessary, which includes the reliving of our behavior, our feelings, and fantasies at the time—what matters is to find out why Hitler had such an unbelievable influence upon us, most Germans, to pervert our consciences with false judgments . . . [p. 982).

> The working through of that which led to National Socialism . . . the psychological and spiritual identification of the individual with that time [is needed]. . . . Today's 20-year-olds, whose parents transmitted to them their warding off of the past, live still in the shadow of denial and repression of events, which can't be undone. . . . The alternative to working through is neglect through rendering the labor of mourning obsolete. [But] such happenings, in my opinion, cannot be considered obsolete . . . certainly not while victims or their children are still alive. . . . Also, the offspring of those who were the evil-doers and fellow travelers have, as we know, considerable psychological problems. The positive identification with their parents and their feelings of self-worth are extremely disturbed, or, the denial of these problems by means of lack of affect and alienation, is often the consequence [p. 983].

The Jerusalem Congress became the catalyst that caused a storm against the German analysts' own teaching analysts. This manifested itself particularly at the time of the Congress of the Middle European Association in 1980 in Bamberg, Germany. Here there were open and bitter accusations against the stonewalling resistance of the teaching analysts. And additionally, the overall theme of the congress "Die Wiederkehr von Krieg und Persekution" (The Return of War and Persecution) brought to the surface for the first time that those, who as children, had been exposed in Germany itself to war and flight, had their own agenda. They did not wish to speak of the victims of persecution alone.

Grubrich-Simitis (1979) described at the beginning of this stormy period how difficult it was for psychoanalysts to stay empathic with the deep misery of the survivors of the Holocaust. Then especially between 1980 and 1985 we find the pages of *Psyche*, the oldest postwar German psychoanalytic journal, filled with controversies about cooperation of German psychoanalysis with the Nazi regime. The controversy is at times very sharp, at times ad hominem. Research is earnest and impartial as well as biased and emotional, at times so dry and affectless that it becomes confusing. The disputes spill over into special mimeographed editions by the editors of *Psyche* (April and May 1984) and by the presidium of the German Psychoanalytical Association itself (September 1984). The voices heard in this dispute were at times shrill and accusing and at times defending and forgiving. They are too numerous to be singled out here. I am inclined to see this extended period in German psychoanalysis as a manifestation of a paranoid–persecutory phase (to use Kleinian terminology) corresponding to the self-accusations and self-justifications which Freud commented on in "Mourning and Melancholia" (1915).

After some deliberations the leadership of the International Psychoanalytical Association came to a compromise decision: The 1985 congress of the IPA (i.e., the return to Germany) would take place in the Free Hanseatic city of Hamburg. With some knowledge of the acute and intensive preoccupation in the German Psychoanalytical Association with the working through of the Nazi prehistory, I proposed during 1982 and 1983 that the major theme of the Hamburg Congress be precisely this issue. While young German colleagues and many of their elders were eagerly agreeing with me, to my surprise the president of the IPA, himself an Italian Jewish refugee in England, together with his staff(!), placed themselves in opposition to such a proposal. "How could we," he wrote me, "go to Hamburg and be so offensive to our hosts?! . . . It would be tactless. . . . How would it be if he came to Israel and spoke there about the war in Lebanon?" Despite my inherently pacifist inclinations, maybe built on reaction formation, I was shocked by his placing on a par the Shoah, the genocide of the Jews, and of so many other completely disarmed and helpless people, with the fight against the constantly attacking and armed Palestine Liberation Army (PLO). Quite antianalytically, the president of the IPA proposed to sweep under the rug what had been experienced worldwide with profound psychopathological consequences. I should not have been so astounded. The wish to deny, to have done with what is a traumatic overload, demonstrably extends itself to the persecutors and the persecuted alike. In a further compromise the Program Committee for the 1985 Congress set aside one day for the discussion of the "Nazi Phenomenon." I take exception to this label too: a "phenomenon" is a meteoric manifestation, it suddenly appears and equally fast it disappears. The Nazi ideology and actions took a long time in preparation, and as we see their psychological consequences have not yet vanished.

But as those who attended the Hamburg Congress will remember, the discussions did not take the foreseen, restrictive course. First of all the participants found in Hamburg an extraordinary picture-and-word exhibition (Brecht, Friedrich, Hermanns, Kaminer, and Juelich, 1985) about the development and liquidation of the German Psychoanalytical Society, and second, the greeting address by the Hamburg Mayor, Klaus von Dohnany (1986) drew all our attention forcibly to the Nazi catastrophe and its consequences. He criticized psychoanalysis for its previous political disengagement and for its present attempts in the same direction. In consonance with Mitscherlich's thesis of missing mourning, he declared: He who says "our Bach" and "our Beethoven" has also to say "our Hitler."

In 1989 a meeting of psychoanalysts took place in Jerusalem. Its theme was: "The Meaning of the Nazi Holocaust to Those Not Directly Affected. A Psychoanalytic View." The meeting had been arranged by the Freud Centre of the Hebrew University, under the leadership of Rafael Moses, together with the Israel Psychoanalytic Society. Here, the late Gottfried Appy (1986, 1989a,b), then the president of the German Psychoanalytical Association, took up the just-cited words of Dohnany as the motto for his presentation entitled: "Collective Guilt and Responsibility." Following the psychoanalytic formulations of Melanie Klein, he delineated the way German psychoanalysis could accomplish the end of mourning over its lost, and at the same time hated, Nazi ideals.

> "We have to reappropriate these ideals," he said, "that means to recognize them once more as our inner objects . . . we have to admit that these representatives of these ideals had been loved by us, although they were also hated, and that they are still parts of ourselves. To declare them only as being 'out there' denies our identification with them. . . . Only after this sort of recognition of an inner conflict, can a renewed separation from them take place.

> "As of now it is a conflict which has to be tolerated. It is a constant process. In order to maintain a degree of health, despite the depression which necessarily has to occur because of the loss of an ideal, the process is slowed up by resistance [my addition]. The road of depression over the loss of an ideal goes through what Melanie Klein calls the 'paranoid phase' of development. The paranoia manifests itself in a defensive arrogance: 'we consider ourselves to be free of guilt or shame and we push these onto others.' "

Such shifting occurred, according to Beland (1988), when in 1949 and 1950 the German Psychoanalytical Association split off from the German Psychoanalytical Society, and thereby obtained recognition by the IPA.

In my opinion, the phenomenology of a paranoid phase became quite clear about 1980, during and after the Bamberg Congress. There were sharp attacks against the teaching analysts for their silence about their own teachers' Nazi past. This silence fixed the scotomata, which the new generation now gradually uncovered in itself. Against these accusations in writings and words, there were other voices, which tried to defend the elders, praised their courage for having gone into "inner emigration" during the Nazi time. "We should be thankful to them that any traces of psychoanalysis had remained." What also became clear during these disputes in Bamberg was that those who wanted to be heard included the offspring of survivors of the Shoah, but also those who had passed as children through the terror of war on the side of the evil-doers. They too accused their parents and were full of self-pity (self-pity always contains an accusation against someone who has done one damage). All these were, in my opinion, signs of a paranoid-persecutory phase. This phase, however, is also the threshold to the depressive phase, which opens the way to accomplish mourning.

No matter how difficult it may be for us analysts to be empathic with those whom we feel to be exclusively evil, outer objects, we have to acknowledge them also as inner objects. We have to examine in which historical setting they belong; we have to uncover what led them into being National Socialists or their fellow travelers. We also have to grasp the personal fear in which they lived to the degree to which they secretly wanted to uphold individualism as against conformity. We have to try to sense the humiliation brought to them by their dependency on Freud, from whom they sought approval for their betrayal of their Jewish colleagues. We also have to follow their inner degradation through their submission to Hitler and his delegates.

We all are tempted to embrace either of the alternatives, idealization or total repudiation. Appy, however, held that we have to live with the persistence of ambivalent feelings, those of love and hate toward inner objects—mirror images of outer ones—and that depressive feelings, which always occur when a separation takes place, have to be tolerated. Only slowly can new ideals be assimilated in order to reconstitute a less conflict-laden identity. It is then also probable that creative activities may develop out of the mourning, including all the aspects of the events of the past.

An example of such working through of mourning was presented in December of 1990 at the meeting of the American Psychoanalytic Association in Miami, Florida. The title of the presentation was: "Dilemmas in Identifications for the Post-Nazi Generations: 'My Good Father was a Bad Man?' " (Tessman, 1990). The patient was a daughter of a high Nazi official. He was arrested by the Russians on his flight West with his family. He died somewhere in Russia. The daughter remembered his proud bearing when he was arrested. She was quite conscious of the fact that she came to therapy—it was now thirty years later—in order to finish her mourning for the then rejected father, whose arrest caused her mother and her considerable material hardship, and exposed them to much sexual temptation. To turn to a German-speaking, Jewish female therapist and to be accepted by her into treatment, contained hope for forgiveness. Ten years after the therapy ended the therapist heard that the patient was now much happier and that she had found a way to express in a special form of artwork, which she had invented for herself, the pleasurable childhood memories with her father, her unconscious sexual fantasies about him, and burial rituals for him, whose grave was nowhere.

I proceed now to a proposal that aims at alleviating to some degree the burden of shame and guilt which rests upon the shoulders of the post-Nazi, post-Shoah generations of both the offspring of the evil-doers as well as those of the victims. I have already spoken of the self-consciousness with which they encounter each other, when and if at all they meet. The "never again shall happen what has happened" of which Adorno wrote upon his return to Germany, which is in the mind of many of today's Germans, and the "never again" of the Israeli Jews (enunciated not only by those on the political right), may sound alike, but they don't have the same perspective. One sensed this at the International Congress in Jerusalem in 1977, in Hamburg in 1985, and again in Jerusalem in 1988. The German psychoanalysts came to these meetings in expectation of being accused, and the Jews had to overcome unconscious fear, mistrust, or reactive defiance. The latter often left these encounters with a feeling of dissatisfaction and incompletion. Both sides have not yet ended the mourning which parents or grandparents had delegated to them.

My proposal refers to *these* generations (and *not to mine,* in which guilt, shame, or pain are still too alive and potentially too acute). I suggest that they who so unjustly have taken upon themselves a feeling of guilt, a need for penitence, or a reactively heightened fight or flight readiness, that they should meet two or three times a year in the coming years, in order to specifically explore, with and before each other, the identifications and signs of their missing mourning which the parental silence delegated to them. This would facilitate as well a degree of liberation from the mutual prejudices which automatically surface in each other's presence.

The situation that exists between German and Israeli psychoanalysts (and other Jewish psychoanalysts elsewhere as well) may be considered prototypical for the German and the Israeli populations. Psychoanalysts, who are by their training and inclination introspective and empathic, could in such a group-exploration serve as models for the work that remains to be done by the people to which they belong. Neither penitence, nor reactive courage, nor reversal by domination of another group can lead to an end of mourning. We have to find ways which permit creative sublimation for what has happened between us.

ADDENDUM

In the meantime a first intergroup meeting between members of the German mental health community and its Israeli counterpart has already taken place. It was organized by the Sigmund Freud

Center for Psychoanalysis of the Hebrew University, Jerusalem, in collaboration with OFEK: Organization, Person, Group. The Israel Association for the Study of Group and Organizational Processes.
The German Psychoanalytic Association (DPV)
The Israel Psychoanalytic Society (IPS)
The German Psychoanalytic Society (DPG)
The Israel Association of Psychotherapy (IAP)
Its name was: A Working Conference, "Germans and Israelis: The Past in the Present." It took place in Nazareth, Israel, from June 1 to June 6, 1994. Rafael Moses was one of the meeting's consulting staffers. It was a good beginning, which will, of course, need follow-up in order to deepen the personal searching and the mutual understanding.

REFERENCES

Adorno, T. W. (1970), Die Freudsche Theorie und die Struktur der Faschistischen Propaganda. *Psyche,* 24:7, 494–495.

Ahlheim, R. (1985), Bis ins dritte und vierte Glied. Das Verfolgungstrauma in der Enkelgeneration. *Psyche,* 39:330–354.

Antonovsky, A. M. (1988), Aryan analysts in Nazi Germany: Questions of adaptation, desymbolization, and betrayal. *Psychoanal. & Contemp. Thought,* 11:213–231.

Appy, G. (1986), Podium discussion: Psychoanalyse Unter Hitler—Psychoanalyse Heute. H. Beland et.al. *Psyche,* 40: May 86, 55:437–440.

——— (1989a) Kollektivschuld und Verantwortlichkeit. Klinische Ueberlegungen zur Destruktivitaet und deren Abwehr. *Zeitschr. Psychoanal. Theorie und Praxis,* 4:199–223.

——— (1989b), The meaning of "Auschwitz" today, Clinical reflections about the depletion of a destructive symbol. Paper presented at the Fourth Conference of the Sigmund Freud Centre of the Hebrew University of Jerusalem.

Baeyer, W. R. von, Haefner, H., & Kisker, K. P. (1964), Psychiatrie der Verfolgten. In: *Psychopathologische und gutachtliche Erfahrungen an Opfern der Nationalsozialistischen Verfolgung und Vergleichbare Extrembelastungen.* Berlin: Springer Verlag.

Beland, H. (1988), How they know themselves: Confronting the past—A contribution to the history of the German Psychoanalytic Association. *Psychoanal. & Contemp. Thought,* 11:267–283.

Boehm, F. (1951), Angst und Schuldgefuehl im Leben des Einzelnen und der Gemeinschaft. *Psyche,* 5:451–462.

Bowlby, J. (1960), Grief and mourning in infancy and early childhood. *The Psychoanalytic Study of the Child,* 15:9–52. New York: International Universities Press.

——— (1961), Process of mourning. *Internat. J. Psycho-Anal.,* 42:317–340.

——— (1963), Pathological mourning and childhood. *J. Amer. Psychoanal. Assn.,* 11:500–541.

Brecht, K., Friedrich, V., Hermanns, L. M., Kaminer, I., & Juelich, D. H. (1985), Hier geht das Leben auf eine sehr merkwuerdige Weise weiter . . ." Zur Geschichte der Psychoanalyse in Deutschland. ("Thus life goes on in a very peculiar way." To the History of Psychoanalysis in Germany.) Hamburg: Michael Kellner.

Deutsch, H. (1937), Absence of grief. *Psychoanal. Quart.,* 6:12–22

Dietrich, D. R. (1989), Early childhood parent death, psychic trauma and organization, and object relations. In: *The Problem of Loss and Mourning,* ed. D. R. Dietrich & P. Shabad. Madison CT: International Universities Press.

Dohnany, K von (1986), Eroeffnungsrede zum 34. Kongress der Internationalen Psychoanalytischen Vereinigung am 28. Juli 1985 (Stimmen zum Hamburger IPA-Kongress). *Psyche,* 40:860–863.

Draeger, K. (1971), Bemerkungen zu den Zeitumstaenden und zum Schicksal der Psychoanalyse und der Psychotherapie in Deutschland zwischen 1933 und 1949. *Psyche,* 25:255–268.

Freud, S. (1915), Mourning and melancholia. *Standard Edition,* 14:243–258. London: Hogarth Press, 1957.

Grubrich-Simitis, I. (1979), Extremtraumatisierung als Kumulatives Trauma. *Psyche,* 33:991–1023.

Juelich, D. (1992), Die Wiederkehr des Verdraengten. Soziologische Aspekte zur Identitaet der Deutschen nach Auschwitz. In: *Das Echo des Holocaust, Paedagogische Aspekte des Erinnerns,* ed. H. Schreier & M. Heyl. Hamburg: Kraemer, pp. 70–71.

Loch, W. (1983), Alexander Mitscherlich und die Wiedergeburt der Psychoanalyse in Deutschland. *Psyche,* 37:336–345.

Loewenstein, R. M. (1951), *Christians and Jews. A Psychoanalytic Study.* New York: International Universities Press.

Mitscherlich, A. (1967), *Die Unfaehigkeit zu Trauern, Grundlagen Kollektiven.* München: Verhaltens Piper.

——— (1982a), Geschichtsschreibung und psychoanalyse. Bemerkungen zum Nuernberger Prozess. *Psyche,* 36:1082–1093.

——— (1982b), Wissenschaft ohne Menschlichkeit (1947; 1949). *Psyche,* 36:1094–1109.

——— Mielke, F. (1947), *Das Diktat der Menschenverachtung, eine Dokumentation.* Maerz: Lambert Schneider.

——— (1989), The inability to mourn—today. In: *The Problem of Loss and Mourning. Psychoanalytic Perspectives,* ed. D. R. Dietrich & P. C. Shabad. Madison CT: International Universities Press, pp. 405–426.

——— (1992), Die (Un) Faehigkeit zu Trauern—Deutschland 1992. *Psyche,* 46:406–418.

Mitscherlich, M. N. (1979), Die Notwendigkeit zu Trauern. *Psyche,* 33:981–990.

Moser, T. (1992), Die Unfaehigkeit zu Trauern—eine taugliche Diagnose? *Psyche,* 46:389–405.

Parin, P. (1985), Die Angst der Maechtigen vor oeffentlicher Trauer. *Psyche,* 37:52–72.

Schreier, H., & Heyl, M. (1990), Brief (Letter) Maerz 26, 1990 / 3.26.90 Institut fuer Didaktik der Georgraphie, Geschichte, Politik und des Sachunterrichts, Universität Hamburg.

Shakespeare, W., Henry VI, Part 1. Arlen Shakespeare. New York: Routledge.

Tessman, L. H. (1990), Dilemmas in identifications for the Post-Nazi generations: My good father was a bad man? Paper presented at the American Psychoanalytic Association Meeting, Miami, FL, December.

Thomae, H. (1963), Die Neo-Psychoanalyse Schultz-Henkes, *Psyche,* 17:44–128.

Wangh, M. (1962), Psychoanalytische Betrachtungen zur Dynamik und Genese des Vorurteils, des Antisemitismus und des Nazismus. *Psyche,* 5:273–284.

——— (1964), National socialism and the genocide of the Jews. Psychoanalytic study of a historical event. *Internat. J. Psycho-Anal.,* 45:387–395.

——— (1968), A psychogenic factor in the recurrence of war. *Internat. J. Psycho-Anal.,* 49:319–323.

——— (1985), The nuclear threat: Its impact on psychoanalytic conceptualizations. *Psychoanal. Inqu.* 6:251–266.

Wolfenstein, M. (1966), How is mourning possible? *The Psychoanalytic Study of the Child,* 21:93–123. New York: International Universities Press.

THE WRITINGS OF RAFAEL MOSES

1951 *Psychological Aspects of Bronchial Asthma.* Doctoral dissertation, University of Zurich, Switzerland.

1957 Discussion. "On treatment of a kibbutz patient," by J. Mann. *Ofakim,* 11:433–434.

1958 A crisis in group therapy (with D. Schwartz). *Internat. J. Group Psychother.,* 8:445–458.

On attempted suicide (with R. Rubenstein & T. Lidz). *AMA Arch. Neur. & Psych.,* 79:103–112.

Trademark functions of symptoms in a mental hospital (with D. Freedman). *J. Nerv. & Ment. Dis.,* 127:448–457.

Problems in the adaptation of immigrants. *The Nurse in Israel,* 8:24–28.

1959 Trends in psychiatry and the medical framework (Hebrew). *Harefuah (J. Isr. Med. Assn.)* 56:3.

1960 Psychological aspects of breast feeding (Hebrew). *Briuth Hatsibur* (Public Health), 3:247–250.

Problems in the application of psychotherapeutic principles to a general medical setting (Spanish, with A. Hoek, R. Grushka, & S. Hoek). *Scientia: Revista de Psiquiatria,* 4(5):12–14.

About the problem of medical certificates (Hebrew, with A. Hoek). *Monthly J. Isr. Min. Labor,* 12(8):18–20.

Social background and intake procedure in a psychiatric out-patient clinic (Hebrew, with J. Shanan). *Megamoth,* 11(1):52–57.

1961 Uses and abuses of medical certificates (with A. Hoek). *Isr. Med. J.,* 20:95–102.

Problems in introducing group psychotherapy into a psychiatric outpatient clinic. *Acta Psychother.,* 9:227–280.

Psychiatric outpatient clinic: An analysis of a patient sample (with J. Shanan). *AMA Arch. Gen. Psychiatry,* 4:60–73.

The readiness to offer psychotherapy: Its relationship to social background and formulation of complaint (with J. Shanan). *AMA Arch. Gen. Psychiatry,* 4:212.

Psychosomatic problems of a patient with gastrointestinal disorders (Hebrew). *Harefuah,* 60:253–356.

1963 Parental education as part of a program for prevention of delinquency. In: Tel Aviv: Israeli Ministry of Welfare / Council for Problems of Delinquency, pp. 237–240.

Report of proceedings of the 12th international course in criminology. *Isr. Ann. Psychiatry,* 1:160–162.

Causation and prevention of crime: An Israeli psychiatrist's point of view. *Proc., 12th Internat. Course on Criminol.,* 11:225–245.

1964 Bureaucracy: A Social and psychological analysis. *Isr. Center of Man. Bull.,* 5:37–50.

Causation and prevention of crime in developing countries. *Corrective Psychiatry & J. Soc. Ther.,* 16:74–79.

The image and function of the psychiatrist in Israel (with J. Zellermayer). *Briuth Hatzibur* (Public Health), 7:2–3, 285–291.

Dangers inherent in the widespread use of group psychotherapy in Israel (Hebrew). *Megamoth,* 13:3–6.

1965 An analysis of the factors influencing psychiatric consultations in a general hospital (with P. Noy, A. Kaplan de Nour, & S. Wollstein). *Harefuah,* 68:18–20.

The general practitioner and present day civilization (Hebrew). *Briuth Hatsibur* (Public Health), 8:16–22.

Recognized emotional disorders in an Israeli immigrant community (with A. Hoek). *Med. Care.,* 3:230–239.

Emotional disorders in an Israeli immigrant community (with L. Terespolsky & A. Hoek). *Isr. Ann. Psychiatry,* 3:220–228.

1966 The discrepancy between expectation and services in psychiatric consultation (with P. Noy & A. Kaplan de Nour). *Arch. Gen. Psychiatry,* 14:651–657.

Different levels of awareness of illness: Their relation to some salient features in cancer patients (with N. Cividalli). *Trans. NY Acad. Sci.,* 984–994.

The institutionalization of mental health values. *Isr. Ann. Psychiatry,* 4:148–161.

1967 Psychiatric consultation in a general hospital (with S. Barzilai). *Comprehen. Psychiatry,* 8:16–26.

Training for community psychiatry (Hebrew). *Symposium on Psychiatric Education.* Tel Aviv: Israel Neuropsychiatric Society, pp. 80–85.

1968 Form and content. An ego psychological view. *The Psychoanalytic Study of the Child,* 23:204–223. New York: International Universities Press.

1969 Recognized emotional disorders in an Israel immigrant community (with A. Hoek). *Social Psychiatry,* Vol. 1, ed. A. Kiev. New York: Science House, pp. 183–196.

Mental health in Israel. In: *Perspectives on Mental Health*. New York: Grune & Stratton.

1971 Psychopathology of children raised in the kibbutz: A critical review of the literature (with A. Kaplan de Nour & J. Rosenfeld). *Isr. Ann. Psychiatry*, 9:68–106.

Family therapy in Israel. *Isr. Ann. Psychiatry*, 9:132–137.

Family psychotherapy—Its development and place in Israel today (Hebrew). *SAAD—Soc. Workers' J.*, Nov: 3–7.

1973 *Psychological Bases of War* (with H. Z. Winnik & M. Ostow, Eds.). New York: Quadrangle Press; Jerusalem: Academic Press.

Summary and outlook, an Israeli view. In: *Psychological Bases of War*, ed. R. Moses, H.Z. Winnik, & M. Ostow. New York: Quadrangle Press; Jerusalem Academic Press.

Psychiatric aspects of juvenile probation (Hebrew). In: *The Juvenile Probation Service*. Tel Aviv: Israel Ministry of Welfare, pp. 19–23.

1974 Psychological reactions to sensory deprivation (with H. Klein). *Psychother. & Psychosom.*, 24:41–52.

On the treatment of combat reactions in the Yom Kippur war (Hebrew). *Harefuah*, 87:569–572.

1976 A rear unit for the treatment of combat reactions in the wake of the Yom Kippur war. *Psychiatry*, 39:153–162.

1977 Community mental health services in times of emergency. *Isr. Ann. Psychiatry*, 15:177–288.

1978 Welcoming address. Thirtieth International Congress of Psychoanalysis. *Int. J. Psycho-Anal.*, 59:3–5.

Adult psychic trauma: The question of early predisposition and some detailed mechanisms. *Internat. J. Psycho-Anal.*, 59:353–363.

The emancipation of war-bereaved widows, a two-step role (with K. Moses). In: *The Child in His Family*, Vol. 5, ed. E.J. Anthony & C. Chiland. New York: John Wiley.

1980 Psychoanalytic perspectives of the Middle East peace process: Obstacles to peace, with special reference to narcissism. *Samiksa, J. Ind. Psychoanal. Soc.*, 34:117–129.

1981 Community mental health services in emergency and war (Hebrew). In: *Community Mental Health in Israel*, ed. U. Aviram & I. Levav. Cherikover, Tel Aviv: Goma Science & Research Books, pp. 379–396.

1982 The group self and the Arab-Israeli conflict. *Internat. Rev. Psycho-Anal.*, pp. 55–65.

Denial and projection in reaction to violence. In: *Violence and Non-Violence* (Hebrew). Tel Aviv: Social Workers' Union, pp. 48–51.

Ideological polarization in Israel—Psychological aspects. In: *From Crisis to Opportunity* (Hebrew). Tel Aviv: National Union of Social Workers in Israel, pp. 186–189.

A therapeutic community program for a multi-cultural adolescent population (with S. Schneider). *Isr. J. Psychaitry Rel. Sci.*, 19:81–92.

1983 Emotional response to stress in Israel—A psychoanalytic perspective. In: *Stress in Israel*, ed. S. Bresnitz. New York: Van Nostrand Rhinehold.

Guilt feelings in political process (German). Annual Sigmund Freud Lecture. *Sigmund Freud House Bull.*, 7 / 1:2–14.

The personal factor in education—The contribution of a psychoanalytic approach (with R. Hrushovski-Moses). *Iyunim Behinuch* (Studies in Education), 37–38: 31–40.

A fifty year span—Some reflections on Israelis and Germans. *Isr. J. Psychiatry* (Spec. issue) 20:155–168.

1984 An Israeli psychoanalyst looks back in 1983. In: *Psychoanalytic Reflections on the Holocaust: Selected Essays*, ed. S. Luel & P. Marcus. New York: Ktav Publishing, pp. 52–70.

Understanding and treatment of combat reactions: The Israeli experience (with I. Cohen). In: *Psychotherapy of the Combat Veteran*, ed. H. Schwartz. New York: SP Medical & Scientific Books, pp. 269–303.

North of Eden: The evacuation of Ophira, Sinai (with J. Rosenfeld, R. Hrushovski, & R. Beumel). *Jerusalem Quart.*, 33:109–124.

1985 Empathy and disempathy in political process. *Pol. Psychol.*, 6:135–140.

The psychiatric case register and confidentiality (with S. Schneider). In: *Psychiatry, Law and Ethics*, ed. A. Carmi, U. Hefetz, & S. Schneider. Heidelberg: Springer.

A psychological view of the forced evacuation of a small town at the southern-most tip of Sinai in April 1982: A case study (with R. Hrushovski-Moses, & J. Rosenfeld). *J. Soc. Psychiatry*, 5 / 4:31–38.

Emotional perception of the Arabs by Israeli Jews and their view of the Arabs' perception of them. In: *Jews and Arabs—Mutual Images and Psychological Aspects.* Jerusalem: Israel Interfaith Association.

Psychological aspects of Arab-Jewish meetings. *Inst. Ed. for Co-Existence between Jews & Arabs*, pp. 1–11.

1986 Steps in self development (with R. Hrushosvski-Moses). *The Psychoanalytic Study of the Child*, 41:491–514. New Haven, CT: Yale University Press.

A form of partial denial (with R. Hrushovski-Moses). *Internat. Rev. Psycho-Anal.*, 13 / 1:175–180.

Psychiatry, psychotherapy and world peace. *Internat. J. Soc. Psychiatry*, 32 / 1:76–79.

Psychoanalysis as method: Psychohistorical relationships. In: *Psychoanalysis as Method,* Monogr. No. 3. Frankfurt: Sigmund Freud Institute, pp. 151–164.

Watergate as a universal phenomenon: Some social aspects of the bribing of the superego and the subverting of the ego ideal. In: *Psychoanalyse Heute* (Psychoanalysis Today), ed. H. Lobner. Vienna: Verlag Orac, pp. 185–204.

Denial in non-psychotic adutls. Some adaptive and maladaptive aspects. *Samiksa, J. Ind. Psychoanal. Soc.,* 40:79–93.

Facing the threat of removal—Lessons from the forced evacuation from Ophira (with J. Rosenfeld & R. Hrushovski-Moses). *J. Appl. Behav. Sci.,* 23 / 1:53–71.

Projection, identification and projective identification and their relationship to the political process. In: *Projection, Identification and Projective Identification,* ed. J. Sandler. Madison, CT: International Universities Press, pp. 133–150.

What audience does the political psychologist address? *Pol. Psychol.,* 8 / 4:667–671.

1988 The defense mechanism of denial in non-psychotic adults: An overview (German). *Psyche,* 42:753–768.

1989 La desmentida en los adultos no psicoticos. Algumos de sus aspectas adaptivos y no adaptivos. (Denial in nonpsychotic adults). (Spanish). *Rev. de psicoanalisis* (Buenos Aires), 46 / 1:133–146.

Denial in political process. In: *Denial: A Clarification of Concepts and Research,* ed. E.L. Edelstein, D.L. Nathanson, & A.M. Stone. New York: Plenum Press, pp. 287–297.

Shame and entitlement: Their relation to political process. In: *The Psychoanalytic Core,* ed. H. Blum, E. Weinshel, & F.R. Rodman. Madison, CT: International Universities Press, pp. 483–498.

1990 The self, self-view and identity. In: *The Psychodynamics of International Relationships,* ed. V.D. Volkan, D.A. Julius, & J.V. Montville. Lexington, MA: Lexington Books, pp. 47–55.

On dehumanizing the enemy. In: *The Psychodynamics of International Relationships,* ed. V.D. Volkan, D.A. Julius, & J.V. Montville. Lexington, MA: Lexington Books, pp. 111–118.

The leader and the led: A dyadic relationship. In: *The Psychodynamics of International Relationships,* ed. V.D. Volkan, D.A. Julius, & J.V. Montville. Lexington, MA: Lexington Books, pp. 205–217.

Reflections on the sense of entitlement (with R. Moses-Hrushovski). *The Psychoanalytic Study of the Child,* 45:61–78. New Haven, CT: Yale University Press.

An Israeli psychoanalyst speaks to the German Psychoanalytic Society (German). In: *Hassen und Versoehnen, Psychoanalytische Erkundigungen,* ed. E. Herdieckerhoff, D. v. Ekesparre, R. Elgeti, & C. Marahrens-Schuerg. Goettingen: Vanderhoeck & Ruprecht, pp. 18–27.

Acknowledgement—The balm of narcissistic injuries. *Austen Riggs Center Rev.,* 3 / 2:4–8.

Review. Anita Eckstaedt's *National Socialism in the "Second Generation."*

Suhrkamp. *Isr. J. Psychiatry & Allied Disciplines,* 28:49–51; *Zeitschrift fur Psychoanalaytische Theorie und Praxis,* 5:384–386.

1991 Preparing for the negotiating process: The psychological dimension. *Jerusalem J. Internat. Rel.,* 13 / 1:77–89.

1992 Israel: Internal and external conflicts. In: *Social Psychiatry and World Accords,* ed. J. Masserman. New York: Gardner Press, pp. 180–186.

Discussion. Transmission of Holocaust trauma—The second generation. *Isr. J. Soc. Work Pract. & Policy,* 5–6:107–114.

The Meaning of the Holocaust: Its Meaning to Those Not Directly Affected (German, with F.-W. Eickhoff, Eds.). Stuttgart-Bad Cannstatt: Frommann-Holzboog.

A short history of psychoanalysis in Palestine and Israel. *Isr. J. Psychiatry & Rel. Sci.,* 29 / 4:289–238.

Deployment—As a form of defensive character organization (with R. Moses-Hrushovski). *Samiksa, J. Ind. Psychoanal. Soc.,* 46 / 3:79–100.

1993 *Persistent Shadows of the Holocaust: Its Meaning to Those Not Directly Affected,* Editor. Madison, CT: International Universities Press.

Violence—A view from Israel. *Mind & Hum. Interact.,* 4 / 3:135–140.

German version: Aggression at the end of the century. *Psychoanalytische Blatter,* 1:62–75.

"Deployment: as a form of defensive character organization (with R. Moses-Hrushovski). *Psychoanalyticky Sbornik* (Prague), 5 / 1:7–22.

Doing first and thinking afterwards: The psychoanalyst, the individual and society (German). In: *Die klugen Sinne pflegend. Festschrift for Hermann Beland,* ed. J. Gutwinski-Jeggle & M. Rotmann. Tuebingen, Germany: Discord.

1994 Polarization in Israel—Can it be remedied? In: *Group Process and Political Dynamics,* ed. M.F. Ettin, J.W. Fidler, & B.D. Cohen. Madison, CT: International Universities Press, pp. 63–68.

Foreword: The pitfalls and promises of group psychotherapists addressing the political process. In: *Group Process and Political Dynamics,* ed. M.F. Ettin, J.W. Fidler, & B.D. Cohen. Madison, CT: International Universities Press, pp. xiii–xvii.

The PLO-Israel handshake—A view from Israel (with R. Moses-Hrushovski). *Mind & Hum. Interact.*, 5 / 2:45–50.
Psychotherapy toward the year 2000. *Proceedings A psychoanalytic view of group psychotherapy.* Presentation at Annual Meeting of Israel Association of Psychotherapy, September (Hebrew).
1995 The perception of political enemies—A psychological view. *Palestine-Israel J.*
A psychological view of the enemy. Presented at the second international conference on Palestinians in Transition: Rehabilitation and Community Development, at the Gaza Community Mental Health Center, September, to be published as proceedings of the conference
A psychoanalytic view of the enemy. To be published in *Mind and Human Interaction.*
Denial and psychic reality. *Samiksa, J. Ind. Psychoanal. Soc.*, in press.
Internal and external hostility in groups. *J. Group Analysis* (German), in press.
Attraction and repulsion in inimical groups. Invited paper to the International Working Group of Group Analysts, Altaussee, October.
Psychological aspects of the process of peace and conflict between Palestinians and Israelis. Invited presentation to conference on the psychology of peace and conflict organized by the Truman Center for Peace, Hebrew University, the Palestine Consultancy Group and the Konrad Adenauer Federation in October, to be published as conference proceedings.

Newspaper Articles 1977–1984

1977 Guilt feelings and Palestinians. *Jerusalem Post,* November 17:p. 8.
Rashumon in the peace process. *Jerusalem Post,* December 19:p. 10.
1978 Peace psychology. *Jerusalem Post,* December 8:p.6.
1979 Psychological barriers to peace. *Jerusalem Post,* February 11:p. 8.
An end to mourning. *Jerusalem Post,* September 7:p. 6.
1980 Psychological responses. *Jerusalem Post,* September 4:p. 6.
Peace and mourning (Hebrew). *Ma'ariv,* October 21:p. 7.
The problem of trust. *Jerusalem Post,* December 27:p. 8.
1981 The voter and peace psychology. *Jerusalem Post,* February 17:p. 8.
Love, hate and mourning (Hebrew). *Ma'ariv,* March 21:p. 5.
Peace and mourning (Arabic). *Al Ghomoriyah* (Cairo), p. 7.
How nations mourn. *Jerusalem Post,* October 28:p. 6.
The need to have an enemy. *Jerusalem Post,* December 28:p. 10.

1982 Psychology of the home front. *Jerusalem Post,* June 17:p. 8.
The right to be afraid. *Jerusalem Post,* July 28:p. 10.
1984 Psychiatry and politics. *Jerusalem Post,* November 6:p. 8.

Unpublished Writings

1954 The psychotherapeutic treatment of a drug addict. 17 pp.
1963 Psychiatric education in Israel. Presented at joint meeting of American Psychiatic Association and Israel Neuropsychiatric Association, May.
1964 A case of homosexuality. Presented at Israel Psychoanalytic Society, January.
1965 Some comments on mental health values, cultural values and the individual (with D. Kligler). Department of Psychiatry, Albert Einstein Medical College, New York, mimeographed.
1968 Report on research of Palestine Refugees and United Nations Relief and Works Association (with A. Doron & J.M. Rosenfeld). Hebrew University for Professors' Committee on Held Territories. Mimeographed.
1970 Report on Arab refugees in administered territories (with A. Doron & M. Rosenfeld), mimeographed.
1971 The defense mechanism of projection (with H. Halevi). Presented to Israel Psychoanalytic Society, mimeographed.
1972 The structural elements of the organizing processes of the ego (with P. Noy and E. Gumbel). Presented to Israel Psychoanalytic Society, mimeographed.
Some aspects of teaching family therapy. *Proceedings of 4th International Congress for Social Psychiatry,* Jerusalem.
Psychopathology of Children Raised in the Kibbutz: A Symposium, co-Editor with J. Rosenfeld & J. Bowlby, and participant.
1975 Psychological aspects of aggression. Lecture to Second Conference of Israel Psychiatric Association, October, mimeographed.
1990 Children in war: Some cautions about policy decisions, presented at Children in War Conference of Sigmund Freud Center for Psychoanalysis, Jerusalem, June.
Particularism and Universalism—The three great monotheistic religions—and Peace: The case of Israel. Paper presented at the 12th Congress on Social Psychiatry, Washington DC, October.
1991 Nationalism and chauvinism—their relation to the Palestinian–Israeli conflict and to political conflict generally (with R. Moses-Hrushovski). Invited lecture to Israeli Mental Health Professionals for the Advancement of Peace (IMUT), Bi-annual meeting, Jerusalem, June.

Conflict. Aggression and violence—A possible contribution by psychiatry: The Arab-Israeli conflict as illustration. Presented at First scientific symposium of Section on Conflict Management and Conflict Resolution of World Psychiatric Association, Budapest, August.

1994 Psychological difficulties in the transition to the PLO-Israel peace process (with Rena Moses-Hrushovski). Paper presented at the International Conference: The PLO and Israel—From Armed Conflict to Political Settlement, May.

The function of a director of psychotherapy in a psychoanalytically oriented hospital.

Review. Alice Platen-Hallmund, *The Killing of Mental Patients in Nazi Germany. Isr. J. Psychiatry.*

NAME INDEX

Abraham, K., 290
Adivar, A. A., 275
Adler, G., 169
Adorno, T. W., 201, 203, 290, 292
Agnew, S., 232
Akhtar, S., 260
Altan, 274
Andreas-Salomé, L., 138*n*
Antonovsky, A. M., 288–289
Anzieu, D., 95
Apprey, M., 257, 259
Appy, G., 296–297, 298
Arlow, J., 78
Arvanitaki, K., 175
Ast, G., 258, 260
Atwater, L., 225
Aulagnier, P., 95

Baeyer, W. R. von, 292
Bak, R., 51
Balint, A., 101
Balint, M., 53–54, 101, 110, 111, 112, 113–114
Barron, A., 186
Barron, F., 17
Beethoven, L. van, 57–58*n*
Begin, M., 182–183, 248
Beland, H., 13, 297
Beland, R., 193–195
Bene-Moses, A., 239–240
Bergman, A., 44
Bergmann, M. S., 51–52
Berkes, N., 274
Berlioz, L .H., 57–58*n*
Bernays, M., 23
Bettelheim, B., 105–106
Bianchedi, E. T. de, 191
Biden, J., 223
Bion, W. P., 95–96, 107, 112, 197
Blass, R. B., 53–54, 134, 135
Blatt, S. J., 53–54, 65
Bleger, J., 86–87
Blos, P., 265, 274
Blum, H., 12, 46
Boehm, F., 288, 290
Bollas, C., 49–50
Bowlby, J., 73, 284
Boxer, B., 227, 229
Braun, C. M., 227, 229
Brecht, K., 296
Brenner, C., 74, 76, 79, 81
Brunswick, R. M., 204
Burlingham, D., 257
Bush, G., 214, 221, 222, 225

Cain, A. C., 258
Cain, B. S., 258
Carpy, D. V., 108, 109
Carter, J., 182–183, 220
Caruth, E., 144
Cassius, 219
Charnov, E., 77
Chasseguet-Smirgel, J., 246
Choisy, M., 47
Clinton, B., 214, 228, 229, 232
Cobb, S., 277
Cohen, Y., 12
Coleman, J., 5
Colson, C., 159–160
Coltart, N., 12
Cooper, A. M., 72, 166
Cremerius, 292

Dahl, 76

Dare, C., 28, 105
Darrow, C., 230
Davis, H. B., 57
Dean, J., 218
Deutsch, H., 284
Dietrich, D. R., 284
Dixon, A., 227
Dohnany, K. von, 296
Dole, R., 232
Draeger, K., 292
Dukakis, M., 223, 225
Dulles, J. F., 219

Easterbrooks, M. A., 257
Eifermann, R. R., 13, 133, 140
Einstein, A., 95
Eisenhower, D., 219
Eissler, K. R., 207*n*
Eitingon, M., 288, 290
Ekstein, E., 144
Elbirlik, K., 266
Elon, A., 17
Emde, R. N., 76, 257
Emery, F., 232
Erikson, E. H., 241
Estes, D., 77

Fairbairn, W. D., 72, 75, 79
Fedue, S., 232
Feinstein, D., 229
Feldman, M., 165
Fenichel, O., 7
Ferenczi, S., 111, 113
Filelfo, G. M., 274
Ford, G., 217
Fosshage, J., 69
Freud, A., 13, 105, 133–144, 217–218, 257, 265
Freud, S., 7–8, 12, 13, 23–24, 26–27, 35, 47, 50–51, 69–81, 71, 74, 78, 85, 87, 95–96, 99, 107, 113, 120, 134, 135, 137–141, 143, 148–150, 152, 154, 157, 159, 161, 190–191, 192, 203, 204, 230, 244, 246–250, 271, 278, 284, 288, 290, 298, 299–300
Friedman, L., 78
Friedrich, V., 296
Fromm-Reichmann, F., 5

Gampel, Y., 12, 90, 93, 95, 96
Gardiner, A. B., 276
Gardner, W., 77
Gediman, H. K., 52
Goethe, J. W. von, 13, 189, 190, 191–205
Golding, W., 149
Goldwater, B., 215
Göring, M., 289–290
Gray, T., 121
Green, N., 258
Greenberg, J., 72, 73–74, 77, 80
Greenson, R. R., 103
Greenspan, S. I., 257
Greer, W., 257
Grinberg, L., 108, 191
Grossman, D., 183–184
Grubrich-Simitis, I., 294–295
Grunberger, B., 168

Haefner, H., 292
Haldeman, H. R., 232
Hanly, C., 13
Hareven, S., 252
Harris, M., 259, 271, 277, 279
Hartmann, H., 24
Haynal, A., 252
Hearst, W. R., 230
Hegel, G., 157, 158
Heimann, P., 107
Hendrick, 73
Herman, J. L., 174
Hermanns, L. M., 296
Herzfeld, M., 277
Herzog, J. M., 198*n*
Hill, A., 221–222, 223
Hitler, A., 290
Holder, A., 28, 105
Holt, R., 70
Horkheimer, M., 201, 203, 292
Horney, K., 72
Horowitz, N., 185
Hössler, K., 196*n*
Hussein, King, 4

Hussein, S., 225, 247

Itzkowitz, N., 270, 272, 276, 278

Jacobs, T., 46
Jacobson, E., 24, 31, 289
Jodoin, R. M., 175
Joffe, W. G., 31
Johnson, A., 44
Johnson, W. I., 257
Jones, E., 7–8, 199*n*, 230, 232, 288
Joseph, B., 105
Juelich, D. H., 296
Julius, D., 279

Kahn, M. R., 144
Kaminer, I., 296
Kant, I., 189–190, 207
Kaufman, M., 5
Keats, J., 112
Kennedy, E., 225, 226
Kennedy, J., 233
Kernberg, O., 53, 76, 260
Kestenberg, J. S., 90, 96
Khan, M., 102
King, R., 225–226
Kisker, K. P., 292
Kissinger, H., 232
Klein, G., 70, 73
Klein, M., 9, 51, 103, 204–205, 284, 296–297
Kriegman, D., 80

Lacan, 95
Lachmann, F., 69
Lamb, M., 77
Laplanche, J., 50
Lester, E. P., 175
Levi, G., 185
Levin, S., 168
Lewis, H. B., 168
Lichtenberg, J., 69, 75–76, 77–78
Lidz, T., 5
Limentani, A., 99
Lincoln, A., 213
Little, M., 111
Loch, W., 293

Lussier, A., 175

MacFarlane, R., 220
Mackay, N., 78
MacKinnon, D. W., 18
Mahler, M. S., 44, 214
Margolis, G. J., 144
Markides, K. C., 278
Marx, K., 154, 158
Masri, A., 257
Matusow, A. J., 219
McCarthy, J., 218–219
McGovern, G., 232
Mehmet II, 274–275
Meissner, W. W., 242
Menninger, K., 218
Mitchell, S., 70, 72, 74–75, 77, 78–80
Mitscherlich, A., 283, 284, 285, 287–288, 292, 293, 296
Mitscherlich, M., 285, 287–288, 293
Mitscherlich-Nielsen, M., 293–294
Molnar, M., 252
Montesqieu, 160
Montville, J., 279
Moran, P., 214–215
Morris, X., 80
Morrison, N. K., 168
Moses, R., 4–14, 10, 14, 17, 19, 81, 185, 237, 238, 239–240, 242–243, 245, 246, 247, 248–249, 250, 251, 252
Moses-Hrushovski, R., 11, 13, 19, 165, 167, 182, 186, 246
Motolinía, T. de, 277
Mozart, W. A., 64–66
Müller-Braunschweig, C., 288
Murat II, 274–275
Murrow, E. R., 219

Nebel, G., 203
Nixon, R., 11, 159–160, 213–214, 216–221, 229–230, 232
North, O., 219–220, 227
Novick, J., 181
Novick, K. K., 181

Ogden, T. H., 63, 80

Pasha, H., 275
Paskauskas, R. A., 8, 232
Perot, R., 214, 228
Person, E. S., 51
Pick, B., 108
Pine, F., 44, 72–73, 77
Plato, 156
Poindexter, J., 220
Pontalis, J. B., 50
Poznanski, E. O., 258
Puget, J., 86, 95–96
Puymege, G., 252

Quinodoz, J.-M., 242

Rabicovitch, D., 18
Rabin, I., 4
Rangell, L., 10, 36, 71–72, 81, 153, 178, 213, 217, 218, 228, 229–230, 269
Rapaport, D., 69–70
Reagan, R., 220, 221
Richards, A., 12
Robertson, B. M., 175
Romney, G., 214
Roosevelt, F. D., 160
Rosalato, G., 95
Rosenbaum, M., 5
Rosenblatt, D., 70
Rosenfeld, H. A., 204
Rycroft, C., 100–101

Sadat, A., 182–183
Sandler, A.-M., 12
Sandler, J., 12, 28, 30–31, 58, 71, 105, 238, 241
Schafer, R., 70
Schoebel, R., 273, 274
Schreber, D. P., 203–204
Schubert, F., 196
Schultz-Henke, 293
Schwartz, 76
Segal, H., 191, 192, 205, 207
Setzman, E. J., 57
Shakespeare, W., 286–287
Sheleg, D., 184
Shevrin, H., 76
Simpson, A., 226–227
Simpson, O. J., 232–234
Slavin, M. O., 80
Sloan, H. Jr., 217
Smith, W. K., 225
Solan, R., 14, 239, 240–241, 243, 246, 252
Solnit, A. J., 241, 258
Sophocles, 202*n*
Sor, D., 191
Spector, A., 227, 229
Spitz, R., 257
Steiner, J., 166
Stern, D. N., 52
Sterren, D. van der, 202
Stevenson, A., 230
Stewart, H., 12, 100, 112, 113
Stolorow, R., 76
Strachey, J., 109
Sullivan, H. S., 72, 75, 79
Suphi, M., 276–277
Symington, N., 107

Tal, Y., 249–250
Tessman, L. H., 298
Thickstun, J. T., 70
Thomae, H., 288, 290, 292–293
Thomas, C., 221–222, 223
Thompson, R., 77
Totenberg, N., 223
Truman, H., 219, 249–250
Trunz, E., 190*n*
Tsongas, P., 230
Tyson, M., 225

Volkan, V. D., 10, 14, 58, 175, 182–183, 257–260, 266, 269–273, 276–279

Waelder, R., 4
Wallerstein, R., 71
Wangh, M., 14, 286, 289
Weber, M., 250–251
Weiker, L., 230
Weinreich, 177
Weinshel, E. M., 165
Weinstein, L., 77, 78
Welch, J., 219

Whelan, M., 105–106
White, R. W., 69, 73
Wieland, C. M., 199*n*
Winnicott, D. W., 62–63, 94–95, 101–103, 109, 110–111, 113, 197
Wolfenstein, M., 284
Wright, A., 224
Wurmser, L., 168, 181

Yeakel, L., 227, 229
Yerushalmi, Z., 96
Young, K., 278
Young-Bruehl, E., 133, 135, 137

Zaleznik, A., 250–251
Zintl, E., 273
Zuckerberg, J. O., 51

SUBJECT INDEX

Abuser position, 176
Accountability, 231
Acting out, 35
  of analyst, 108–109
  parental incitement to, 43–44
Actuality, versus symbolic meaning, 94–97
Adoption Service of the Ministry of Welfare, 6
Affect, in motivation, 75–76
Affective investments, 24–25
Affective state, conveyors of, 100–101
Afterlife, 121–122
Aggressive behavior. *See also* Violence; Violent behavior
  CNS disorders and brain damage in, 36–37
  versus love, 12
Aggressive drive, 74
Aggressor, identification with, 217–218
Ambivalence, 36
American Constitution, 160
American Psychoanalytic Association, 1990 conference of, 298
Analyst
  appearance and personality of, 104
  behavior and setting of, 101
  as container, 107–108
  emotional response to patient, 105–108
  empathy of, 103
  idolization of, 152–153
  nonverbal communication to patient of, 99–114
  silences of, 104
  verbal communication of, 103–104
Analytic dyad. *See* Patient-analyst relationship
Analytic setting, 100–101
  maintenance of, 111–112
Angry persons, 167
Anti-Semitism, 276–277
Arab-Israeli conflict, 7, 9
Arglos, 113
Athenian democracy, 160
Attachment
  infant, 77
  motivation for, 75
  primary bond of, 60–61
Attachment behavior, 24–25
Attitudes, assumption of, 176–177
Aversive reactivity, 75

"Bad seed" fantasy, 41
Ballads, dreamlike quality of, 193
The Basic Fault (Balint), 110
Basic Instinct, 221
Bataan Death March, transmission of trauma of, 257–269
"Beating Fantasies and Daydreams" (A. Freud), 13, 133–144
Beating fantasy, of siblings, 138–140
Bereavement counseling, 121
Berlin Psychoanalytic Institute, 288–289
  integration into Deutsches Institut für Psychologische Forschung, 289–290
"Beyond the Pleasure Principle" (Freud), 23–24
Black sheep role, 176
Blind Ambition (Dean), 218
Borderline personality, 37
Brain damage, violence and, 36–37
Breakdown, fear of, 62
Buddhism, beliefs regarding death, 122

Bulimia, 260
Bush-Clinton campaign, 214
Byzantine Empire, 273, 278

Castration wish, 204
Cathexis, 23
affective, 24
Celebrity status, 233–234
Central nervous system disorders, 36–37
Change, resistance to, 239–240
Charisma, 252
Charismatic leader, 251, 252
Children
as deposited representations, 258–259
replacement, 258
Christianity, beliefs regarding death, 121
"Civilization and Its Discontents" (Freud), 23
Clinical theory, 71
Communication
nonverbal, 99–114
verbal, 103–104
Communism
Freud on, 154
inhibited cooperation under, 162
suppression of individual life in, 156–157
Composite theory, 71–72
Compromise formation, 74
centrality of, 81
Compromise of integrity, syndrome of, 218
Concern, 118
Conflict
Arab-Israeli, 7, 9
centrality of, 74
Conscience
balance with ego and, 220
versus self-interest, 220–221, 224
Consensus leader, 251
Conservation of constancies, 238–239, 241–242
Constantinople, fall of, 272–278
Contemptuous position, 176–177
Corrupt, identification with, 217–218
Counteridentification, projective, 108–109
Countershame strategies, 168–170
Countertransference, 28–29, 107
antitherapeutic, 108–109
"Countertransference and Role-Responsiveness" (Sandler), 28–29
Courage, of self-knowledge, 190–192
Creativity, precocious, 198*n*
Criminal tendencies
genetic versus environmental etiology of, 46–47
roots of, 35–47
The Critique of Pure Reason (Kant), 189–190
Crusades, 274
Cultural ambience, 3
Cultural media, leader-led relationship in, 242–243

Daydreams, Anna Freud's, 140–144
Death, 12
anxiety about, 118–119
dealing with, 117–125
denial of, 120–121
middle approach to, 121–122
Death drive, 23
De-differentiation, 31
Dehumanization, 248–249
Delinquency, genetic versus environmental etiology of, 46–47
Delinquent adolescent, 35–47
Delusional crime, 205–206
Demarcation signifiers, 95
Democracy, responsibility in, 230–232
Demonization, 248–249
Denial, of Nazi past, 285–286
Deployed persons, 165–174
family background of, 174–175
Deployment, 13
forms of, 175–182
motivation for, 166–167
pathological, 165–174
in political arena, 182–186
turning from, 179
use of, 165
Deposited representation, 258–259
Deprivation
in hatred, 36

violent behavior and, 37
Destructive aggression, hatred in form of, 35–47
Destructuralization, 86–87
Development, love as outgrowth of, 52
"Dialectic of the Enlightenment" (Horkheimer, Adorno), 201
Disappointment, 244–250
Disasters, black humor regarding, 271–272
Distrust, 39
Don Giovanni (Mozart), 64–66
Dreams
function of, 192–193
interpretation of, 191, 192
Drive, Ego, Object, Self (Pine), 72
Drive psychology, 78–79
Drive theory, 74, 81
of motivation, 73–74
Drivenness, 79
Drive / relational dichotomies, 72
Drives, versus drive derivative, 77–78
Dual-drive theory, 74
Duality, 199–201

Eastern Europe, centrifugal forces of, 161–162
Eclecticism, 72
Ego
boundary of, 31
destructuralization of, 86–87
differentiation from self, 24
functioning of, and group formation, 148–149
Egolessness, 122
Ego-superego conflict, 218
Emotionality, split from reason, 198
Empathic experience, 76
Empathy, 103, 108
failure of, 174
jointness and, 242–243
Endings, 12, 117–129
Enemy-neighbor, 248
Enlightener, courage of, 189–195
Enlightenment, rationality of, 197–198
"The Erlking" (Goethe), 13
duality in, 199–201
identification in, 206–207
Oedipus myth and, 201–203
paranoia in, 203–206
psychoanalytic observations on, 189–207
questions in, 193, 195–199
Erlking syndrome, 198*n*
Eros, 23
Eschatology, 121–122
Ethnic conflict, psychoanalysts' participation in, 14
Ethnic group, link with individual psychology of, 257–279
Ethnic identity, threats to, 270–271
Ethnic tents, 271
European Psychoanalytic Federation (EPF), 162
Exploration-assertion motivation, 75
Extremist groups, 184–185

Family
contribution to delinquent behavior of, 41–45
of deployed persons, 174–175
Fantasy
being drawn into, 177–178
love object, 25–26
Father
empathy of, 197
good and evil, 200–201
idealization of, 196
rivalry for love of, 136–140

Father hunger, 198*n*
Father-son relationship, 196–197
rivalry in, 42
Fear, of love, 49–66
Fear of Breakdown (Winnicott), 62
Feelings
transforming roles into states of, 176
turning into facts, 169
Feminist issues, 225
Ferdinand, Archduke, assassination of, 271
Followership, internal representations in, 237–240

Forces of Destiny (Bollas), 49–50
Formal signifiers, 95
Freedom, responsibility and, 230–231
Freiburg, aerial bombing of, 285–286
Fusion, 53–54, 64–66

General theory, 71
German Psychoanalytical Association, 295
German Psychoanalytical Society
development of, 296
liquidation of, 288–290, 296
Nazi experience of, 284–299
"Germans and Israelis: The Past in the Present," 299–300
Germany. *See also* Nazi Germany
manic rebuilding of, 284
psychoanalysis in postwar years in, 292
World War I experience of, 286–288
Global defense, 13
Global rationalization, 213–214
Glory, chosen, 272
Good guy role, 175
Government, public trust in, 215–216
Grandiose self, 260
Gratification
object seeking and, 79
of patient's instinctual wishes, 111–112
Greek War of Independence, 277
Greeks
chosen trauma of, 278
identity of, 277
Group
deployment of, 183–185
inability to mourn, 271–272
intrapsychic conflict within, 12–13
regression to violence of, 149
schism of, unconscious powers of, 189
Group formation, 12, 148
libidinal identificatory bonds in, 159–160
psychoanalytic explanation of, 156–157
"Group Psychology and the Analysis of the Ego" (Freud), 26–27, 148
Guilt
borrowed, 46
over liquidation of psychoanalysis under Nazi Germany, 290–291, 298
overcorrecting, 170
Gulf War, 247
absence of leadership in, 250
media of, 249

Harmonious mix-up, 54
Hatred
in delinquent adolescent, 35–47
as ego response, 35
seeds of, 12
Heaven, 121–122
Hebrew University in Israel, Sigmund Freud Professorship of Psychoanalysis at, 4, 6–7
Heimlich, 85, 87, 88–89
Helpless self representation, transmission of, 257–269
Here and now, living in, 122–123
Hero, unconscious identification with, 219–220
Hill-Thomas affair, 14, 214–215, 221–225
aftermath of, 227
Holding, 101–103
Holocaust, 226
feelings of uncanniness in survivors of, 86–87, 90–97
working through in German psychoanalytic community, 283–300
Holy Wars, 249
Homosexual love, 27
Homosexual seduction, 199
fear of, 197–198
Homosexuality, paranoia and, 204–205
House Un-American Activities Committee hearings, 218–219
Humiliation, 10
delinquency and, 35
refuge from, 168–170
Humor, black, 271–272
Hunting, urge for, 261–269

Idealization, 150
as defense, 27
of leader, 247

of love object, 26–27
Identification, 30–31
fleeting primary, 31
healthy, 268–269
idealizing, 157–158, 160–161
indiscriminate, 58
projective, 30–32, 103, 205–207
Ideology
critique of, 153–154
definition of, 147
ego functioning and, 148–150
polarity of, 147–148
Impulse-ridden character disorders, 37
The Inability to Mourn (Mitscherliches), 285, 293
Individual freedom, 160
Individual responsibility, 230–231
Individuality, suppression of, 156–157
Infant, inner life of, 76
Infant-caregiver experiences, 76–77
Infant-mother dyad, 241
Inferiority feelings, 35
Injustice, sense of, 173
Inner life
balance of, 220
of infant, 76
Inner rules, 169–171
Integrity, syndrome of compromise of, 10
Intentionality, 78
Internal fantasy figure, 27
Internal objects, externalization of, 25–26
Internal representations, role in choosing leader, 237–240
International Psychoanalytic Congress
of 1977, 293–295
first, 9
International Psychoanalytical Association (IPA), 7, 158, 162
1985 congress of, 295–296
Bamburg Congress of, 297
Hamburg Congress of, 296
Jerusalem conference of (1989), 296–297
Jerusalem Congress (1977), 299
International scientific conferences, 7
Interpretation
as detoxification, 107–108
of dreams, 191, 192
therapeutic value of, 110
Interpretation of Dreams (Freud), 159
Intersubjective experience, 76
Intimacy, 241
Intrapsychic conflict, 10, 11, 12–13
in groups, 12–13
in hatred, 36
war and, 11, 12
Introjective identification, 30–31
Iran-Contra scandal, 215, 219–220
Israel
during Gulf War, 249–250
programs for change in, 186
terrorism in, 17
The Israel Annals, Samiksa, The International Journal of Psycho-Analysis, 7
Israeli settlers, group deployment of, 183–185

Jerusalem, fall of, 273, 277
Jews, persecution of, 276–277
Jointness, 240–243, 252
pleasure of, 244–245
Justice, miscarriage of, 222–224

Knight story, 141–143
Knowledge, requests for, 196–199
Kosova anniversary, 271

Leader
Freud on, 249
General Tal on, 249–250
idealization of, 247
idealizing identification with, 157–158
intrapsychic needs for, 14
lost faith in, 253
omnipotent, 247–248
representations in choice of, 237–240
as target for projection, 238
Truman on, 249
trust and disappointment between followers and, 244–250
trust of, 252
"The Leader and the Led: A Dyadic Relationship" (Moses), 240

Leader-led object relation, 240–243
Leadership
within bounds of narcissism, 250–253
rigid, 249
types of, 250–251
Leopold and Loeb case, 230
Liberal democracy, psychoanalysis and, 158–159
Libidinal energy investment, 23–24
Libidinal identificatory bonds, 159–160
Libido, aim-inhibited, 23–24
Life force, 23
Live Forevers, 121
"Living Statue" (Volkan), 175
Lord of the Flies (Golding), 149
Love
as aim-inhibited libido, 23–24
archaic, 63
attachment and, 60–61
as conflict between separation and merger, 53–57
falling in, 25, 63
fear of, 12, 49–66
Freudian theory of, 50–51
frustration of, 206–207
as incorporation of other, 64–65
narcissistic root of, 30
as outgrowth of development, 52
as psychic phenomenon, 50
psychoanalytic theories of, 23–32, 51–52
self expansion and self-identity in, 57–62
separation from mother and, 51
special forms of, 26
structural elements of, 52
Love object
choice of, 29
destruction of, 206–207
finding of, 51
idealization of, 26–27
merging with, 52
Love relationship
development of, 28–30
reciprocal, 32

Magical nature ballads, 190
Manzigert, battle of, 272–273
Marxism, critique of, 154
McCarthy era, 14, 215, 218–219
Media
friendly, 249
of Gulf War, 249–250
leader-led relationship in, 242–243
mature representations of, 252–253
shared investment in, 244
Megali Idea, 278
Memoirs of a Neurotic, Freud's analysis of, 203–204
Merger, 53–54, 64–66
Merging
narcissistic, 245
regulation of, 243
Metatheory, 71–72
Middle East. *See also* Arab-Israeli conflict; Gulf War; Israel; Jerusalem, fall of
conflicts in, 4
peace negotiations in, 4
psychoanalysis of, 4–14
Middle European Association, Congress of (1980), 294
The Mind of Watergate (Rangell), 217
Misery, holding onto, 167
Moderate leader, 251
Moral conflict, in political process, 213–234
Moral courage, 190–192
Moral sensibility, 148–149
Moses, Rafael
analytic orientation of, 7–9
contributions of, 18
influences on, 10
life of, 4–7
scientific contributions of, 8–9
Mother
empathic, 242–243
inability to mourn lost child, 258
overprotective and overstimulating, 42–44
split image of, 199–201
Mother-child relationship, fluidity of psychic borders in, 257–269
Mother-infant unit, undifferentiated and differentiated, 63–64

Mother-son incest, 202–203
Motivation
  affects in, 75–76
  of deployed persons, 166–167
  drive theory of, 73–74
  factors in, 79
  Freudian theory of, 69–81
  Lichtenberg's theory of, 75–78
  postclassical theory of, 80–81
  in psychoanalytic theory, 12
  Rapaport's theory of, 69–70
  relational and self psychological theories of, 78
  relational matrix and, 79–80
Motivational principles, 74
Motivational systems, 75–78
Mourn, inability to, 258, 271–272, 284
Mourners, perennial, 273
Mourning, 12
  of Nazi experience, 283–300
  for object-complementary aspect of self, 30
  of representation, 267–268
  by weak ego, 284–285
"Mourning and Melancholia" (Freud), 284
Multidetermism, 74
Multiple function principle, 81

Narcissism, 26, 51
  leadership in bounds of, 250–253
  malignant, 260
  mourning of, 267–268
Narcissistic entitlement, 43–44
  violent behavior and, 38
Narcissistic fantasy, acting out of, 35
Narcissistic injury, 246–247
  balm of, 10
Narcissistic object love, 26
National asocialism. *See* Nazi Germany; Nazism
National trials, 214–234
Nationalism, 161–162
Nazi Germany, 14. *See also* Holocaust; Nazism; Shoah
  cooperation with, 294–295
  individual freedom in, 160
  psychoanalysis in, 158–159
  psychoanalytic view of, 296–297
Nazism, 87
  suppression of individual life in, 156–157
  working through in Germany psychoanalytic community, 283–300
"The Necessity to Mourn" (Mitscherlich-Nielsen), 294–294
Negative affects, 25
"Never again" creed, 298–299
Nightmares, 192
Nixon funeral, 232
Nocturnal panic states, 198*n*
Nonverbal communication
  of analyst to patient, 99–114
  effects of, 12
  Freud on, 99
  parapsychological, 113–114
  Rycroft on, 100–101
Not-I, 246–247
  threatening, 248

Object constancy, 36
Object relationships
  jointness and, 240–243
  motivation and, 73
  scanning of, 28–29
  therapeutic value of, 110
Object seeking, 75, 79
  motivational valence of, 78–80
Object-complementary aspect of self, 29–30
Oedipus and Beyond: A Clinical Theory (Greenberg), 73–74
Oedipus complex, predecessors of, 13
Oedipus myth, 13
  in fall of Constantinople, 274–276
  "The Erlking" and, 201–203
Offended person position, 177, 179
Omnipotence
  with feelings of inferiority, 35
  narcissistic, 245
Omnipotent narcissism, mourning of, 267–268
Omnipotent self representation, 264–265

Oneness, state of, 32, 53
Organizing activity, 238
Other, inclusion within self boundaries, 52
Otiot, 184
Ottoman Turks, 273–278
Outrage, 216–217
  after Rodney King decision, 226
Overdetermination, 81

Panic state, freezing in, 169
Paranoia
  delusional crime and, 205–206
  Freud's formula on, 204
  homosexual wishes and, 204–205
Paranoid conflict, unconscious powers of, 189
Paranoid thinking, 207
Paranoid-homosexual delusional behavior, 190
Parapsychological communication, 113–114
Parent representation
  externalization of, 27
  refinding of, 51
Parents. *See also* Father; Mother
  excessive shaming by, 174
  good and bad, 41
Past injuries, "correcting" of, 166
Patient, regressed, 109–112
Patient-analyst relationship
  cultural ambience and, 3
  interaction in, 28–29
  nonverbal communication in, 99–114
  physical contact in, 113
  positive feelings toward, 49–50
  post-therapy, 125–126
Peace, deployment as obstacle to, 184–186
Perceptual-affective-action patterns, 75, 78
"Persistent Shadows of the Holocaust: The Meaning to Those Not Directly Affected," 9
Personality disorders, violent behavior and, 37–38
Peter Pan position, 176
Peter the hunter case, 259–269
Physical abuse, 175
Physical contact, in analytic setting, 113
Physicalism, 78
Physiological needs, 76
  psychological regulation of, 75
Pictogram, 95
Political campaign
  candidate personalities in, 227–228
  issues in, 228–229
Political candidates
  character traits of, 229–230
  public response to, 227–228
Political conflict, 11, 12
Political correctness, 214
Political process, moral conflicts and public opinion in, 213–234
Politics
  analysis of, 3–14
  deployment in, 182–186
Positions, rigid, 176–177
Positive feelings, lack of attention to, 49–50
Post-therapy relationship, 125–126
Potential space, 63
Power, origins of, 157–158
Prehistoric psychology, 203
Prejudice, seeds of, 42
Premature antifascists, 213–214
Prepared, being, 169
President, protection of, 219
"Pride" (Rabicovitch), 18
Projective counteridentification, 108–109
Projective identification, 30–31, 32, 205–207
  empathy and, 103
Propaganda, 201
Pseudocompliance, 39
Pseudoimbicility, 213–214
Psyche, 294–295
Psychic borders, fluidity of, 257–259
Psychic change process, 109–110
Psychic determinism, 74
Psychic energy, 69–70
Psychic space, shared, 241
Psychoanalysis
  under Hitler, 292–293
  ideology of, 150–162
  liberal democratic principles of, 158–159

liquidated in Nazi Germany, 285–287, 288–289
nationalism and, 162
Psychoanalysis and Motivation (Lichtenberg) 69
Psychoanalytic Dialogues (Mitchell), 70
Psychoanalytic education, personal analysis in, 150–151
Psychoanalytic theory, classical, 70–71
"On the Psychoanalytic Theory of Motivation" (Rapaport), 69–70
Psychological genes, 14, 258, 270–271
Psychopathology
false selves in, 124
groups and, 12
Psychopolitical border, 13–14
Psychosomatic disease, in postwar Germany, 292
Public opinion, in political process, 213–234

Questions, phenomenon of, 193, 195–199

Racism, 247
Radioactive historical social identification, 93–97
Rape cases, nationally televised, 224–225
Rapist position, 176
Rapprochement, struggle for, 52
Rationality, 149, 197–198
Real, 95
The Real Turk (Cobb), 277
Reality testing
compromise of, 150
freedom for, 159–160
of leadership, 252
superego formation and, 149
Reason-emotionality split, 198
Regression
benign, 112
to group violence, 149
during termination of therapy, 126–127
in therapy, 109–112
Reincarnation, 122
Relational Concepts in Psychoanalysis: An Integration (Mitchell), 72
Relational matrix, 78–79
motivational principles and, 79–80
Relational models, 70
Religious beliefs, regarding death, 121–122
Repetition compulsion, 226–227
Replacement children, 258
Representations
deposited, 258–259
familiar, 248
function of, 238–239
images arousing chain of, 245–246
intergenerational transmission of, 257–269
loss of ability to realize, 246–247
regulation of, 239
role in choosing leaders, 239–240
of separateness / jointness, 252–253
The Republic (Plato), 156
Responsibility, individual, 159–160
Rodney King case, 14, 225–226
Role
deployment into, 175–176
relationship, actualization of, 29
Rules, deployment into, 169–171

Safe place, search for, 93–97
Safety, 25
Sameness, safety in, 239–240
Scanning, 28–29
Schreber case, 203–204
Secrets, concealment of, 178
Secure identity, search for, 93–97
Security, 25
Seductive overprotection, 43–44
Self
conflict between wish to expand and preserving self-identity, 57–62
differentiation from ego, 24
empathic experience and, 76
false, 124
fragmented, 76
loss of, in pathological deployment, 165–174
object-complementary aspect of, 29–30
representation of, 24

Self and Motivational Systems: Toward a Theory of Psychoanalytic Technique (Fosshage), 69
Self boundary, 31
  fear of losing, 64
  safeguarding of, 52
Self organization
  constant attention to, 170–171
  false, 111
Self psychology, roots of, 76
Self-definition, exaggerated, 58
Self-esteem, threats to, 10
Self-identity
  wish to expand versus preservation of, 57–62
  fear of losing, 64
  preservation of, 52
Self-inflicted not-coming-of-age, 189–190
Self-interest, versus moral conscience, 220–221, 224
Self-knowledge, 190–192
Self-object
  confusion of, 31–32
  interaction of, 27–29
Sensual enjoyment, 75
Separateness
  mastery of, 252–253
  regulation of, 243
Separation, 12
  capacity for love and, 51
  jointness and, 242
  undoing of, 52
Separation-merger conflict, 52, 53–57
Serbian identity, 271
Sexual abuse, 175
Sexual drive, primacy of, 74
Sexual issues, in conquest of Constantinople, 274–276
Shame, 10
  arousal of, 246
  in deployed persons, 168–170
  over liquidation of psychoanalysis under Nazi Germany, 291, 298
Shaming, excessive, 174
Shoah, 86–87
  working through in Germany psychoanalytic community, 283–300
Siblings
  ambivalent rivalry of, 133–144
  beating fantasies of, 138–140
Sigmund Freud Center for Psychoanalysis, Hebrew University, German-Israeli
  meeting of, 299–300
Signs, 100–101
Silence, 104
  conspiracy of, 285
O. J. Simpson trial, 14, 232–234
Sincerity, in political candidate, 229–230
Sleeping Beauty position, 176
Social collectivity, 156–157
Social media, leader-led relationship in, 242–243
Social violence, dread and horror of, 85–87. *See also* Uncanniness
Sociocultural world, 3–14
Sociopolitical conflict, 14
Solitude, taming of, 242
Sophisticated work group, 252
Soviet Union, disintegration of, 271
Spain, expulsion of Jews from 276–277
Sphinx
  riddle of, 192–193
  "The Erlking" and, 201–203
"Strum and Drang" ballads, 190*n*
Stuck patients, 166
  factors in, 177
Substance abuse, superego regulation and, 36–37
"Suehne-bewegung" movement, 291
Superego
  fear of, 119
  formation of, 148–149
  wish to overcome, 217–218
Supreme Court judges, 231–232
Survival instinct, 50–51
Survivors
  arousal of uncanny feeling in, 87–93
  children of, 96–97
Symbiosis, 242–243
Symbiotic phase, recalling of, 52

Taxidermy, meanings of, 266–267
Team task experience, 244–245
Tension reduction, 78
Terminal illness, acceptance of, 128–129
Terrorist bombings, 17
Terroristic deployment, 181–182, 185
Thanatos, 23
Therapy termination, 125–129
Thing representations, 95
Totalitarianism, 156, 157
Training analysis, 150–151
Transference, 28–29, 105
  idealized, 13, 151
  intense, 181
  mutative interpretations of, 100
  residual, 125–126
  to theory, 153
"On Transference and Counter-transference" (Balint), 101
Transference relationship, lack of understanding of, 108–109
Transitional object, 94–95
Transsexuals, intergenerational transmission of, 257
Trauma
  "chosen," 270–272
  intergenerational transmission of chosen, 257–279
  transmission to third generation, 269–270
Traumatic events
  defense against repetition of, 62–63
  delusional acts and, 195–196
  in deployed persons, 174–175
  uncanny feelings and, 88–93
Traumatic overstimulation
  in hatred, 36
  violent behavior and, 37
Trust
  blind, 252
  excessive, 245
  between leader and led, 244–250
Turks
  Seljuk, 272–273
  stereotyping of, 276–278
Tyson case, 225

Uncanniness
  applied to Shoah, 86–87
  in clinical psychoanalysis, 88–89
  feelings aroused through child's behavior, 90–93
  Freud on, 85
  radioactive historical identification and, 93–97
Uncanny, 12
  definition of, 85
Unconscious
  acknowledgment of, 190
  road to, 191
Unconscious fantasy, 77
Unconscious motivation, 74
Unconscious wishes, 28, 79
Understanding, holding function of, 103
Unhemilich, 85, 87, 88–89
Union
  based on fusion, 64–66
  types of, 53–54
Unity, false, 201
"The Use of an Object" (Winnicott), 109

Values, of patients, 154–156
Verbal communication
  holding function of, 103
  tone of voice in, 104
Verbal interpretative techniques, 100
Victim position, 176
Vienna Psychoanalytic Society meeting, A. Freud's presentation to, 134–135
Vietnam War, divisiveness of, 215
Violence
  group, 149
  social, 85–87
Violent behavior. *See also* Aggressive behavior
  CNS disorders and brain damage in, 36–37
  hatred as root of, 35–47
Voice, tone of, 104

Watergate, 11, 216, 217–218
Watergate burglary, 14

Watergate complex, 10
Watergate scandal, 215
Watergate syndrome, 249
Western Europe, centripetal forces of, 161–162
"Whatever Became of Sin?" (Menninger), 218
"Wiedergutmachungsgelder," 291
William Kennedy Smith case, 225
Wishful fantasy, 28
Work rhythms, 244
  lack of consideration for, 245
World War I, 286
  postwar economic crises, 286–287
Worry, 118
Worst, being prepared for, 169

Yom Kippur War, 8